THE BAD BOHEMIAN

BY THE SAME AUTHOR

MEMOIRS
The Tightrope
The Serpent and the Nightingale

TRANSLATION
The Good Soldier Švejk

The Bad Bohemian
The Life of Jaroslav Hašek Creator of the Good Soldier Švejk

Cecil Parrott

BH

THE BODLEY HEAD
LONDON SYDNEY
TORONTO

To Dana

Copyright © Cecil Parrott 1978
ISBN 0 370 10344 0
Printed and bound in Great Britain for
The Bodley Head Ltd
9 Bow Street, London WC2E 7AL
by Redwood Burn Ltd
Trowbridge & Esher
Set in Monotype Baskerville
by Gloucester Typesetting Co Ltd
First published 1978

I went into a forest. Spring was singing.

But the fresh grass had all been
   trampled down

By people looking for flowers.

And I recalled how in my life I too

Had trampled down all sorts of things.

JAROSLAV HAŠEK
Cries of May

CONTENTS

RUSSIA IN EUROPE

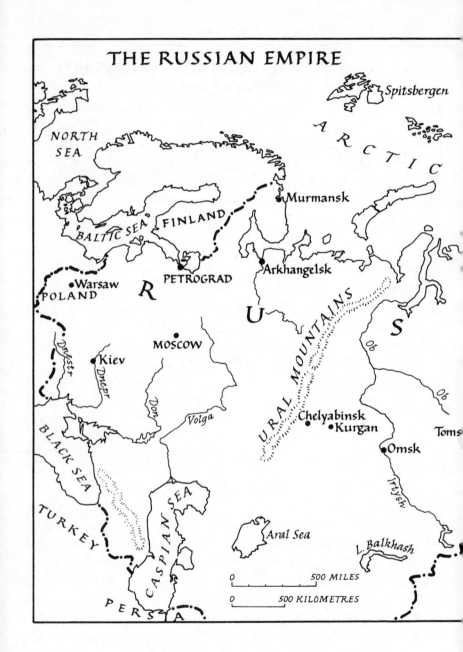

THE RUSSIAN EMPIRE

Spitsbergen

NORTH
SEA

A R C T I C

•Murmansk

BALTIC SEA FINLAND

•Arkhangelsk

•Warsaw
POLAND

PETROGRAD

R

U

S

U R A L   M O U N T A I N S

MOSCOW

Ob

•Kiev

Don

Volga

•Chelyabinsk
•Kurgan

Toms

BLACK SEA

•Omsk

Ob

Dnestr

Dnepr

T U R K E Y

CASPIAN SEA

Aral Sea

L. Balkhash

Irtysh

P E R S I A

0   500 MILES

0   500 KILOMETRES

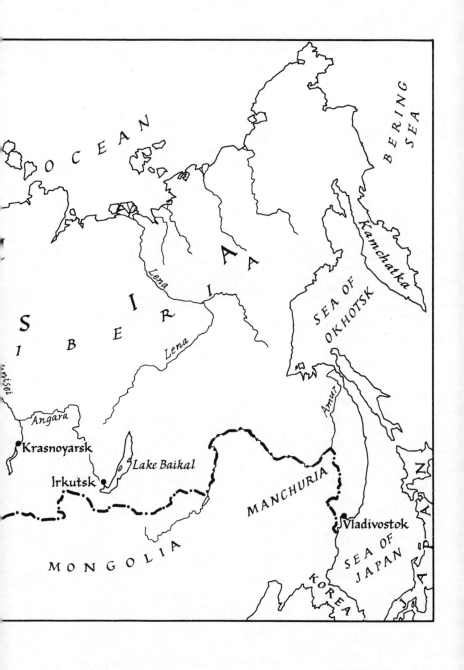

PREFACE

No one outside Czechoslovakia has so far attempted a full-scale biography of Jaroslav Hašek, the author of *The Good Soldier Švejk*. When I first embarked upon the task I was puzzled that I should be the only foreigner to do so in the fifty years or more which had elapsed since his death. But as I proceeded further, the reasons became clearer to me.

It must be rare to find a modern writer who was so reticent about himself, and this in spite of the fact that he was a very sociable and gregarious individual who had a host of friends. Throughout his life he poured out a steady stream of short stories, sketches, satires and press articles, and enjoyed within his circle the reputation of being almost as garrulous as his inspired creation, Josef Švejk. But for all this he seems to have left posterity next to no autobiographical material. He never or very rarely wrote or spoke to his friends about his parents, his childhood, his school-days, his years of wandering, his thoughts and writings. The autobiographical allusions in his works, in so far as they exist at all, offer few clues to what he really thought and felt. His stories and sketches provide bare evidence of where he may have gone on his various peregrinations, and what may have happened to him, but even this is not conclusive, because he was always capable of writing about a place or subject on no better authority than an article in a newspaper or an encyclopaedia which he had just read, and of presenting it as though it was his own experience. He was a very accomplished and persuasive hoaxer. The only times when he seems to have opened up on his personal experiences or feelings were when he wrote to Jarmila Mayerová, his wife-to-be. Unfortunately, relatively few of these letters have been preserved.

We are equally short of material from reliable sources close to him. Jarmila herself wrote nothing biographical about him. His younger brother Bohuslav appears not to have seen much of him after his early manhood. His cousin, Máňa,[1] who lived with his parents during his childhood days, has written her reminiscences of that time, but they have not been published and were not available to me.

Most of the members of his bohemian set, like Longen,[2] Kuděj,[3] Sauer[4] and Opočenský,[5] who wrote copiously about him, are unreliable witnesses. In 1928 Longen wrote and illustrated his memoirs of Hašek in *Jaroslav Hašek*, but they only go back to 1911 when Hašek was twenty-eight. Although very much written up, they contain some useful confirmatory material, especially on the period after Hašek's return to Prague. Kuděj published two rambling books of reminiscence about Hašek and the Prague *Bohème—It's Better When There Are Two of You*[6] (1923–24) and *When the Mighty Four Get Going*[7] (1930). They are of little value as source material. Franta Sauer ('František Kyselý') published two books—one in 1921 in collaboration with Ivan Suk, *In Memoriam Jaroslav Hašek*, and the other in 1924, *Franta Habán from Žižkov*.[8] Some of his stories about Hašek are amusing and probable, but they are mostly chronologically vague, inaccurate or of doubtful veracity. Opočenský published in 1948 a memoir of Hašek, *A Quarter of a Century with Jaroslav Hašek*,[9] which is confined to details of Hašek's bohemian life and contains very little hard information even on that topic. Since they were all writing at a time when Hašek was not taken seriously and was regarded as something of a fabulous animal, none of them ventured any serious character portrait of him. One is tempted to believe that their main motive in writing was to exploit their friendship with him and draw attention to themselves. The financial reward was no doubt an inducement too. Most of them were just as hard up as the author himself.

A valuable, if often unreliable, source is the actor and author Václav Menger, who claimed to have known Hašek from his childhood and was later with him in the Czech Legion. He was for a time the custodian of most of Hašek's and Jarmila's papers and published two biographical books about him, *Jaroslav Hašek, Prisoner No. 294217*[10] (1934) and *Jaroslav Hašek at Home*[11] (1935), which was issued in a revised version in 1946 under the title *The Human Profile of Jaroslav Hašek*.[12] Both books were based on a series of articles he had published in the *People's Newspaper*[13] in 1933. Menger planned to write a third book—*Jaroslav Hašek, the Commissar*, but failed to do so. His two books are indispensable sources of information for the earlier part of Hašek's life. Jan Morávek's[14] reminiscences of Hašek's enlistment and his journey to the front which were published in the *Evening Czech Word*[15] in 1924 were never published in book form but have been extensively drawn on by Czech biographers.

The more reliable, if less well-informed sources are Hájek,[16] Lada[17] and Langer.[18] Hájek, who was at the Commercial Academy with Hašek and was the companion of his youthful days, wrote *From My Memories of Jaroslav Hašek*[19] two years after Hašek's death, so the recollections in it are the freshest. Lada, the illustrator of *The Good Soldier Švejk*, wrote *The Chronicle of My Life*[20] as late as 1942 during World War II, but at that time, presumably for reasons of censorship, did not include in his book his memories of Hašek. These were not published until 1947— nearly twenty-five years after Hašek's death. Langer published his account of the Party of Moderate Progress within the Bounds of the Law five years after the author's death, but it was not until 1958 that he wrote his more personal reminiscences of the author, *They Were and It Used to Be*,[21] which were first published in 1963. Distance of time makes them less reliable than they might otherwise have been.

Finally, like so many Czechoslovak personalities, Hašek ran the gauntlet of differing assessments according to the prevailing political doctrines of the time. From his death until 1939 he was looked on as a 'bad bohemian'; from 1939–45 (under the Germans) he was outlawed and his books burnt; from 1945–48, thanks largely to Communist influence, he was rehabilitated to a limited extent; and since 1948, after a brief period of uncertainty, he has been almost canonised. The attempts by Czech writers to fit their assessments of him to the prevailing political judgements of the time have not made his biographers' task any easier.

The fact that Hašek has been given an honoured place in the Czechoslovak and Soviet Communist pantheons has undoubtedly facilitated the task of scholars, because so much valuable work has been done in the last quarter of a century in collecting his works and editing and publishing them. While the earlier biographical material has not been reissued, it is still obtainable, and there has been in addition an abundance of new books about Hašek and his works which tell us almost everything that is known on the subject. None the less, there still remain periods in his life where first-hand evidence about him is meagre.

We are, for instance, short of information about how he lived during his years of forced separation from Jarmila, about his wedding and the short period of his married life, about the breach with Jarmila and the life he led afterwards. We should like to know much more about the time he spent in the Austrian army from 1915–16, where he seems to have attracted little attention. The period from his return to Prague to his death is, on the other hand, very well documented.

There are also certain periods for which the only information is to be found in the valuable biographies of Hašek published by Ančík[22] and Pytlík,[23] and in Křížek's *Jaroslav Hašek in Revolutionary Russia*.[24] This applies especially to Hašek's life in Russia after he deserted from the Czech Legion. Pytlík's *The Wandering Gosling*[25] proved particularly valuable and if I have appeared to follow this source too closely here and there, it is because if I had not done so I should have had to leave blank passages in my book.

I was fortunate enough to be a guest of the Czechoslovak Academy of Sciences in Prague in the autumn of 1975 and to be permitted to examine much material about Hašek in the Academy's Literary Institute. I also had the inestimable benefit of the advice of Dr Pytlík himself, who is the leading Czech expert on Hašek today and to whom I am considerably indebted. He was also my guide at Lipnice. I should like to express my thanks to the Academy for their hospitality and assistance, and to acknowledge my gratitude for the numerous photographs which they have made available to me for illustration in this book.

It is an advantage and a disadvantage that Hašek has become a 'hero of Communism' and *Švejk* approved reading for the rank and file of the Czechoslovak army. (The book has even been published by *Our Army*,[26] the military publishers.) It means that all source material about him is firmly in the hands of the Czechoslovak or Soviet authorities. I have been assured that practically everything that has been considered essential for a study of Hašek's life has been published and nothing withheld, and that the Czechs have had access to all the material available in Russia. It is always possible that the Soviet authorities may still be holding on to some documents because they reveal 'contradictions' in Hašek's attitude and would, if published, militate against the legend of 'Comrade Gashek', but I doubt it. Of course I have not had the advantage which the Czech biographers have had of examining Party and police archives or of seeing Russian official documents, but any material I have not seen or do not know about would not be likely significantly to affect my judgement at this stage.

There are major disadvantages which confront a foreign biographer of Hašek today. Not only is he necessarily too dependent on books and articles written by Czechoslovak critics and biographers, but the fact that all material about Hašek is in the official domain presents problems of access. Not that I had any difficulties myself—I could count on the maximum of help—but I had to depend too much on others, whereas in the West I could have done much more on my own. As long as I was in Czechoslovakia I had no difficulties and obtained xeroxes of what I asked for, but the problem of sending material out of the country has not yet been solved satisfactorily. Realising what obstacles had to be overcome by those who assisted me, I am all the more appreciative of the efforts made.

A more serious problem was the difficulty of verifying sources of stories about Hašek—a problem under which the Czechoslovak experts laboured as much as I did. Hundreds of anecdotes have long been circulating about him, most of which are more *ben trovato* than true. They cannot be confirmed. What was I to do? Omit everything that could not be verified? That would have made the book very dull indeed. The answer was to be sparing in their use and to leave the reader in no doubt that they might be spurious.

Wherever possible I tried to go back to the original sources before drawing upon the authoritative biographies by Ančík and Pytlík and other important secondary source material, but when there were no traceable sources I often had no alternative but to accept their version of events, and sometimes their conclusions.

Of course I could not always see eye to eye with them on ideological matters. In the West most of us take a different attitude to the events leading up to the Civil War in Russia and we do not subscribe to present Communist views about the Czech Legion or to the current glorification of those who deserted from it. Consequently the interpretation I give of Hašek's activities after the October Revolution sometimes differs noticeably from the accepted version given by the authoritative writers in Prague. But it is based on the same sources, and so readers are free to be as sceptical about it as I am about the version generally accepted in Czechoslovakia.

One should not forget that although Hašek got on well with the Soviet authorities, he was not trusted by the founding fathers of Czechoslovak Communism in Russia, and suspicions of him remained after his return to Prague. Some of those who were against him were later expelled from the Party. Had Hašek not been disillusioned about politics but engaged himself more deeply in Party activities, it is almost certain that with time he would have been expelled from the Party too, because by his very nature he could not be anything but a non-conformist. His experiences in Prague soon after his return cooled his ardour and, paradoxically enough, his subsequent withdrawal from political activity was to prove his saving grace and to earn him later a place in the Communist canon.

I could not have written this book without the invaluable facilities accorded to me by the Czechoslovak State Library and I should like to express my gratitude to the Director and to Mrs Vlasta Volfová. I was lucky to be able to draw on the resources of the Comenius Library at the University of Lancaster, which possesses a collection of works on Hašek unrivalled in Britain. I should like to record my appreciation of the unfailing help of the Assistant Librarian, Mr Peter Burnett.

I am extremely grateful to the British Academy for selecting me as their nominee in their exchange programme with Czechoslovakia.

I should also like to thank Dr Dana Kňourková of the Department of Central and South-Eastern European Studies at Lancaster University for her inestimable help and advice to me in the preparation of this book, Dr A. A. Martin of the Lancaster Moor Hospital for the advice he kindly gave me on Hašek's psychiatric problems and Mrs Betty Graham for her masterly typing of the manuscript—no small achievement considering the very considerable number of difficult Czech expressions. She lived up to the high standard she had set in preparing the manuscript of *The Good Soldier Švejk*. Finally I am eternally grateful to Ellen's forbearance, her readiness at all times to speed on winged feet like the messenger of Jove and her skill in drawing maps of Russia and Austria–Hungary.

NOTE TO THE READER

In the text the names of Czech newspapers and articles have been translated into English. This obviates the inclusion of innumerable Czech names which will mean nothing to most readers and, moreover, the titles when translated can tell the reader something about their contents. The original Czech names will be found in the Notes. Names of streets have been left in the original language except where they are known (Wenceslas Square) or can be easily translated into English (Charles Square). A rough guide to the pronunciation of Czech will be found on page 276.

*

Please note that Švejk is pronounced Shvake. No one pronounces it Shvike—not even in Germany.

[I]

BOHEMIA

(I)

Introduction

It was January 2nd, 1923. The Prague paper *Tribune*[1] had just
received a telephone message that the writer Jaroslav Hašek was
dying. It came from his brother, Bohuslav. Rumour had killed
the author of *The Good Soldier Švejk* so many times already that
no one would believe the news until Michal Mareš, a reporter
who worked on the paper and had been a friend of Hašek's since
his anarchist days, took the receiver. Through the sobs he recognised Bohuslav's voice and knew the report must be true.

Later Mareš related how he wanted to drop everything and
dash off at once to the village of Lipnice, where for a year and a
half Hašek had been living and working on the last chapters of
The Adventures of the Good Soldier Švejk, but his chief editor told
him not to be a fool. 'Hašek is an old hoaxer. If you insist on going, you'll have to do so at your own expense. You won't get any
travel money out of us!' And so the next day Mareš paid his own
fare to Lipnice and arrived there shortly after four o'clock in the
afternoon, when it was already getting dark. The door of
Hašek's house stood open and he went inside. The house was
practically empty but upstairs a glimmer of light shone from a
room sparsely lit by a few candles. Inside, on an old table, lay
Hašek's body, in a white shirt with an open collar and dark
trousers with patches on them. His face was unnaturally still and
pale, and his hands lay on his rounded belly like a child's pudgy
fists.

Mareš was given two mementoes of the dead writer—the
most recent photograph of him, where he sat portly and sedate
in a white shirt, and a copy of the last telegram he had sent to
Prague. He took them with him and rushed back to Prague to
write the obituary notice. But when it eventually appeared, no
one paid any attention to it; it was killed by a bigger sensation.
The Finance Minister in the Czechoslovak Government, Alois

25

Rašín, had been assassinated by an anarchist. Mareš commented: 'This was of course a much more important and interesting event than the passing away of the father of the Good Soldier Švejk, that character who was to outlive so many ministers, governments and acts of state. But of course no one suspected that in 1923. Jaroslav Hašek died, but his Švejk lived on.'[2]

Hašek's death had more than a touch of the irony of one of his own stories. Learning that he had died, his good friends, the local innkeeper and his wife, rushed to his house and saw outside it two men loading a cupboard and chairs on to a little cart. It was the carpenter taking away the furniture. 'He hasn't paid for it all,' he explained, 'and the bed belongs to me too.'

Some said that on the day of the funeral it was impossible to carry the dead writer's body, swollen to a weight of twenty stone, down the narrow stairs, and it had to be pushed through the window instead. Very few of his old friends and acquaintances and none of his family came from Prague to the ceremony, except for the solitary, pathetic figure of his eleven-year-old son, Richard, who had only seen his father two or three times in his life. Bohuslav had made one hurried visit to Lipnice and then was seen no more. Menger says he borrowed money to pay for his brother's cremation and then spent it all on drink. The local priest would only allow the body to be buried alongside the cemetery wall among the unbaptised and suicides, but he did the dead man an injustice: Hašek had never left the Catholic Church since he rejoined it for his marriage thirteen years before. The whole funeral ceremony was arranged by the local branch of the Sokol, the Czechoslovak patriotic organisation, many of whose members were ex-legionaries and would have regarded Hašek as a traitor. It was they who carried the coffin on their shoulders to the cemetery; their local leader delivered the funeral oration; their band played on the way to the cemetery and their choir sang Beethoven's 'Angel of Love' while the coffin was being lowered into the ground. The little village had never witnessed such a grand funeral and people came flocking to it from the whole region.

František Langer, whose cousin was an eye-witness, compared the scene to one of those jokes which the Czechs were always inventing about the immortal Hašek: 'The humour, the irony of it all lay in the juxtaposition of two such incongruous elements as Hašek and the Sokol, which could never have seriously come together in real life. And of all things *over his coffin*!'[3]

As was the custom after funerals, the guests were entertained at the inn and drank to the memory of the departed. Probably most of them had at one time or other been the dead writer's drinking companions, because in his last years, when he could not bear to be without company, he had cast the net of his hospitality far and wide and swept up all and sundry into it.

For lack of money the gravestone had to be a simple one. Later it was converted into something more ornate—an open book of granite with a gilt inscription: 'Austria, never wert thou so ripe to fall, never wert thou so damned.' A group of birches embraced it with their branches until some officious person decided that they obstructed the tourists' view and had them cut down.

On the last occasion when Hašek had been reported dead in Russia, the obituary writers had had a field-day and abused him for all their worth. But Hašek took his revenge on them soon after his return to Prague by publishing in the press a short story called 'How I Met the Author of My Obituary'.[4] With ghoulish delight he pictured himself appearing as a ghost to a former journalist friend of his, Jaroslav Kolman-Cassius, who two years earlier had reported his death under the single headline 'Traitor'. 'Hašek was a clown . . . who sacrificed his life to his art,' he had written. 'He gesticulated with his chubby childish hands and entertained society with his jokes against himself and the whole world. His drunken twaddle was the distorted product of the vilest treason.'

According to the story, Hašek's 'ghost' forced the unfortunate writer to go to his imagined gravestone in the Prague cemetery at a grisly hour of night. There he lectured him until his wails could be heard as far as the most distant suburbs of the city. At length the victim could bear it no longer. Fleeing in desperation, he was held by the guard, who took him for 'some besotted widower' and handed him over to the police to be locked up for the night.

Nearly a fortnight later, smarting under the rumours that as a 'Red Commissar' his hands were stained with blood, Hašek defiantly published in a Prague evening paper his 'autobiography' under the title 'My Confession'.[5]

'At the age of six months I devoured my eldest brother, stole the holy images of the saints from his coffin and hid them in the maid's bed. As a result the girl was hounded out of the house as a thief and sentenced to ten years' hard labour for robbing a corpse. She died a violent death in gaol in a brawl during her daily exercise. Her fiancé hanged himself, leaving behind six illegitimate children, some of whom achieved prominence later as international hotel crooks. One became a prelate of the Premonstrate order, and the last, the eldest, is a contributor to *October 28th*.*[6]

'When I was a year old there was not a single cat in Prague whose eyes I had not gouged out or whose tail I had not docked. When I went for a walk with my governess, all the dogs gave me a wide berth.

'My governess did not go on taking me out for long, because when I was eighteen months old, I took her to the barracks at Charles Square and bartered her away to the soldiers for two packets of tobacco. She never survived the shame and threw herself under a passenger train . . . As a result the train was derailed with eighteen killed and twelve seriously injured . . .

'. . . At the age of four I ran away from home, after having broken my cousin Máňa's head with a sewing machine. As I was leaving I seized and took with me some thousands of guilders, which I squandered in the company of thieves . . .

'Then I was caught and sent to a reformatory in Libeň, which I set on fire. All the teachers perished in the blaze, because I had locked them in their rooms from outside . . .

'Forced to disappear from Prague I went to Polná, and if my confession is to be completely frank, I must state publicly that it was not Hilsner† who murdered that Jewish girl. I did it—and for three guilders! . . .

'I arrived in Prague [again] safe and sound after enticing an elderly lady on to the foot-board of the train, tearing her bag from her hand and pushing her out while we were travelling at full speed. When they searched for her I told them that she had

---

* One of the papers which attacked Hašek after his return to Prague.

† A reference to the famous Hilsner case, in which T. G. Masaryk proved the innocence of a Jewish boy who had been wrongfully accused of ritual murder.

got out at the previous station and wished to be remembered to them all.

'I returned home to find that my parents were no longer alive. Out of grief over my profligacy my father had hanged himself some two months previously and my mother had jumped off the Charles Bridge. When they tried to rescue her she had capsized the life-boat and with it her rescuers, who were drowned too.

'I grew up completely abandoned, because in order to get hold of my uncle's savings-bank books I poisoned his whole family and then forged the numbers to get more money . . .'

But what actually happened to the hero of this present book? Did he resemble the boy in Sacha Guitry's film, who alone of all his family survived death because, as a punishment for his naughtiness, he was forbidden to attend a feast where the mushrooms were poisonous and afterwards drew the conclusion that in this world it is only wickedness that pays?

Not altogether; but somehow or other, when the fairies were invited to his christening, one of them must have been forgotten, because among all the talents and even the few virtues with which he was endowed, one essential quality was conspicuously lacking—a sense of responsibility.

(2)

School Street and School-Days

According to Karel Čapek, if anyone wanted to know the true character of the Czechs, he had only to glance through the pages of a Prague telephone directory, where he would find forty people called 'Merry' (*Veselý*), forty 'Fun' (*Kratochvíl*) and thirty-one 'Happy' (*Šťastný*), as against only four who were called 'Sad' (*Smutný*). He would also soon discover that Bohemia abounded in joke names like 'Scratch-head', 'Cabbage-head', 'Muddy Water', 'Trotters' and 'Uneatable', to mention only a few, while some quite respectable names like 'Hero', 'Nightingale', 'Wise' and 'Humble' were probably only given in jest and were intended to convey the opposite. Moreover the common verbal names like *Pospíšil* ('He hurried'), *Vyskočil* ('He jumped out') and *Nevečeřel* ('He didn't get any supper') might well be the fossilised remains of what had once been funny incidents in the lives of certain individuals.

If this is indeed the case, then it seems quite appropriate that the best-known Czech writer, Jaroslav Hašek, should owe his fame to a humorous book about a comic character, Švejk, who spends a lot of time telling funny stories. Nor need it surprise one to learn that in private life Hašek was an indefatigable jester and hoaxer and that his surname rhymes with the Czech word for 'clown' (*Šašek*).

Many people all over the world have read *The Adventures of the Good Soldier Švejk*, many more have heard of the book and its principal character, but very few outside Czechoslovakia know much about the life of the author, who has become a legend in his own country.

His story has something of the flavour of an eighteenth-century English picaresque novel—a *Tom Jones* or a *Roderick Random*—and one can easily picture the titles running along the top of the pages of such a book: 'How our hero punished his headmaster', 'How he found a job on an animal lovers' journal and came to invent animals' or 'How he was saved from throwing himself off the Charles Bridge'. But it takes place at the end of the nineteenth and the beginning of the twentieth century and is coloured and complicated by some of the phenomena peculiar to the age like anarchism, conscription, world war, revolution and Bolshevism, and its scene is not laid in England but in one of the provinces of the old, ramshackle Austro–Hungarian Empire, so that we can search through world literature in vain to find an exact parallel to it. It is the story of a man who was Bohemian by nationality and bohemian by temperament and habit, something of a Don Quixote and something of a clown, who carried on his own private crusade against the conventions and illogicalities of bourgeois society—a man capable of affection and thirsting for it, but unable to find that life-long love he yearned for.

Jaroslav Hašek was born in Prague in Bohemia on April 30th, 1883. At the time of his birth Bohemia was nothing more than a province of Austria with Prague for its capital. A guide to Prague and Bohemia published in English before the First World War starts with this sentence: 'Of all the extensive and manifold realms ruled by the House of Habsburg no part is perhaps less known in England than the ancient Kingdom of Bohemia.'[1] Indeed outside Central Europe the very existence of the Czechs had long ago been forgotten; they were classed as 'Austrians'. And yet Goethe, who had spent altogether more than three years in Bohemia, had perceptively written some hundred years earlier that Bohemia itself was 'a continent within the European Continent'. And this was indeed true because by language, race, history and traditions the Czechs were entirely different from the other peoples with whom fate had lumped them in that 'prison-house of nationalities'. Proud of the fact that Bohemia was an older kingdom than Hungary and shouldered the burden of one quarter of the taxes of the whole Monarchy, they resented the preferential treatment their Habsburg rulers accorded to the Magyars, who had a position within the Empire almost equal to that of the Austrians. The Emperor Francis Joseph had been crowned King of Hungary in Budapest, but continually postponed his coronation as King of Bohemia in Prague. He cordially disliked the Czechs but was not afraid of them, whereas he had a morbid fear of the Hungarians, although he liked them just as little. An even more serious cause for grievance and disloyalty to the Monarchy on the part of the Czechs was the presence in Bohemia of a minority of Germans who had inherited a position of power out of all proportion to their numbers and who enjoyed the special support of their fellow nationals in the central government in Vienna.

And so Hašek was born into a city and a country which were part of the realm of a German dynasty, where Germans held most of the ruling positions and where German was the official language. Any hope of greater autonomy for his countrymen was doomed to frustration as long as the minority held power and continued to show its contempt for them. The boy was quick to see that his people felt no sympathy for the Germans and little loyalty to the Crown. It was an atmosphere not just of ordinary estrangement, but of illogical and unreasonable alienation, in which the young people of the majority race had every temptation to rebel against foreign authority and those of their countrymen who did its bidding.

Hašek had inherited from his southern Bohemian peasant ancestors their spirit of independence. Hašeks had been prosperous farmers in Mydlovary for three centuries at least, and according to Menger, Hašek's grandfather, František Hašek, had been important enough to take part in the Prague Rising of 1848 and be a member of the Austrian Parliament at Kroměříž (Kremsier) which followed it—the only hopeful and progressive institution which the Monarchy briefly permitted to exist throughout the whole of the nineteenth century. He no doubt experienced the shock of its forcible dissolution.

Jaroslav's father, Josef Hašek, was born in 1843. While studying at Písek, a small town about sixteen kilometres north of České Budějovice (Budweis), he got to know Kateřina, the daughter of Antonín Jareš, one of the water-bailiffs on the Schwarzenberg estate at Krč near Protivín, fell in love with her and asked for her hand. Little is known about her except that she took lessons in French from a Písek schoolmaster, Adolf Heyduk, who was afterwards to become a well-known Czech lyric poet.

The Schwarzenbergs, a noble family of German descent, were the most powerful feudal landholders in Bohemia and their vast estates, which were centred in the south, included the famous Bohemian fishponds. Here the carp were reared that provided the obligatory Christmas fare in Bohemia and throughout the Catholic parts of the Austrian Monarchy. Each pond had its water-bailiff, who lived in a log cabin nearby. It was his duty not only to keep off poachers, but to watch over the level of the waters to see that at flood times they did not breach the dam. To forestall this he had to regulate the level by operating the sluices. If we can believe 'Stories from the Water-bailiff's Lodge at Ražice',[2] which Hašek published in the humorous weekly *Merry Prague** in 1908, Jareš was a very competent and resourceful water-bailiff. Once, at the seasonal draining of the fishponds, when the level of the water had to be gradually lowered so that the fish could all be caught in big nets, some miscreant surreptitiously opened the sluices and, before the fishermen could prevent it, the whole catch lay gasping high and dry on the mud. In this crisis Jareš showed great presence of mind. He immediately brought up horse-drawn water tanks and poured enough water on the fish to revive them and bring them in alive. But to his fury the land agent blamed the accident on his negligence and when he tried to defend himself he was told rudely to clear off. Never able to tolerate an injustice, Jareš tore off his fishing boots and flung them on the ground in front of his superior. This gesture of defiance and his subsequent refusal to apologise for it cost him his job. His water-bailiff's station was abolished and his log cabin given over to one of the gamekeepers on the estate. On an earlier occasion, when he believed himself to have been unjustly accused by another land agent, he had even threatened to throw him into the water. If these stories are true they show that Jareš, like his grandson, was a man who had little fear of authority or respect for it.

Josef Hašek, Jaroslav's father, failed to obtain the required qualifications to teach in state secondary schools. This unfortunately restricted him to posts in private teaching establishments, where the pay was low. In 1877 he came to Prague and took the only job available to him, teacher of mathematics and physics at a private German *reálka*.†

After thirteen years of waiting, he and Kateřina were at last

* Veseál Praha
† The rough equivalent of a secondary modern school.

able to get married. The wedding took place at Protivín in 1879, and not long afterwards they left for Prague and settled in a flat in Školská (School Street) in the house of a family relative, a well-known advocate and Prague alderman, Dr Jakub Škarda. Ironically enough it was at this address that in 1883 the future truant and *enfant terrible* Jaroslav Hašek was born. He was the second child. The first, Josef, had died soon after birth.

Jaroslav was christened at the nearby Church of St Stephen,[3] a Gothic basilica built by the Emperor Charles IV in the middle of the fourteenth century. The godmother was the daughter of the German proprietor of the school where Josef taught.

In the same year the household was enlarged by the arrival of Josef's niece Máňa, who had been tragically left orphaned at the age of fifteen months. A year later, when Grandfather Jareš became a widower, he came and joined the family too. And then in 1886 a second son, Bohuslav, was born. With a family of six to maintain Josef was obliged to rely on private coaching to supplement his meagre income.

Old Jareš did not remain a burden to the family for long. He had already been ill when he came to Prague and died there three years later in 1887. There is a story that shortly before he died he used to take the four-year-old Jaroslav for walks. One day he found he had lost him and, after searching for him up and down Charles Square[4] all day, he finally discovered him late in the evening outside the gates of the military hospital, talking as bold as brass to the soldiers, who had stuck a pipe in his mouth and were having fun with him.

In 1890, by the time Jaroslav was seven, Josef had left his job at the German school and accepted a more remunerative and secure one as an actuary in the Insurance Bank of Slavie. If we are to believe Menger, he had taken to drink soon after leaving the university, and by the time he married was already a confirmed alcoholic. Few knew or suspected this, because he did not normally drink outside, but consoled himself at home. Menger hints that this was why he looked for a job in a bank; with his weakness for alcohol he could hardly hope to secure advancement as a teacher. Other biographers have disputed this, and we shall never know for certain whether Jaroslav inherited his propensity to alcohol from his father or acquired it by habit, although the fact that he could not break himself of it towards the end of his life and that his brother Bohuslav died of drink seems to suggest a family weakness.

In 1891, when Jaroslav was eight, the time had come for him to go to school, and he was sent to the nearby St Stephen's together with Bohuslav and Máňa. According to Bohuslav, Jaroslav was a lazy and naughty, if clever, pupil. Complaint followed complaint, and he was often stood in the corner or sent to the bottom of the class. He was 'a regular little bandit, never still for a moment', but at the same time 'a perfect scream'. During the very first lesson he started a rebellion. The teacher was allotting seats to the boys and asked: 'Who's got good eyesight?' (This meant, who wanted to sit in the back row which was reserved for the worst rascals.) Jaroslav was the first to volunteer. 'All right then, Hašek, sit down next to Kruliš!' 'Please, sir, I'm not going to.' 'And why not?' 'Because he stinks!' 'Hold your tongue and sit down.' 'I won't.' 'Then get out, you disgraceful, insolent puppy!' Jaroslav's reply was to seize his spelling book and throw it at the teacher's head.

There was one master whom Jaroslav is said to have particularly hated—the Catholic catechist, who gave the boys scripture lessons. This was not so surprising since the catechist in Bohemia was at that time regarded by many as the watch-dog of the regime, which was based on the 'alliance of altar and throne'. Jaroslav got very low marks in scripture and was allegedly once tied to the foot of a bed for half a day as a punishment. If this is true, it may explain his later virulence against the Catholic Church. On the other hand we know that the catechist recommended him as server in various churches and monasteries in the neighbourhood, and it seems improbable that he would have done so if their relations had really been so bad. These duties were an asset to Jaroslav, because they not only earned him some money or rewards in kind but—more important— gave him that knowledge of the Catholic ritual which he was able to exploit in his irreverent accounts of the services held by the drunken chaplain in *The Good Soldier Švejk* and elsewhere in his works.

Some of Jaroslav's biographers have dwelt on the straitened circumstances in which he was brought up and blamed his later eccentricities on these. But although the family were certainly not well off, they do not appear to have lived in penury. It is true that they moved very often—seven times in the first ten years of his life—which may have been made necessary by the growing size of the household. But on two occasions they found accommodation with the help of influential benefactors and in any case, if they changed the street, they did not change the quarter in the New Town, which was a very select one.

Školská was a respectable enough address; the Masaryks were to live there ten years later. Jecná housed at one time two of the best-known Czech writers, Božena Němcová[5] and Eliška Krás-nohorská.[6] Charles Square, which was planned to be the central park of the New Town,[7] was beautifully laid out with gardens. In Lipová where they moved in 1893, they took a flat in a house belonging to a family friend, the deputy mayor of Prague. The view all around was particularly beautiful and consisted of academic buildings, churches, monasteries and gardens. It lay near the lunatic asylum and the German Anatomical Institute—a juxtaposition which would most certainly have appealed to the adult Jaroslav's sense of the ridiculous, which was directed just as often against certified or uncertified lunatics as against Germans. The asylum, today the neurological clinic, and then popularly known as Kateřinky,* occupied what had formerly been the Convent of St Catherine,[8] founded by Charles IV for Augustinian nuns in celebration of the victory at the battle of San Felice in Italy in 1355. Its church, which had been rebuilt in 1737 by the Czech architect František Maximilián Kaňka, is one of the finest examples of Prague baroque. In the neighbouring street of Na Slupi† is still to be found the baroque church of Our Lady of the Nuns of Elizabeth of Thüringen,[9] the work of the famous Bohemian architect Kilián Ignác Dienzenhofer, and today part of the whole complex of the Prague General Hospital.

All these streets and the buildings around them were part of the so-called New Town, the quarter of Prague founded in the fourteenth century and richly endowed with monasteries. When the monasteries were dissolved by Joseph II in the eighteenth century, many of them were turned into hospitals or scientific institutions, and so the neighbourhood in which Jaroslav lived

---

* 'The Kitties.'

† 'At the Fish-trap.' The trap was made of wattle and fastened in the River Vltava.

and was brought up was a very select part of Prague, remarkable not only for its academic and civic importance, but also for its beautiful historic monuments, which in his time were certainly being well maintained by the various religious orders and academic authorities. He was lucky to have lived in such a fine quarter, conveniently near his school as well as the churches and monasteries where he attended services and even for a short time acted as a server. The Gymnasium and Commercial Academy where he was later to be sent were also close at hand.

However, this concentration of German academic buildings could not fail to have its effect on the ten-year-old boy. In the atmosphere of Prague in the nineties, when members of the German student corps were for the Czech students 'public enemy no. 1', it is easy to imagine how Jaroslav itched to climb over the railings of the building bearing the proud title 'German Anatomical Institute' and steal the apples in its grounds.

On May 15th, 1893, the police found a hangman's noose round the neck of the statue of the Emperor Francis I on the Francis Embankment.[10] When on August 17th, the eve of the birthday of the ruling Emperor, military music was interrupted and subversive leaflets distributed, the authorities staged a trial of the members of the *Omladina*.* On grounds of false evidence provided by a police informer, sixty-eight were sentenced to terms of imprisonment varying from seven months to eight years. Among them were the future Finance Minister in the Czechoslovak government, Alois Rašín, who received two years, and the future poet, S. K. Neumann, who received fourteen months. Jan Ziegloser, who had prepared the leaflets, was given eight years. He was amnestied three years later only to be imprisoned again during World War I. Ziegloser and Neumann were only eighteen years old at the time.

During the violent disturbances between Czechs and Germans in Prague which took place at this time, there were continual scuffles between young people of both nationalities. The boys of the various streets formed gangs and Jaroslav was said to have been one of the most active leaders. At a later period he was to describe these scuffles in two of his short stories— 'Baluška's Treason'[11] and 'The Greatest Day of Folimanka'.[12]

By now he had finished his primary schooling and, after

* 'Progressive Youth.' An association of young radicals.

passing a stiff entry examination, was accepted into the Imperial and Royal Junior Gymnasium. As long as his father was alive and reasonably well, discipline at home was strict, even if the times were too disturbed for this discipline to prevail on the streets. He was among the top pupils and had excellent reports after his first and second years at the Gymnasium. But during his third year his father became worse and took to his bed for good. The responsibility for looking after the son was henceforth to devolve entirely on the mother. One tragic day Jaroslav returned from school to see a priest leaving their home. He had just administered the last rites to his father.

Whether, as Ančík claims, Josef Hašek's death was the result of an epidemic of 'flu, or whether, as Menger has it, it was due to a long and lingering cancer, aggravated by alcoholism, Jaroslav was left at the impressionable age of thirteen without a firm parental hand to guide him. This, more than anything else, was to leave its fatal mark on his development. That same year he had to re-sit his mathematics, and the following year saw worse failures: he had to re-sit all his subjects. The results were a complete fiasco and all the hopes his adoring mother had set on him came to nothing.

Kateřina was not only prostrate with grief but destitute, because after only six years' service in the bank her husband had no pension rights. She received nothing more than a small *ex gratia* payment, which at least enabled her to take the children to southern Bohemia to visit her family and that of her husband. It was probably on the basis of this journey that Jaroslav was able to write some of his later stories about this region and describe in detail Švejk's 'anabasis'.*

Times grew more and more disturbed and the mother was quite unable to cope with her wayward son. There were daily scuffles on the streets between Czechs and Germans, and Jaroslav could not go out without getting into one scrape or another. The situation became so serious that posters were put up proclaiming a state of emergency. One evening Jaroslav found himself standing in front of one of them and could not resist tearing it down. After that, he and others of his gang went round pulling down all they could find and setting fire to them. The streets swarmed with police, gendarmes and troops. When armed

* *The Good Soldier Švejk*, p. 241.

dragoons with drawn swords chased the adult demonstrators, Jaroslav and his gang threw paving stones at them from behind. He succeeded in escaping by climbing over walls and hiding away in the gardens of some of the academic institutions, but not before he had thrown a large paving stone through the window of the German Institute on the other side of the road. There is a story that he was stopped by a police officer and made to turn out his pockets, which were full of stones. When asked for an explanation he replied with aggrieved innocence that they belonged to the school mineral collection and he had only borrowed them for the purpose of study. But the official complaints arising out of these escapades and excesses were too much for the Gymnasium and Jaroslav was finally expelled.

In desperation the mother turned to her brother-in-law, Jan Hašek, who was a master-printer and managed to get Jaroslav an interview at a printing works, but he was turned down on his bad school record, poor physique and ignorance of German. On the way back he saw a notice in a shop window advertising a vacancy in a chemist's shop, the Three Golden Balls. At his mother's prompting he immediately applied for it and was taken on. He was later to record his experiences in it in some of his early stories called 'From an Old Pharmacy'[13] and to refer to them again in *The Good Soldier Švejk*.

The owner of the shop, Ferdinand Kokoška, would not let Jaroslav serve at the counter but made him spend most of his time in an attic mixing drugs. This gave him the spare time he needed for his first literary efforts. Seeing him bent over a sheet of paper, Kokoška was afraid he might be copying down drug recipes and, knowing very little Czech and being short-sighted as well, he made Jaroslav read out to him what he had written. Without flinching, Jaroslav at once took up the sheet and began:

'Dear Uncle and Aunt,

'First of all, love from all of us. As you probably know I am now assistant at Mr Kokoška's pharmacy. He took me on and has become a second father to me. Indeed my own father could not have treated me better. I am very happy to be with him. I am learning very well and I already know *aqua destilata* (sic) and *spiritus veni*.* Soon I shall learn even more.'

* *Veni, Sancte Spiritus*—the words of the Mass.

Kokoška was touched. He patted Jaroslav paternally on the head and said: 'You're a good boy, and, if you show your worth, you could work yourself up to being manager with me. But you must do your writing at home. While you're here you must work and show you've really learnt something.'

Kokoška's chief assistant soon became jealous of the favour the proprietor showed Jaroslav and stirred up the rest of the staff against him. Jaroslav found that he was being given the worst jobs, but he was quite able to pay his enemy back in his own coin. Among other 'dirty tricks' he prepared fly-papers for him to get stuck in and emptied three Seidlitz powders* into the beer which he was made to fetch.

He was obviously not destined to stay long at the shop. There are two versions of how he got sacked. One was that Kokoška fancied himself as an artist and had covered the walls of his office with paintings of alpine landscapes. One day, when his chief was asleep, Jaroslav crept in and with a few strokes turned the face of one of the cows into the spit image of Kokoška himself with his pince-nez and square beard. According to the other version, while up in the attic one day, Jaroslav heard the sound of singing and the stamping of feet outside. Sticking his head out of the window, he saw a procession of striking bakers. Anxious to show his sympathy for them, he tore down the red petticoat of Kokoška's maid, which was drying in the attic, and hung it out on the roof. The strikers broke into thunderous applause, shouting out the Czech patriotic greeting of '*Nazdar*' and singing 'The Red Flag'. The police came swarming round and insisted on questioning Kokoška. This was too much for the chemist, who asked Jaroslav's guardian, Dr Škarda, to take the boy away.

Dr Škarda then found a job for Jaroslav with another chemist named Pruša. He was an easy-going man who had progressive ideas and could appreciate Jaroslav's gifts, and so, after a year, he succeeded in convincing Kateřina that a boy with such talent should not spend all his life at a shop counter. It was therefore decided to send him to the Czechoslavonic Commercial Academy[14] for his further education.

---

* A mild aperient.

(3)

The Literary Vagabond

It may seem odd that Jaroslav was sent to what sounded like a business school. He had shown no interest whatsoever in commerce; what he had shown was evidence of literary talent. But the Commercial Academy, which still exists in Prague today under the name of the Higher Economic School, had a high reputation at that time, not only as a commercial college but as a general secondary school as well, and many of its pupils were later to distinguish themselves in the field of literature, such as S. K. Neumann, the poet; Vladimír Neff, the novelist; and, in more recent times, Jan Otčenášek, author of two novels, *Citizen Brych*[1] and *Romeo and Juliet and the Darkness*.[2] In Prague at the turn of the century middle-class business circles were beginning to set the tone and a commercial school had become socially respectable, particularly when it provided a high-class general education as well. The Commercial Academy had on its staff some very distinguished teachers, including Alois Jirásek, the Czech Walter Scott; J. V. Sládek, the leading translator of Shakespeare; Ferdinand Schulz, the historian and journalist; Hanuš Jelínek, a leading scholar of French literature; and last but not least, V. A. Jung, the compiler of the standard large Anglo–Czech dictionary.

The years from 1899 to 1902 which Jaroslav spent there might well have advanced his career if he had made better use of the advantages it offered. It is true that he worked hard and passed his final examination with distinction, collecting four 'Excellents' (the highest of the traditional Czech five grades of merit) in National Economy, Commodity Studies, Chemistry and Chemical Technology. But he had little respect for the Commercial Academy as an institution and conceived a violent hatred for its Rector, Dr Řezábek. Indeed, years after he had left, he still felt animosity towards him and longed for an opportunity to vent it on him. This was not long in presenting itself. In 1908 another state of emergency had been declared in Prague; the streets were empty but Schäffer's café-bar was full, with the police drinking beer in its back-room. Jaroslav's mischievous eye lit on their greatcoats, sabres and feathered hats hanging in the lobby.* In a flash he had dressed himself up in them and dashed round the corner to a restaurant where he knew Řežábek was in the habit of taking his meals. Striding past the tables, as though chasing a criminal, he stopped in front of his unsuspecting victim. 'Are you Government Counsellor† Řežábek?' he asked in a deep official-sounding voice. The Rector, alarmed by the sudden appearance of this unknown representative of the law, could do nothing but nod affirmatively. 'Then you are under arrest. You must follow me and come quietly!' Refusing to answer his startled victim's questions, Jaroslav conducted him to the nearest police station. When they reached the entrance, he adroitly pushed him inside and shut the door behind him. Then he tore back to Schäffer's, divested himself of the borrowed plumes and went into the back-room to sit with the police. During the subsequent alarm, when all the police were suddenly recalled to the police station, he was able to feign complete surprise.

A year later he published in *Caricatures*‡[3] a short piece called 'The Commercial Academy', which began:

'Because my relations wanted to make a businessman of me, they sent me to the Commercial School. They might as well have sent me to a school for farriers. It would have been just as good.

'The Rector of this institution is Government Counsellor Jeřábek. The man was once in the service of the Tsarist régime in Russia and is one of the Black Hundred.§ He loves the nation and the government, and lives for Austria, thanks to which he obtained his title by special dispensation without having to pay for it. In Russia he pledged his life to his Little Father, the Tsar

* An Austrian policeman wore a black homburg-shaped hat with a big black plume sprouting out of it.

† A rank in the Austrian civil service equal to an assistant-secretary.

‡ A cheap satirical magazine.

§ *Chernosotenets*, the name given to the anti-revolutionary groups in Russia, 1905–7.

. . . (Here six words were obliterated by the censor.) He says himself that you ought to feel personal affection for rulers . . . He comports himself like the governor of one of the Russian state prisons. Not that there is anything dishonourable about that, of course.'

Jaroslav's sarcastic article throws a revealing light on the snobbish way Řežábek apparently ran the Commercial Academy.

'Although he knows he is a government counsellor and understands the full significance of this title, yet none the less he condescends occasionally to talk even to the junior teachers. Of course he shouts at them from time to time, but again there's nothing wrong in that, because he is rector, government counsellor etc. etc. . . . He obtained the title for his merits, his pedagogical and literary activity and his knowledge of twelve languages. But because twelve is a large number, it occasionally happens that he forgets that there is a certain language he does not know.

'For example, years ago, when he was appointed Rector, he wrote an article in a respectable paper praising himself and boasting that he could speak Persian. Later it turned out that his knowledge of Persian was limited to naming a few towns in Persia. He knew the Persian for Teheran, Tabriz etc. Anyone can know that, but not every one knows that Teheran, Tabriz etc. are in Persia. But the Rector does, and that is why he got the title of government counsellor . . .

'His watchword is: "No one is to be let off school fees. They are 120 guilders a year, and anyone who cannot pay that is a pauper and cannot be of any benefit whatsoever to the Czech nation as a businessman . . ." It often happened that if anyone was actually let off school fees, he was told by the Rector on various occasions: "Now then, remember. You have been let off school fees, and therefore you must tell us the name of the culprit." But there is nothing dishonourable in using various means of compulsion in the course of an interrogation. The Government Counsellor spent a long time in Russia—and that's the long and the short of it.'

Řežábek's insistence that the students should greet him from a long way off recalls Colonel Kraus von Zillergut in *The Good*

43

Soldier Švejk.* Woe betide anyone who failed to notice him! The culprit was given a dressing down before the whole class and his crime was recorded in the class book. In addition his marks for good behaviour were slashed and he was led off to the Rector's office, where he got a second dressing down and his parents were told of his unheard-of behaviour.

The editor of *Caricatures* at this time was the artist Josef Lada, later famous for the illustrations he made for *The Good Soldier Švejk*, but the magazine was under the general direction of the Nationalist Socialist Party and the deputy Stříbrný[4] was the responsible editor. The issue carrying Jaroslav's article was a great success, especially with the pupils of the Commercial Academy, and was quickly sold out. But Stříbrný was soon sued for libel by Řežábek and had to appear in court together with Jaroslav. When the judge asked Jaroslav what he had against the Academy, he replied defiantly that he was against all schools. When he heard this Stříbrný decided to abandon the defence and publish an apology. The task of drafting it devolved on Jaroslav, and he formulated it so ambiguously and ironically that Řežábek could have had little satisfaction from winning his case.

Not content with lampooning the Rector, Jaroslav poked fun at many of the other teachers too, although he does not appear to have got on at all badly with them. He never forgot the way they taught him to write business letters. 'With your esteemed letter to hand I beg to inform you that your esteemed sack of coffee reached us in good order', was, he maintained, an example of the style. But he had one great admirer in the lexicographer Jung, who prophesied with rare foresight that Hašek would one day become the Czech Mark Twain.

Meanwhile Jaroslav was turning his attention to what were to become the two main occupations of his life—writing and vagrancy.

In January 1901 the oldest and most important Prague daily, the *National Newspaper*,† published his first story 'Gypsies at their

* *The Good Soldier Švejk*, pp. 201–206.

† *Národní listy*, at this time the principal organ of the Young Czechs, the progressive national Czech party led by Dr Kramář and Dr Václav Škarda (the son of Dr Jakub Škarda). The writer Jan Neruda was previously associated with this paper.

Feast'.[5] In April and June it published two more, 'A Country Idyll'[6] and 'He Came in Time'.[7] These were the first fruits of a walking tour in Moravia, Slovakia and Hungary made during the summer vacation of 1900 in the company of his brother Bohuslav. One can understand how exciting it must have been for these two Czech boys—Jaroslav was only seventeen and Bohuslav fourteen—to find themselves in northern Hungary where the officials might speak Hungarian but all the peasants spoke Slovak, a language so close to Czech that it was understandable and familiar. An exotic feature of this part of Hungary was the colourful gypsy life, which particularly fascinated Jaroslav. Indeed his first published story featured the life of the gypsies on the borders of Moravia and Hungary, their merrymaking and their brawls, which had to be broken up by Austrian gendarmes.

'A Country Idyll' described the grief of a Czech peasant girl and her mother when her bridegroom-to-be suddenly died and his inheritance passed to his brother instead of to her. 'He Came in Time' told a disillusioning story of a Slovak peasant who sold all his property and emigrated to America, only to find that he had been cheated and robbed of his money, first by the Hungarians who arranged his departure and then by his companions in America. He came back a beggar, just in time to warn his cousin against following his example. These sketches show evidence of remarkable literary maturity.

The goal of the two boys' tour was probably the festival of Živena, which was held at Turčiansky Svätý Martin, the centre of Slovak national culture. During this part of the journey they were accompanied by a young Slovak friend, Jan Čulen, who had already fired their imagination with enthusiastic descriptions of his country. He brought them into contact with some of the leading members of the Slovak patriotic intelligentsia, including Dušan Makovický, who was later to become Tolstoy's doctor and one of the most faithful Tolstoyans. They were regaled everywhere with proverbial Slovak hospitality.

As Jaroslav's later writings showed, his feelings were immediately stirred by the fate of this brother people, who were leading a hard life under the oppressive rule of the Magyars. He inscribed a little poem in the autograph album of the daughter of a Slovak schoolteacher, in which he expressed the hope that she would always remain a Slovak patriot.

This was the time when the Czechs were beginning to waken to the beauties of Slovakia and the wretched plight of its peasants, an awakening akin to the sudden romantic interest in the Lake District taken by English poets at the beginning of the nineteenth century. Just about the same time the composers Vítězslav Novák and Leoš Janáček were jointly collecting Moravian and Slovak folk melodies. In Novák's case this was to culminate in his beautiful symphonic poem *In the Tatras*[8] and his *Slovak Songs*.[9]

During the summer holidays of the following year, 1901, the two brothers went off once more in the company of two or three of Jaroslav's fellow pupils, this time to explore the Polish-inhabited northern slopes of the Tatras. They met in Galicia and made extensive tours all over it. On the way they reached Zakopane on the borders of Hungary (Slovakia). It lay in a broad sunny valley along the river Dunajec and commanded a magnificent view of the Tatras from the Galician side. It was even then a favourite excursion point for tourists, especially for Poles. From these the boys crossed over to the Hungarian side of the mountain ridge. Jaroslav was immensely proud of their feat of crossing the 6,500-foot-high passes without a guide in spite of the severe cold.

He did not confine his tramps abroad to the immediate neighbourhood of Bohemia but penetrated as far as the Balkans and the Turkish frontier. The titles of his stories give a fair indication of the range of the countries he visited. In 1902 the *National Newspaper*[10] published several more of them, some of which foreshadowed the true Hašek style and introduced for the first time an anti-romantic, cynical and challenging note. One, 'The End of the Monkey',[11] described the heart-rending lamentations of a group of gypsies over their pet monkey, which had just died. The death struggles of the unfortunate animal were vividly reproduced, followed by the crying and weeping of the gypsies, which lasted only until they began to feel hungry, when they all at once forgot all about their grief and decided to cook and eat it.

This was the perverse and tasteless strain in Jaroslav which was to be a feature of some of his writings from then on. Some biographers have attributed it to the difficult circumstances of his life, his frustrations and failures. But here we find this streak coming out in him when he was no older than eighteen or nineteen and could feel proud at having had so many of his stories accepted by a paper like the *National Newspaper*. It published four more in 1901 and twenty in 1902. The Social Democrat paper the *People's Right*[12] published two in 1902 and the *Illustrated World*[13] two in 1903.

At the Commercial Academy Jaroslav formed a close friendship with Ladislav Hájek, who was a budding writer like himself. Together they used to go to the literary club Syrinx, of which various future leading Czech writers and dramatists were members, such as K. H. Hilar (later to become director of the Prague National Theatre under the Republic), Josef Mach (a publicist who went to America and became an ardent propagandist there for the Czechoslovak cause), Jiří Mahen (afterwards a leading playwright), Rudolf Těsnohlídek (the author of the story of Janáček's opera *The Cunning Little Vixen*[14]), and Jaroslav's friend, the poet Opočenský.

He liked the members of the club and enjoyed sharing their bohemian life, taking an active part in the rowdy evenings they held at the beer-house U Fleku, which is well known to tourists in Prague today. The tone of their conversation can be judged by the words which one of the members, a sculptor, is said to have once addressed to Jaroslav: 'Come here, you hairy bastard, and let me tear all those lice off you!' But, as time went by, Jaroslav came to the club less and less, because, never a serious student of culture in any form, the 'modern art' which its members professed meant nothing to him.

In June 1902 he completed his studies at the Commercial Academy and went off on his third holiday in Slovakia. On his return his mother persuaded him to apply for the post of clerk in the Insurance Bank of Slavie. He was accepted on October 1st, 1902 and started work there. But he did not hold the appointment long. According to Bohuslav he could not stick the head of his section. 'He's such a donkey,' Jaroslav told him. 'He's always asking me where the various districts are, as if he didn't know anything about Bohemia at all. "Pluhařovice—in which district is that, Mr Hašek? Žitnoves—where is that? Do you know in which district Dešenice is?" I can't bear breathing the same air as a cow like that. He makes me mad!'

Bohuslav described how his brother came to part company with the bank in the spring of 1903:

'One day Jaroslav had a special errand to perform at Vyše-hrad. On the way he stopped at a pub and took a decision. He packed up his ledger, put his visiting card inside and sent it by messenger to the bank. The message on the card was short and sweet:

"I'm not baking today!*
Jaroslav Hašek"

'At home he didn't say a word about it and got up early the next day to go to the office as though nothing had happened. "Please come back to lunch, Jaroslav," his mother urged him. "Today we're going to have goose liver!" "Of course I shall," he said, licking his lips, because it was his favourite dish. But two o'clock passed and the evening and the next day, and there was no sign of him. A few weeks later we received a letter from him. He was tramping about Slovakia without a farthing in his pocket. And how did he manage it? Quite simply. He always fell on his feet. In each village he would apply to the Catholic presbytery and ask for hospitality, casually remarking that he had applied to the Protestant vicarage and been turned away. The Catholic priest, with an eye to competition, took him in and sometimes even gave him something for his further journey. The next day he applied to the Protestant vicarage, saying that he had been turned away at the Catholic presbytery. And so the Protestant vicar felt obliged to give him hospitality too.'

Bohuslav relates how after a considerable interval—he says ten months but it could only have been a few weeks—Jaroslav turned up again in the doorway of their home, wearing his eternal smile. 'Well, what about it, Mama?' he burst out before she could get a word in. 'Where's that liver? I'm terrifically hungry!'[15]

After this escapade—his fourth visit to Slovakia—the bank was generous enough to take him back, but when at the end of May 1903 he took French leave once more, he was finally given the sack.

* This expression means in Czech 'I'm downing tools'.

A few months previously Hájek and Jaroslav had published a volume of poems together, *Cries of May*,[16] in which their verses appeared on alternate pages. Jaroslav had promised the publisher that he would help to find purchasers in the bank, but the book appeared the day after he had walked out and so there was no one there to help with its promotion. One of Jaroslav's poems 'In the Garden in Spring',[17] described a group of 'pale maidens' who, entranced by the tulips and hyacinths in a garden, dreamed ecstatically of the 'handsome young gardener' who had planted them. But the gardener turned out to be a grey-haired old man who, when he was planting the bed, had 'grunted, spat and cursed like a madman, rubbing his red nose with his sleeve'. 'Hell,' he had sworn, 'if I were master here today I'm damned if I'd plant any of these tulips. Blast every one of them!'

These lines made the publisher see red. ' "Hell" and "Blast"!' he shouted. 'Is that poetry? No, there's only one word for it. Muck!' However, when the critic in *National Policy*[18] wrote approvingly of the volume and said that it augured well for the authors, he was pleased as Punch and quite forgot what he had said.

Gradually Jaroslav was earning a small income through his literary contributions. Apart from one or two published poems, we know of five stories dating from 1901, twenty in 1902, twelve in 1903 and thirteen in 1904—fifty in four years. This was quite a respectable quantity for a beginner, but not nearly enough to pay for his keep or contribute to the family funds. His mother, who was in severe financial straits, was desperate.

Hájek has left us a portrait of what Jaroslav looked like at the age of eighteen and we can compare it with his photograph. He describes him as a bright, intelligent boy, with dark brown sparkling eyes and unruly chestnut curls falling in disorder over his face. Rosy-cheeked, the dark down under his nose was the only jarring element in his otherwise completely girlish face. He had inherited his mother's finely moulded mouth but not her bright and intense blue or grey eyes. He probably had his own dark eyes and pensive, rather melancholy look from his father.

Hájek mentions that during his time at the chemist's shops Jaroslav was taught how to make fireworks and it became a hobby of his to make Roman candles and Bengal lights. His room was full of 'stinks' bottles. (As we have read, he had obtained an 'Excellent' in chemistry at the Commercial Academy.) Once when Hájek visited him in his mother's flat, he found him busily mixing something. 'What are you doing?' 'I'm making a bomb,' Hašek replied. Not long afterwards there was an almighty explosion and several window panes were shattered. His mother came rushing out of the kitchen in alarm, but Jaroslav disarmed them all by saying with his captivating smile: 'I mixed it too well.' He rushed up to his scared mother, kissed her and begged her not to be angry, saying he would repair the window out of the fees he got for his stories.

At this period he fancied himself as a revolutionary, and grew enthusiastic about Russian writers. In his tramps about the country he liked to model himself on Gorki and wanted Hájek and himself 'to live like Russians'. He also picked up a little Serbian, was in contact with many Serbian students and began to wear a red and black cap of Serbian type. Whenever there was any demonstration he was sure to be found in the front ranks. Fortunately Police Commissioner Fahoun, whom he got to know through tutoring his son, helped him out of many a scrape. Later another police officer, whom he met through one of his fellow ex-employees at the chemist's shop, held a protecting hand over him too.

He and Hájek used to visit the lowest haunts they could find in old Prague, Jaroslav dressing up in tattered clothes, an open shirt and a peaked cap. He had developed not only a taste for 'the lower depths' but a strange and persistent penchant for hoaxing people as well. Once, while he was walking in the evening in the busiest part of the town, he suddenly stopped, stooped down and lit a match, anxiously searching the ground and audibly lamenting. Eventually a crowd gathered round him and searched in sympathy. Finally one of them asked him what he had lost. Jaroslav rose and smiled. 'You didn't really think I was searching for something? Oh, no, I just got rather bored and made a little light here.'

Hájek had a room opposite the Týn church in the house of his uncle, a painter of stained glass and a crusty old bachelor, who lived with his aged mother. Because of his whiskers Jaroslav nicknamed him 'the Monarch' after Francis Joseph. When the moon shone through the window at night it lit up the coloured figure of a grey-bearded St Peter holding an enormous key in one hand and raising the other in solemn warning. It gave the whole room an ecclesiastical, almost ghoulish air. Sometimes, when Jaroslav returned late with Hájek after their night wanderings, he did not want to go home but slept the night in Hájek's bed, gazing long at the stained glass and making ribald remarks about the saint.

One morning they both slept late. The Monarch was highly suspicious. Deceived by the sight of Jaroslav's curls and youthful girlish looks, he walked through their bedroom several times, muttering in his beard and staring furiously at the bed where Jaroslav and Hájek lay curled up together. Then he slammed the door and could be heard snorting angrily: 'The monstrous impudence of it! Bringing a woman into his uncle's flat and sleeping with her in his bed!'

When they got up and dressed, there was the Monarch waiting outside to give his nephew hell. But Jaroslav met him with the disarming remark: 'Mr Pazdera, I'm not a girl, you know. I'm a man like you are. I'm Jaroslav Hašek, the writer.'[19]

He was certainly not a girl, but he was in no sense a responsible adult.

(4)

The Would-Be Anarchist

The period of unemployment for Hašek which followed his departure from the bank was a bad beginning for him. He quickly became involved in scrapes and minor conflicts with the police. Details of his disorderly and sometimes violent behaviour were being collected and recorded in a fairly voluminous file at police headquarters. It is true that the charges against him were mostly minor breaches of the law, but they caused the authorities a lot of trouble and they were remarkably tolerant to him, all things considered, as one typical instance revealed:

'On October 6th, 1903, at 9.15 p.m. Police Sergeant V. S. brought in the twenty-one-year-old writer, Jaroslav Hašek, domiciled at Vinohrady No. 195, because, while in an intoxicated state, the above-named had performed his lesser bodily needs in front of the building of the main police station . . .'

An indulgent official had crossed out the end of the sentence which had originally read: '. . . which caused considerable indignation among the passers-by.'

He was sentenced to a paltry fine for damaging the pavement and to six hours' imprisonment, should the money be unrecoverable. In the event it took the court three years to get the fine out of him. First he was untraceable and then, when the police finally got on to his address, he had no money to pay it. In fact the artful young man made a profit out of the incident by writing a humorous sketch on the subject, which earned him a modest fee. Indeed so many of his pranks provided source material for his literary work that one is tempted to think that this could have been one of his main motives for playing them.

Early in 1904 the Russo–Japanese War had broken out. This inevitably stirred up feelings in Prague, the Right supporting the Tsarist government and the Left hoping for its defeat. On February 22nd the members of the Prague Civic Council held prayers for the victory of the Tsarist troops in front of the Church of St Nicholas in the Old Town Square, at that time serving as a Russian Orthodox church. The Anarchist and Social Demo-cratic youth tried to break up the ceremony with shouts of 'Down with the Tsar!'

On that day Hašek was among these young and noisy demon-strators and was arrested and held for questioning. In the course of the disturbances he met the Anarchist Václav Křížek, who persuaded him to be co-author of a radical pamphlet attacking the 'reformist' policy of the Social Democratic Party and brought him into contact with a branch of the Anarchist movement led by Karel Vohryzek, the director of *Progressive Youth*, and with Bedřich Kalina, its editor.

Hardly had a month passed when a further brush with the police was recorded: 'Jaroslav Hašek was brought in . . . be-cause on the night of March 31st, 1904, while in a slightly inebriated condition, he damaged two protecting fences round the trees.' While loitering about with a group of rowdies, he had suddenly noticed that the fences round the trees were not placed at the same height and insisted on adjusting them 'on aesthetic grounds'.

Then came a fourth arrest, this time on April 27th, 1904, for lying about on the ground in a state of drunken torpor at about 10.30 p.m. On the back of the report another tolerant police official had minuted: 'Was celebrating and drank himself blind. Can be released.' The next day at twelve noon he was dis-charged.

After all these incidents, petty as they were, Hašek felt it wiser to disappear from Prague for a while. The police were still chas-ing him in the hope of recovering the fine of two crowns for the damage to the pavement. In July 1904 his mother told them that his last address had been Lom (Bruch) near Duchcov (Dux). Both these places lay in northern Bohemia in the heart of the brown coal country, the so-called Most (Brux) basin. Hašek had chosen to go there with Kalina and Křížek (presum-ably in May 1904), because the Anarchist movement had a firm foothold among the miners in that region.

It was only natural that Hašek should be attracted towards

Anarchism. Not that he had any deep-seated radical convictions:
he was quite happy to offer his stories and *feuilletons* to a leading
bourgeois daily like the *National Newspaper* or to the journals of
the Otto publishing house and try to extort advances from their
cashiers. It was just that he was 'agin the government'—opposed
to authority, whatever form it took, and instinctively up in arms
against those who tried to discipline him, whether they were
his employers, superiors, teachers, the bureaucracy or the
police.

Most of us, at least those of us who have been used to living
under stable governments, can with difficulty repress a shudder
when we read the word 'Anarchist'. This is partly because
'anarchy' in its sense of the collapse of law and order has for us
a particularly sinister ring: when we say a country is on the
verge of anarchy, we mean that it is on the brink of disaster, and
of course we associate Anarchism with political assassination and
terrorism.

But to the younger generation of Czechs the word did not
conjure up this frightening spectacle. Although they had been
living under a stable government ever since 1849, they regarded
not only that government but the whole constitutional system
in the Monarchy as anti-Czech. In Bohemia the Anarchist
movement was for a time the only substitute for a radical Left,
since there was then no Communist Party and the programme
of the Social Democratic Party was too moderate, cautious and
constitutional for the taste of the radical youth. The Social
Democratic panacea for all the injustices of society was universal
franchise, which the young radicals dismissed as nothing more
than a perpetuation of the existing system, especially as the
Party, being composed of both Germans and Czechs, was international rather than national in outlook and saw better pro-
spects for the movement within a larger conglomeration than
within the narrower confines of Bohemia alone.

Naturally the older generation judged Anarchism by the recent wave of political assassinations which had horrified the
world and in which Anarchists had had a hand. Two years
before Hašek's birth the Russian Tsar Alexander II had been
assassinated, and in the next twenty years a President of France,
the Empress of Austria and the King of Italy had all fallen victims
to murderous attacks. But these were not necessarily the blind

and senseless crimes they were usually taken for. They were, the Anarchists maintained, no more than a retaliation for the acts of torture and the executions perpetrated against their followers (notably the execution of four Chicago Anarchists in 1887).

But the Czech bourgeoisie had the uncomfortable feeling that the Anarchist campaign was directed just as much against them as against the Habsburgs and Romanovs. Moreover they held fast to the precepts of their former leaders, Palacký and Havlíček, who had always maintained that the Czech people would have more to lose than gain from violent revolution.

When a judge once reproached a French Anarchist for jeopardising the lives of innocent men and women, he replied: 'There can be no innocent bourgeois.' A philosophy which professed and justified complete disregard for the rights, principles and self-respect of the bourgeoisie was naturally anathema to the respectable citizen. But it was likely to have a strong appeal for Hašek, who seldom wrote of anyone in authority, Czech or German, with respect. Men of public affairs, church leaders, doctors, historians, archaeologists, romantic writers, were for him nothing more than rogues, impostrs or figures of fun. The bourgeoisie was a class which it was necessary and right to shock—perhaps even to blow up! It certainly needed a 'good hiding'.

Some twenty years earlier the workers in the north Bohemian brown-coal fields and the north-eastern textile mills had fallen for a time under the very strong influence of the German proponent of 'individual Anarchism', Johann Most, whose radical journal *Die Freiheit* was then being smuggled into Bohemia from England, where he was living in exile, until he was sent to prison for eighteen months for praising the assassination of the Tsar. But with his subsequent emigration to America the Anarchist movement in Bohemia dropped political assassination from its programme and concentrated on the 'economic' or industrial struggle (such as the reduction of working hours, revision of wages etc.). Its chief weapon of 'direct action' was the general strike, which it propagated as a more attractive and effective slogan than 'universal suffrage'. It still preserved the concept of 'individual Anarchism' in the sense that it was opposed to most forms of organisation or collective action, such as contact with Anarchist movements abroad. It opposed the dictatorship of the proletariat and denied the right of any party to speak for the working man.[1]

In Prague, however, and in its most radical suburb, Žižkov, another branch of the movement had developed under S. K. Neumann.[2] It too denied the necessity for the existence of the state but believed in political action in the form of anti-militarist, anti-religious and anti-clerical agitation. While the Anarchists in the north were led by a doubtful character called Vohryzek and were in fact Anarcho-syndicalists, the Prague branch under Neumann were supporters of Collective Anarchism, later to be called Anarcho-Communism. A feature of their philosophy was 'the revolutionary liberation of the individual'. The idea of achieving this by 'personal involvement in the social struggle' stirred the hearts of many idealistic young poets and writers of the time. At the café-bar 'At the Otčenášeks' in the Prague suburb of Vinohrady, Neumann collected around him some of the most gifted young poets, like Karel Toman, Fráňa Šrámek and František Gellner. As a young writer in touch with some of his contemporaries, Hašek was drawn towards the abstract philosophy of Anarchism which fascinated Neumann's circle and, as a born rebel against society, warmed to the idea of 'direct action' which was popular with the workers in the north.

Neumann as a poet with a wide cultural spectrum was able to attract young intellectuals thanks to the various Anarchist periodicals he edited. (Their lease of life was always short and they were speedily replaced by other journals with different names—partly to escape censorship difficulties.) These journals and the lectures he gave in his house at Olšany at Žižkov kept up with contemporary developments in art and literature abroad.

Neumann, who was of aristocratic descent on his father's side but whose mother was the daughter of a shoemaker, started his literary activity by contributing to the anti-realist, symbolist and 'decadent' journal *Modern Review*.[3] Later he took over the editorship of the *New Cult*[4] and made it the vehicle for his own ideas. He was also responsible for its satirical supplement *Gallows*[5] which began to appear in 1906. He had, as we have seen, been imprisoned at the age of eighteen for his alleged part in the 'Progressive Youth' 'conspiracy' and combined a flair for the decadent verse of the *fin-de-siècle* with radical social views. His poem 'I Am the Apostle of the New Life' was much in vogue at the time. He was an outstanding poet and the only personality of any dimension in the Anarchist movement. His influence on the younger generation of his time was very considerable indeed.

And so, to judge from police reports and his story 'A Fairy Tale from the East',[6] Hašek was to be found in the summer of 1904 in Lom, working in the day and sleeping at night on a straw mattress in the office of *Progressive Youth*.[7] It had been recently taken over by the Czech Federation of Trade Unions[8] as the group of 'individual and economic' Anarchists had called themselves. Originally founded in Prague in 1893, the journal had moved around to various towns in Bohemia. At one time it had been edited by Neumann but now it was under the direction of Vohryzek and the editorship of Kalina.

One night, an hour after Hašek had gone to sleep, someone started to kick at the door. Gendarmes broke in, woke him up roughly and began to interrogate him. Others searched the premises, examining even the spittoons and the perambulator of the Kalina family who lived in an adjoining room.

Hašek did not allow himself to be intimidated by police raids but carried on with his job. He attended Anarchist meetings and gave lectures on geographical and political themes. Riding on a bicycle he distributed newspapers and leaflets to the miners. According to Kalina he even worked for a short time in the *Barbra* mine in the neighbourhood.

Hašek also contributed to the paper, writing in 'Aesopic language'* to escape intervention by the censors. Sometimes he made use of Arabian or Assyrian names as in the 'Cuneiform Inscription'[9] or 'A Fairy Tale from the East', where he used *Idalmo* as a partial anagram for *Omladina*. According to the bibliography of Hašek's works he published half a dozen articles or poems during the short time he worked in Lom.

One of his reasons for joining the Anarchists was that he was finding it increasingly impossible to work for anyone at all. Soon he began to realise that he could not work for them either. He grew dissatisfied with conditions on the paper and thought he was being cheated. It was not long before he reached the conclusion that the whole Anarchist 'conspiracy' was 'boundlessly

* Political writing disguised as a fable – a technique employed by Russian writers.

naive, transparent and primitive'. To his mind the Anarchists were not one whit better organised than the political parties. And so, as soon as he had scraped together enough funds, he gave up the job. He left Lom early in July, having arrived there little more than a month previously.

The Anarchists on their side were just as suspicious of him. One day he borrowed the office bicycle to visit supporters and subscribers and collect money. A few days later he was found with a bandage on his head suffering from a bad hangover. (A bicycle story crops up repeatedly in his biography: it is part of the Hašek legend.) When one of the staff of the paper remonstrated with him, he angrily left Lom for good. In due course Vohryzek went to Prague and tried to claim the money back from his mother.

Quite apart from the fact that Vohryzek's enthusiasm for 'economic Anarchism' based on a federation of Anarchist-directed Trade Unions was not likely to appeal to Hašek, there was some justification for his suspicions of the Anarchist movement as a whole. Some of the leaders were very queer fish indeed. Vohryzek had been mixed up in various scandals including smuggling and embezzlement, and it did not help the cause when he was finally arrested and sentenced for robbing a jeweller's establishment. There were also grounds for suspecting that the movement had been infiltrated by the Austrian police and that Vohryzek was one of their agents. It was odd, to say the least, that on the outbreak of war he was taken into the accountancy branch of the army in spite of his history, and his records were not marked 'Politically unreliable', as was normally the case with Anarchists. Austrian police attempts to penetrate the movement were colourfully described by Hašek in a *feuilleton* called 'On the Tracks of the State Police in Prague'[10] which he published in the Czech newspaper *Čechoslovan*[11] in Russia in 1916. According to his account, at the time of a forthcoming visit of the Emperor Francis Joseph to Prague, the editorial staff of *New Progressive Youth*[12] (the successor to *Progressive Youth*), where Hašek was working, received a visit from a Pietro Perri, purportedly a member of the Italian Anarchist movement who had just arrived from Russia with an article written against the Emperor in bad German. When Hašek noticed that the visitor's Italian and German sounded like a literal translation from

Czech, he naturally smelt a rat, and said loudly to the others in Czech: 'Let's take him to the bathroom and cut his throat.' 'Pietro Perri' turned white with fear and was taken away trembling to stay the night with another of the editorial staff. The next day he absconded with all the private papers he could find in the house. Fortunately they were quite unimportant.

The Anarchists burnt the article which 'Perri' had left in their office. It was a seditious document which could have cost them twenty years' imprisonment if it had been found in their possession. It was as well they did so, since there was a prolonged police raid on the office that very evening.

According to Menger, Hašek and his friends took their revenge on 'Pietro Perri'. He cites *National Policy* as having published an article as follows: 'Yesterday at 8 p.m. ... three Prague revellers, one of them dressed in women's clothes, stopped in a cab in front of the police station. The other two, apparently in an intoxicated state, pretended that the third, who was so drunk that he lay unconscious on the pavement, was a serious case of spotted typhus. Both the others disappeared in the Prague streets without paying for the cab ...'

The one left on the pavement was none other than 'Pietro Perri' whom the others had beaten, chloroformed and dressed in women's clothes. He was found to have a note pinned to him:

'I present this monster to the men of the secret political department, Messrs Gellner and Slavíček, for the zoo in the Emperor's palace in Vienna.

Hagenbeck'*

This did not prevent the appearance at the editorial office of another odd visitor who offered his services in connection with the Emperor's visit. This time it was a man whose head was covered with bandages and who told an affecting story of how he had worked politically among the miners in Lom and had been beaten up by German nationalists. But there was something strangely familiar about his voice and handwriting, and at Hašek's prompting the editor tore off the bandages and found 'Pietro Perri' again, who, now under a final threat of death, confessed that he was in reality Alexander Mašek and worked for the Austrian police. Mašek happened to be in Russia when

* The owner of a famous zoo in Hamburg.

Hašek's *feuilleton* about the Austrian Secret Police appeared and *Čechoslovan* saw to it that he was caught and gaoled. He was later shot without trial by the Czech legionaries.

The Austrian police were by no means always as clumsy and crude as this. They may have had their Brettschneiders,* but some fifty years earlier they had suborned the leading Czech radical Karel Sabina, the respected librettist of *The Bartered Bride*.[13] Sabina was probably in touch with all the Czech anti-Austrian elements and it was not until the end of his life that he admitted to having been in Austrian pay during most of his career. His merits as the librettist of the famous Czech national opera were deemed by his countrymen to have partially atoned for his treason. So devoted are the Czechs to the music of Smetana! Another notorious case of the successful bribing of Czech politicians was that of Karel Šviha, the president of the club of the deputies of the National Socialist Party, who in a famous trial was accused of acting as a paid police informant. When the archives were opened in 1918 he was shown to have been working for the Archduke Francis Ferdinand for many years!

It is quite possible that from their penetration of all possible subversive movements the Austrian police were satisfied that Hašek presented no danger to them and that this accounts for their lenient treatment of him. Alternatively, their policy may have been to give him as much rope as possible in the hope that he would one day put the noose round his own neck, just as his young fellow-Anarchists had once put it round the neck of the old Emperor 'Franz'.

By now Hašek was beginning to feel that Prague had become too hot for him again, so he decided to disappear on another of his tramping trips in Europe, but in spite of his disillusionment with the Anarchists at Lom he did not break with the movement and continued to work for it in Prague when he returned.

From Lom he appears to have gone to Bavaria. Somewhere in the plain between Spalt and Nuremberg he took a job as a hop-picker. He received money, either from his wages as a labourer or from the newspapers he wrote for, and with it was able to see more of Bavaria and even range further afield, possibly to Switzerland. The sketches he wrote about this journey

* *The Good Soldier Švejk*, p. 6.

are interesting for the contrast they present with his usual writings about Germans.

The title of one, 'Justice in Bavaria',[14] is ironical but not unkind. He tells how he was arrested in Hochstadt on the Danube when on his way to Dillingen to collect fifty marks from the post office there. In spite of his explanations he was put into gaol, because he only had eight pfennigs on him at the time and was therefore technically a vagrant. If he had had two marks ninety-nine pfennigs it would have been just the same. Three marks was the minimum to avoid arrest. It took forty-five days for the court to reach a verdict, but during that time he was kept in a very cosy prison and well looked after by his gaoler, who even took him with him on a family outing. The only disturbing feature of his stay in prison was that he had to be confined in the tower, because the lower rooms could not be used. 'You see, the building is on the verge of collapse,' the gaoler told him. A minor disadvantage was that he had to be continually taking his shoes on and off, changing from the slippers he wore in the 'preserved' part of the castle into ordinary boots when he had to appear before the authorities. After he had been held in detention for a month and a half, he was finally sentenced to three days' imprisonment and on his discharge was paid one mark twenty pfennigs per day for all the excess forty-two days he had spent in prison, i.e. a total of fifty marks forty pfennigs. Finally he was escorted to the town by the judge, the gaoler and his family, who wept as they took leave of him. Another example of how Jaroslav always fell on his feet! 'That was justice in Bavaria,' Jaroslav concluded. Very different from justice in the Monarchy!

He certainly made fun of the Bavarians in 'The Tourist Guide in the German Town of Neuburg',[15] but again he did so with indulgent humour and sympathy. He related how the guide, Jogelli Klopter, offered him his services for 'four marks and food and drink'. But anxiously eyeing his belly, which was gargantuan even by Bavarian standards, Hašek said: 'You're rather too good a trencherman, I fancy. If you had been leaner ...' 'Christ Jesus,' replied the guide, 'you should have seen my late father! And what about my late grandfather? Why, he ate a whole ham, a bowl of dumplings and a pot of cabbage just as an appetiser!'

Normally Jaroslav reserved his bitterest sarcasm for the German Austrians, especially the Germans in Bohemia. Witness his stories 'How Hans Hutter and Franz Stockmaynegg Defended Vienna's German Character'[16] or 'Adele Thoms from Haida, the German Schoolteacher'.[17] Why then was he suddenly so indulgent to the Bavarians? Probably the explanation was that at the time, when he had to leave Prague to escape the attentions of the Austrian police, he felt violent bitterness against everything Austrian. The Bavarians were not Austrians and for once appeared in a better light than his fellow-citizens.

Judging from the motifs of some of his alpine stories ('The Little Donkey Guat')[18] Jaroslav reached Switzerland and wandered about near Lake Constance or somewhere on the foothills of the Bernese Alps. He apparently reached Bolzano in the Tyrol (referred to in 'The Affair with the Telescope')[19] and from there he went back to the Regensburg road.

His story 'The Great Day'[20] provides evidence of his return from his Bavarian expedition. Here he described how on his way back he stopped at Domažlice and stayed with Hájek on his sister's birthday. He was looking so down and out by this time that he thought it prudent to warn the Hájeks of this before his arrival, for Hájek senior was a director of the local credit bank and a man of some position in the town.

'I am in a rather odd condition [Jaroslav wrote] because my shoes are torn and the rest of my outfit doesn't make a particularly attractive impression. I am writing to you to make sure that I shan't be thrown out, if by any chance you're not at home when I arrive. Please explain to all at your home that if a low character appears with the suspicious look of a vagabond, he can be identified as me by the felt hat on his head. It has completely lost its shape and has three long crow's feathers sticking out of it.'

And it was just as he had described. He appeared in torn rags and in baggy grey trousers he had got from a Bavarian gendarme. But the stories he told about his eccentric experiences fascinated the respectable Hájek family none the less. Difficulties arose only when he started to drink. He behaved as if he thought he were half-gypsy and half-Hungarian; he started to

swear like a real tramp in three languages—German, Hungarian
and Czech—rolled his eyes and refused to stop drinking. Finally
one of the guests who was a doctor seized an enormous old key
and pointed it at him, pretending it was a revolver. Then he
allowed himself to be put to bed like the Chaplain Katz.*

The next day he was, as usual, abjectly sorry for what he had
done and started to cry and ask for forgiveness. But this did not
prevent him continuing to sponge on the family. He spent about
a fortnight in Domažlice and gave a lecture to the local academic club about his various journeys. When his host at last
hinted to him in the friendliest possible way that he might perhaps be being expected at home, he suddenly took umbrage,
borrowed money from a local musician and left for Prague.

But there he was soon in trouble again. The police report
states that on January 1st, 1905, in spite of frequent warnings,
Hašek continued to wave his arms about violently among the
passers-by, and so caused a breach of the peace. 'The arrested was
very drunk and assaulted German students at the police station
here.' He was detained and released again. On the back of the
report there was again an indulgent comment written in another
hand: 'Hašek states that he was very drunk and only remembers
that he had a quarrel with someone in Na Příkopě.† He was unable to state anything more. The case is unimportant . . .' On
June 20th he was brought in again for lighting three street
lamps which were out and for reacting violently to his arrest.
He was put into solitary confinement for a short time.

During the rest of 1904 and 1905 he published no more arti-
cles in Anarchist journals. Instead his contributions appeared
in the more remunerative bourgeois papers like the *National
Newspaper*, the *Illustrated World*, *Horizon*,[21] the *People's Forum*,[22]
Illustrated Czech Humorous Stories,[23] *National Policy*, *Neruda*, *Merry
Prague*, *New Neruda*[24] and *Lantern*.[25] It was a good crop indeed.

---

* *The Good Soldier Švejk*, p. 117.

† A fashionable street in Prague resembling Am Graben (On the Moat) in
Vienna and meaning the same.

(5)

Jarmila

Up to now the only feminine influences in Hašek's life had been his mother and his cousin, Máňa. He was devoted to the former, who spoiled him, and on very good terms with the latter, who had her own money and often helped him out with loans when he was hard up. At school he had an occasional rendezvous with a girl, but probably more to demonstrate to his young male friends that he was a normal young man than out of any strong sexual urge.

There is no record of his having had any amorous adventures on his travels in Central Europe and the Balkans (apart from what happened to him in Slovakia, to be described in one of his letters to Jarmila), nor is there any hint of them in his many stories for which his wanderings provided the material. His close companions on these occasions were either his younger brother, Bohuslav, or one of his young friends, the Slovak Čulen or the Czech Janota. There is no evidence that these friendships were more than ephemeral either, although his relations with Hájek, who was his boon companion in his bohemian adventures in Prague, seem to have been particularly close.

One would have expected that at least by the age of twenty-one Hašek would have begun to take an interest in the other sex, but he seems to have suffered from retarded adolescence.

A story told by Menger may throw light on the cause. He claims that when he was in Russia, Hašek told him how as a boy he had met a dissolute young sailor, who took him off on disreputable escapades and encouraged him to watch his sexual orgies. Later Hašek spoke with disgust of this man and the trauma he had caused him.

The first signs of a change in Hašek came when, on his return from his wanderings at the end of 1905 or the beginning of 1906, he made the acquaintance of Slávka Hajnišová, who was the daughter of a schoolmaster at Helfštýn near Přerov in Moravia. When he had a fall she bandaged his leg, after which he stayed with her parents for a few days. Later she came to Prague to study at the Women's Manufacturing Association,*[1] where she met Hašek again and introduced him to four of her friends— Vilma Kokešová, who later became known as the novelist and playwright Vilma Warausová; Helena Milotová; Máňa, the sister of the future writer Lila Bubelová; and Jarmila Mayerová. And so, after having had no girl companions for so long, he suddenly acquired five of them.

In her memoirs, which were published in 1965,[2] Vilma has described Hašek's appearance at this time. He did not seem at all romantic, but was very handsome with his brown eyes and curly chestnut hair. His face was almost girlish with its soft pink complexion. He looked healthy and well nourished and seemed level-headed.

They all went on expeditions in the surroundings of Prague and had refreshments at inns on the outskirts of the city. Not only were they all emancipated young women, some of them privately believing in 'free love'; some were of a literary turn of mind as well, which Hašek as a budding author did his best to encourage and develop. He used to read them his humorous sketches, which were later to be published under the title *The Sufferings of Mr Then*.[3]

Vilma found some of his poems and stories tasteless. She had not changed her mind about this by 1965. They must have talked about the unusual young man at home, because their parents apparently became suspicious of their meetings and for-bade them to have anything more to do with their new acquaintance. It was not long before Hašek had had enough of the flirtatious and feather-brained Slávka, who knew next to nothing about literature and politics and was embarrassed when he talked to her about them, and began to transfer his interest to Vilma instead. He asked her twice to go out with him, but she only agreed reluctantly, because she did not understand him and could not be sure whether he meant what he said or was only pulling her leg. She was after all the baby of the five.

---

* One of the schools set up in Prague to train young women in commerce. The Commercial Academy did not accept them.

Slávka was responsive but unintelligent, Vilma intelligent but unresponsive. Hašek gave up Vilma, looked a little further off and found Jarmila, who satisfied him on both counts.

She was not pretty. Freckled, snub-nosed and so short-sighted that she had to wear pince-nez, she had the appearance of a blue stocking, except that she was elegantly and fashionably dressed. But there was something appealing and tantalising in her sensitive and piquant little face. And her timid look seemed to call for his protection.

The two had a lot in common. She had an ironical, quizzical way of talking, which matched or parried his. They shared a love for literature, studied it together and attended courses in Russian and Polish at the Central Workers' School.[4] She sympathised with his political views and admired his independence. Having four brothers who had had their own studios, painted models in the nude and mixed with bohemian company, she was not alarmed by his hatred of the bourgeoisie, although she was one of them. But in some ways they were contrasting characters. Although she prided herself on being emancipated, she was in fact reserved, timid, conventional in some matters and rather puritanical in most. Her young friend was just the opposite. Above all she was practical and business-like, which he was not.

Her father, Josef Mayer, was a wealthy partner in a firm of plasterers and sculptors, who owned a three-storey house in Vinohrady, a fashionable suburb of Prague next to the New Town. Son of a mill-hand, he had worked his way up to the top and had provided all his children with a good education, insisting that they should learn a craft as well, so that they could maintain themselves by their own hands, if necessary. A self-made man, he was understandably suspicious when his daughter, on whom he doted, became friendly with an impecunious writer and Anarchist.

But Jarmila loved and admired Hašek for being both. She had various pet names for him. Once, when they had gone on an expedition together, she had slipped on a rock and sprained her ankle, and he had to carry her to the nearest station. From then on she called him 'Grýša', which she supposed to be a diminutive of Richard Coeur de Lion, her favourite hero in history, although it was really short for the Russian Grigori. She also used countless variations of the name Míťa, which again she quite wrongly supposed to derive from the Anarchist Mikhail Bakunin. It was short for Dimitri.

During the summer holidays of 1906, when she went away to Libáň[5] to stay with her relations, the couple fell deeply in love, but in the autumn after her return there was a row in the Mayer household and she was told that she must have nothing more to do with her Grýša. She commented on the event to a friend in an elegiac epigram:

> Believe me,
> Grýša is a tyrant to me,
> And yet, he used to love me.
> Since I shut the door on him
> I've only laughed but once.

Meanwhile, after a winter of separation and clandestine meetings, Hašek was back again among the Anarchists. In April 1907 he went to Ustí nad Orlicí in north-east Bohemia to speak at one of their meetings, this time directed against the Catholic Party. He had promised he would bring back as an offering to Jarmila the head of its leader, Dr Václav Myslivec. With a breezy mock-callousness typical of him and not to be taken seriously, he wrote to her in the same paragraph of the beauty of the town and the Anarchists' plans to burn it down.

'Beloved Jarmila,

'I am writing to tell you how much I love you although I am so very far away . . . Today I shall go with about three hundred of our boys . . . to break up a meeting of the Clerical Party. I'm having great success here and on my advice our slogan's going to be: "Force against force."

'The State is force. (Excuse me. As you see, I'm letting myself go and am already orating on paper.) I'm looking forward to what we are going to do with that Clerical Myslivec. The river Orlice is flowing not very far away and I don't know at the moment whether we ought to throw the bastard into it before, during or after the meeting. I'm for giving him a good hiding as well, and the boys are too and only wait for a signal from me. As I write these lines I'm turning over in my mind whether to say yes or not. The meeting will be like nothing seen in the region within living memory. We have very powerful militant organisations here and I'm just now advising them to adopt revolutionary tactics. On May 1st, they want to burn down the town. It's a very nice spot, as you can see. The scenery is beautiful; there are enormous forests which would be all the nicer, if only you were here. I'd show you how the river Orlice flows and roars through the mountains with waters as green and bright as our hopes are of thrashing Myslivec. I'm already thrashing him with words and the boys will thrash him with whatever they can lay their hands on. The priest will be there too, and we'll thrash that servant of God as well. They want to tie a Clerical teacher by the leg to a chair and force him under the threat of a beating to recite the prayer "Our Father" and "Ave Maria" for six hours. Let's hope he'll be utterly sickened by it. Dear Jarmila, my success is your success. I place my triumphs at your feet. On the ground before you I lay the head of Dr Myslivec and kiss you in spirit as I do so . . .

Grýša

'p.s. I've just given permission for Dr Myslivec to get a sound Catholic thrashing.'

Naturally hooliganism of this kind, even if there was more bark in it than bite, was hardly likely to appeal to the Mayers, but fortunately they probably never knew about it. It was lucky too that they were unaware that on April 17th, 1907 the police had ordered Hašek to be put under regular surveillance as correspondent of two Anarchist papers—*Commune*[6] and its supplement *Pauper*.[7]

Frustrated by the continual need for clandestine meetings with his love and her constant fears, Hašek determined to take the bull by the horns, and go and see Mr Mayer. So one day he went to their front door and calmly knocked at it. But his characteristically jocular and jaunty approach did not pay off. Menger tells us: 'When Jarmila's father opened the door and asked him what he wanted, Hašek replied: "I'm coming to ask you for Jarmila's hand, my dear respected father-in-law. I thought a long time beforehand whether I should clean my shoes or put on a clean collar, and finally I plumped for the clean collar. It means less work." But he had no time to finish. Mr Mayer froze him with a withering look and slammed the door in his face.'

68

Under his rather brusque exterior Mr Mayer had a soft heart, and after he had had a row with his daughter or his prospective son-in-law, he nearly always felt pangs of remorse. After all, he told himself, Hašek was not really a bad chap and there was no doubt that Jarmila was genuinely in love with him. Perhaps if he could wean him away from the bad influences to which he was subjected, he would go straight. Of these the first and most important was Anarchism, and so he made it an irrevocable condition of their being permitted to meet that Hašek should quit the movement. For various reasons Hašek was already in the mood to do this, and after he had promised it, Mr Mayer relented and they were able to go about together again. This was decided on May 1st, in any event an unfortunate day perhaps, but this time particularly so because it was the date which the Anarchists had fixed for a mass meeting in the garden of the restaurant Na Slovanech in Prague. It was the culmination of their campaign against the Social Democratic Party's demand for universal suffrage, and the main speaker was Vohryzek himself. Hašek maintained that he himself had only been there to report the events for the paper *Day*[8] and not to participate. But he could never remain a passive spectator.

According to *Commune*: 'About one o'clock in the afternoon a group of some forty participants marched up Ječná, singing various revolutionary songs.' The rest of the article was blacked out by the censor. The official report states that Hašek hit a constable with a stick and shouted out 'Beat him!' when he was trying to disperse the crowd. As a consequence Hašek was remanded until May 14th for 'inflicting serious bodily injury on a constable and for inciting the public to similar assaults'.

This was just what would happen when everything was looking so hopeful for the young couple's future. It was obviously vitally important that the Mayers should not get to know. The censorship no doubt helped to keep the news from them, but as a precaution Hašek decided not to write directly from gaol to Jarmila but to use Helena Milotová as an intermediary:

'Dear Miss Milotová,
'Please do me a kind favour and go and see Jarmila and try to cheer her up. As you see, I am at this very moment in custody and my medical report lies before me on the table. "For the

accused Hašek, Jaroslav, the appropriate punishment should be fasting, irons and manual labour." I am being held here for causing an unlawful assembly and for inciting the crowd to hit a policeman, all of which I was supposed to have done after the popular rally on May 1st ... The remand won't last long, but please ask Jarmila to come and see me in the morning, and please go and see her at once when you get this letter. Tell her that she is always in my thoughts and I am longing for the time when I'll be out again and at liberty. This will happen as soon as they have heard the witnesses ... My life here revolves around brown soup, which I get every day for breakfast, and the *šoule*,* which is the name they give here to their admirable mixture of peas and barley. It's what's called the philosophy of life. I kiss Jarmila and send you my kindest regards.

Jaroslav Hašek

'P.S. Give Jarmila a kiss from me!
Ask her to write to me!'

When Hašek's case eventually came up before the magistrates, he was asked: 'Where is your defence counsel?' Hašek replied: 'Oh dear, I forgot and left him at home'. He tried to defend himself rather unconvincingly by maintaining that he had not shouted 'Beat him!' (*Natři ho!*) as was the charge against him, but 'See him!' (*Spatři ho!*), and the constable had misheard him. He also tried to prove an alibi in an involved way by retelling at length the story of Dostoyevsky's *The Double* until the magistrate stopped him. Reportedly there was laughter in court in which the magistrate joined. But he sentenced him to a month's imprisonment none the less, starting from August 16th.

During the time he spent in gaol in the New Tower in Charles Square Hašek gave Jarmila full powers to collect his fees from the newspapers. He wrote on the back of his visiting card:

'Dear Mr Editor,
'Please be good enough to hand the money orders for my

---

* A Jewish dish made of goose roasted with boiled peas and peeled barley or rice.

work published in your distinguished paper to the bearer of this
card, Miss Jarmila Mayerová.

I remain,

Yours truly . . .

(Valid for all editorial offices.)'

There is a story that when eventually Jarmila came to collect
the money Hašek had already done so, but let us be charitable
and ignore it.

Naturally Hašek's imprisonment eventually came to Mr
Mayer's notice and he resolved to take the severest measures
against his daughter's undesirable attachment. Once more
Hašek had to swear that he would have nothing more to do with
the Anarchist movement. If we are to believe what he wrote in
*The History of the Party of Moderate Progress within the Bounds of the
Law*[9] he received similar advice from the Prague Police Commissioner whose son he had tutored, and who suggested that it
would be wiser for him to get out while the going was good:

'My friend, remember this. The Vienna State Police have
your name down in the Anarchists' register.'

'Surely the Prague police, sir?'

'Both the Vienna and the Prague police.'

'And what about the Brno police, sir?'

'The Brno police is not a state police.'

'Then I'll move to Brno.'

'You will do nothing of the kind. You will stay here in
Vinohrady, like me.'

'But, sir, may not a man be an Anarchist?'

'Why not? Only it's fraught with disagreeable consequences
. . . Get all that petrol and dynamite out of your head. It doesn't
do, you know. You have a mother who is a decent woman. You
have a brother who is waiting for a job in the Bank of Slavie.
Order is order. If you want to join a party where they shout a
lot, join the National Socialists. If you've still got revolutionary
ideas, join the Social Democrats.'

On the back of one of the police reports were written the following words: 'Has left *Pauper* and *Commune* and will try to find
a job on other papers.'

And so, after he had been let out of prison, Hašek looked for employment elsewhere. It was not easy for him, because he already had a bad name and no one wanted to be saddled with him. As usual he did not go the right way about it, as a letter which he addressed to the Director of the Library of the National Museum very well shows:

'Gentlemen,
   'I offer you my services.
   'I have practical experience behind me.
   'I have edited the journals *Commune* and *Pauper* and although I am not an outright Anarchist I edited them in an anarchist way.
   'Would someone of the age of twenty-five suit you?'

As long as Hašek was not able to satisfy the Mayers by getting a job, the lovers had to meet in secret and communicate through friends. At the end of 1907 he tried a little artful diplomacy on Jarmila's parents by writing her a letter which he knew they would read, and in which he addressed her in the more formal second person plural:

'Dear Jarmila,
   'Don't think that I want to spoil the peace of your home. I have the fullest respect for your father's opinion and to avoid further scenes I shall do my best to follow his wishes. I shall give up my membership of the Anarchist movement and occupy my-self exclusively with literature, possibly joining the editorial staff of papers which are agreeable to your father. Then no one will be able to say that he forbids you to talk to me . . .
   'Of course I love you much more than any slogans! And so please tell your father that I entreat him not to talk of the past any more, now that the present is quite different. And ask him if he would please allow you to come to Sokolovna at ten o'clock tomorrow.
   'I shall be really glad when there's an end to your mother's slighting remarks. I respect her very much, although up till now she has never said a word in my favour. I know that she is your mother and your happiness is very important to her, darling,

and so I am giving up those dangerous walks in Anarchist boots and I am going to put on more comfortable shoes, as your father wishes.

'Tomorrow afternoon I would like to have a word with your father and explain to him that I don't want to cause any political disturbances and that I shall henceforth be guided in my behaviour by my last conversation with him. And so come tomorrow at ten o'clock to Sokolovna in Vinohrady. I kiss you,

Your

Jaroslav'

There was more behind this letter than met the eye. Shortly before he wrote it, he had been found completely drunk in the street in the early hours of the morning and detained by the police. It was imperative for him to solve the question of his and Jarmila's future once and for all. And so he resolved to approach Mr Mayer once more.

He plucked up courage and waylaid him one day in the street. Here is the account he subsequently gave to Jarmila of what took place between them:

'In the course of an hour and a half's conversation with your papa we at length got so far that he promised that if I was decently dressed and had a permanent job, even if it was only a modest one, he wouldn't put any obstacles in the way of our friendship. He said that when I have made a clean start, he is going to like me.

'Next he gave me his word that we could correspond and thirdly he promised that he would be nice to you. I, for my part, promised him I would find a job, and the promise is not an empty one this time, as it was in the spring, because then I wasn't really trying, whereas now I truly am.'

If we can believe Hašek, Mr Mayer appears to have been remarkably open-hearted during their talk together.

'Your papa apologised for having lost his temper, said he loved you, loved you very much, and that he could kick himself for being harsh with you, but that he couldn't help it; it

73

suddenly burst out. He said he was sorry for both of us and owned that he'd probably spoken harshly, but your mama was crying all the time and he couldn't stand it . . .

' "Come for her, when you've got a job," he said, "I'll gladly give her to you, but calm down now, and see that she calms down too . . . and don't spend the whole day loafing about. Sometimes it's enough if people see each other for a quarter of an hour, half an hour—God knows—perhaps an hour. But what can people think when you loaf about together the whole day? Tell me, am I not right?

' "The girl loves you," he went on. "I've got nothing against it and can't have anything against it, and if I ever said anything, it was only my nerves. It was nothing more than that."

' "Mr Mayer," I said, "let's regard what's happened as finished and done with, and agree that it'll never occur again. Can I have your assurance on that?"

' "Yes, you can, but see that you keep your word. Don't let me down. My health depends on it. Jarmila needs peace too to get strong again. And we must not overstrain her with work or upset her."

'My darling, believe me, I've never talked to anyone so intimately as I did with your papa. And he spoke intimately to me too. I could hardly hold back my tears. That walk was somehow so strange, so odd, so moving. I trembled with emotion and confessed how frightfully irresponsible I had been.

'And all the time we spoke so tenderly, so warmly, and, I believe, totally seriously.

'Finally we shook hands.

'And so we have won the possibility of corresponding and meeting—it's no longer total separation. Now you must write to me, of course, and tell me when, where and in what circumstances we can be together.

'It must always be a little way from home. And I am going to work, because only by work can I win you. In the olden days knights used to kill dragons, if they wanted to win princesses, and today one unhappy knight errant will have to slay his irresponsibility and laziness.

'Be calm, my princess, be calm as the sphinx when the desert wind blows. I love you inexpressibly. It's not so bad as we thought. Our fight is not lost.

74

'I had to make the most of my meeting with your papa, and do it sensibly, not hastily like before.

'I am learning a little sense after all.

'I must pat myself on the back a little for having talked about things that humiliate me, like when I said I was lazy and irresponsible.

'My darling, my clever one, think out how and where we shall see each other. I kiss you many times. Be very happy! I am always thinking of you. I am already calmer and have a new zest for work.

'I kiss you.' [Here he drew the symbol of infinity.]

One cannot help feeling sympathy for the honest and well-meaning father, who was devoted to his daughter and anxious to protect her from a son-in-law whom he could neither understand nor approve. Moreover, he had had one serious stroke and had to try to spare himself violent emotions. But his unyielding stance during the preceding years certainly helped to drive Hašek deeper and deeper into his bohemian way of life. Whether a more tolerant attitude on Mr Mayer's part would have kept him on the right path during the rest of his life is doubtful, but it seems clear that the immediate cause of his downfall was the bleak period of separation from the person he loved combined with the penury and discouragement he suffered.

Alas, in spite of all his promises to improve (throughout 1908 he received only two police summonses) Hašek soon relapsed again. One morning, returning in a particularly maudlin mood after a night out, he suddenly took it into his head to present himself at the Mayers' house in the small hours. He found no one to open his heart to except the sleepy wife of the concierge, who would not let him go upstairs. After his outpourings, he begged her not to tell anybody, but of course by the next morning everybody knew what state the 'writer gentleman' was in when he came during the night to ask for the hand of Miss Mayerová.

Meanwhile, in spite of having actively campaigned against the Social Democratic Party, he was now making strenuous efforts to obtain a job on one of their papers or at least to make some regular arrangement with them. He wrote to Jarmila on

January 10th, 1908, to say that he had been promised a job on the *People's Right* and that two distinguished members of the Party, Dr Soukup and Dr Winter, had told him that this had not been done out of sentimentality. In his optimistic frame of mind he imagined that he would be writing for all Social Democratic journals. Šmeral, the leader of the Party, went so far as to invite him to come with him to Kladno to attend a conference of editors of all the Party papers, which was a compliment and a promising development. But with his passion for writing for the press of all political shades he was flirting with the National Socialist press as well. This was perhaps a more logical step, because the Party had close connections with the Anarchists and was the moving spirit in the anti-militarist campaign. Discouraged by the failure of the Social Democrats to live up to their promises (if indeed they had ever made them— one never knew with Hašek, because he saw everything through rose-tinted spectacles) he started to try to blackmail them. One day he brought them an article guying the National Socialist leaders. When they hesitated to accept it, Hašek sat down, took out his pen and changed the names in the article to those of the Social Democratic leaders. A few further alterations were required and then the article was ready for the National Socialist press and was in fact published there. However he also made fun of both party papers, offering articles to the *People's Right* and *Czech Word*[10] at the same time and even carrying on polemics between the two papers, writing anonymously both sets of articles himself.

The parents heaved a sigh of relief when the summer came again and it was time for Jarmila to go to stay at Libáň once more. When she had left, Hašek wrote to tell her how much he missed her, parodying the sentimentality of a lover and at the same time making fun of the long and complicated names of Czech villages:

'I've been studying the map, and the day you left I looked at the train time-table to see where you might be—Chvaly, Počernice, Mstětice . . . and I reckoned that my Jariška must be five kilometres away from me. And the more these kilometres piled up, the sadder and sadder I became. No one would believe what those stupid kilometres could do.

'Then I looked at the clock. It was eight. That meant that you were in Nymburk. And so there were now about nineteen kilometres between us and I sent you one more kiss. After that at the stations of Všechlapy, Jíkev-Boben and Ronov-Oskořínek came melancholy reflections on my loneliness together with the wholly appropriate thought of razing those idiotic stations to the ground as a punishment for standing between us. And then at 8.44 I looked at the time-table again. Hello, I thought, by now you will have got to Křinec. When you reached Rožďalovice I kissed your photographs. Finally Kopidlno came and I wrung my hands in despair . . .'

Hašek went to see her at Libáň several times. Otherwise he relieved the sad existence of his 'dear emigrée' by writing her more letters displaying charm and wit expressed in the same inimitable style. Jarmila had scolded him for two misdeeds: he had cheated her by using an enormous envelope and a still larger sheet of writing-paper and then wasting so much of it by leaving it blank; and he had done nothing about the x's in her letter and put none in his own. She threatened to put no more x's on hers if this went on.

In a characteristic reply Hašek separated these two charges into categories (a) and (b):

'I answer ad (a) as follows. That enormous envelope was to show you how much I love you and how much I could have written, if I had wanted you to get the letter half a day later. Didn't you read properly my explanation why I ended the letter before I had filled up the space on the paper and in the envelope? My letter was an answer to your dear letter, which I got at four o'clock in the afternoon. The train to Kopidlno only goes at 5.43 in the afternoon and 5.50 in the morning, and there was nothing for it but to send the answer the same afternoon, that is to say write it and carry it to the station. Well, first I had to read your letter and kiss it all over, and to do all these things I had only an hour and forty-three minutes from the time I received it to the departure of the train. But because letters are collected every half hour before the departure of the train, I had only really an hour and thirteen minutes left. During this time I had to read your letter, kiss it all over, write you a new one and take it to the station. I read the letter in ten minutes and that left me an hour and three minutes. Then I kissed it, as well as your photograph, which took a quarter of an hour (thinking of you and kissing you). That left me forty-eight minutes for writing and carrying the letter to the station. Let's say I'm a mile and a quarter away from Hybernská (which I covered at a speed of two kilometres an hour—that makes twenty minutes). There were now twenty-eight minutes left for writing the letter. Well, it was a long letter for such a short time, proportionately the longest I've ever written, and if we base our reasoning on the following mathematical calculations: 28 minutes, small lettering (16 words a line on quarto format, of which $1\frac{1}{2}$ pages are thickly covered with writing) we come to the surprising result that the letter is proportionately twelve times as long as the longest of yours and confirms what you wrote in your last letter: " . . . You know you can write quickly and fill the sheet completely in a moment." As you see, you were not wrong, even when you wrote that sentence about my cheating you over my "note". You must admit, though, that it was not really a "note" but a letter. Unfortunately, neither Czech nor any other language has a suitable word for such a comparatively long letter. Professor Hron,* who invents words, would probably call it a "thunder-and-lightning-love-letter", which means a letter vigorously dashed off with the speed of lightning and carrying with it all my love to my dear Jarma.

'*ad* (*b*). As far as concerns the x's, after careful consideration I decided they were unnecessary. It would after all be a restriction on your personal liberty if I were to indicate, by inserting them, the places where you are to kiss my letter, my dear Jarmila. I am convinced not only that you love me so much that the number of kisses which you send me cannot be expressed only by those few x's in your letter, but that, when I round my lips and breaths of wind touch them, they bring me lots and lots of your kisses with them. Now don't get worried and think I am wandering about the street with my lips stuck out and astonished crowds of children are running after me. I do it mostly when I am asleep and alone, when I'm dreaming that I have you in my arms etc. etc. (N.B. because you are a Christian you put x's in

---

* An eccentric professor, whose works on astronomy and mathematics were couched in his own idiosyncratic language.

your letter. A Jew would have put stars, a Moslem a crescent and an atheist like me might have put a wild pansy. You must admit that a letter with some twenty signs like that would have looked frightful! You wouldn't have been able to sleep for horror).'

In another letter with fanciful profanity he signs himself with four different names—Jaroslav, Mína, Grýša and Maňousek—and goes on:

'I am greater than the Lord God. I am *four* people in one and this holy mystery sends you I I I I ,,,, I I I I ,,, I I I ,, I I I , I I I I I I kisses, which reckoned up arithmetically (one kiss per second) would be enough for 345,721,804,732 years.'

He adored mathematical rigmaroles.

There is no doubt at all that Hašek's relationship with Jarmila was perfectly normal—not 'platonic' and not 'sensual'—in fact in many respects ideal. It is curious that this should have been the one and only time in his life when he really seems to have longed for physical love. His appetite was whetted by long separation, as the following extract from a letter written to Jarmila at Libáň shows:

'. . . when two people love each other as we do, walk out to-gether, talk together, unbosom themselves to each other, kiss, long for each other, embrace, look for four-leaved clovers together, cuddle up to each other, put their heads on each other's shoulders and in each other's laps, hug each other with a vague idea of how nice it will be when they sleep together, when it's a delight for them to feel each other's warmth and they aren't ashamed of their passionate sighs and understand each other as we do and tell each other everything, which strict moralists would not approve, when each fears for the other and cannot live without the other, then . . . this is real love, not platonic and yet not sensual, but a mixture of both, something, darling, which we both understand so well when we sit side by side and embrace, and you say "Pst!" ' [Jarmila's code warning that Hašek was trying to go too far with her!]

In the same erotic letter written on July 11th, 1908, he confided to Jarmila his innermost secret, an affair on the hills of Myjava in Slovakia which had had an important sequel for him:

'Believe me, my darling, you are the only one I love, Jarmila, and I love you, love you, and have never loved any other woman, neither that gypsy, nor Maryška, even if I did sleep with her on the hay in Slovakia. I never think about her now. I can't even remember her, because I didn't love her and she didn't love me either: she loved the gendarme who married her a fortnight later. You know, my darling, the girls there are very sensual and would like to do nothing else all day but sleep with the boys. The boys work in the fields and don't take much interest in them, but the girls have a strongly developed sensuality and blindly obey their own instincts (I know you'll say "Pst" again when you read this, but don't be cross, my darling).

'Upon my honour I couldn't help it. We only saw each other twice, and, when the second time came, she invited me to sleep with her in the attic of her parents' house. At that time I was such an inexperienced young man that I wouldn't have even dared to go to the attic there. It was she who did it. You know, she had been in service in Vienna, she used to go dancing with the soldiers and certainly was no saint. I don't hold it against her. She wasn't a prostitute who for financial gain abandons her right to choose whether to give herself or not. That is what prostitution is. There's no guilty sensuality there, but only economic slavery. But this girl, out of sheer sensuality, without any idea of financial gain, slept with me, just as she did next day with her fiancé, the gendarme. She didn't love him any more than she did me or anyone else who served her just to satisfy her desires. I certainly wasn't smiling then, my darling, nor was I proud of myself. I was no conquering hero. I was so terribly inexperienced. I was over eighteen, perhaps nineteen, but I had never had a woman with me who was ready to give me everything I already knew about but hadn't actually experienced. I knew the inside of brothels, but I had never once gone upstairs to a cubicle with a creature who hadn't the strength to resist any sexual urge. I didn't love her and she didn't love me either. It was nothing more than a physiological act, and, believe me, since I started going out with you I've never slept with any woman, not for a second, because today no one else exists for me, only you, my love, and as long as you are fond of me and love me, other women mean less than the tiniest patch of your skin. Please, please, my darling, write to me and say you forgive me for that time when I didn't know you. Say that if you had been in my place, my darling, you wouldn't have been able to resist either and might have gone with that gypsy like me at a time when I didn't love any woman and still thought that love was only *coitus*.'*

Meanwhile, in spite of his success in placing his stories in the press of all shades of the political spectrum, he was constantly in debt, borrowing either from Jarmila or Máňa, and because Jarmila only received a pittance at home she herself had to borrow clandestinely to support him. When the time came for him to repay her, he never had enough.

'I was afraid that you wouldn't be satisfied with what I sent you,' he wrote to her. 'I did what I could and I hate not having been able to scrape up more money, heart of gold. Well, for the time being, you are probably satisfied.'

Several of his letters are full of self-reproach: 'You cannot imagine how it tortures me when I think that I was so stupid as to play cards and sit around in taverns. Now I sometimes go to a café or an exhibition and work very hard.' But unfortunately the police records tell another story. Less than three weeks after writing this he was wanted for being involved in a brawl and had vanished without a trace.

If a permanent job still eluded him, he was being given plenty of chances as a freelance.

'Now I am writing another long article for the *Countryside*.[11] I have already written one for *Horizon*. And tomorrow I shall write for the *National Newspaper*. I won't write for *National Policy*: it's sheer idiocy how that man Žák runs his humorous column . . . I am reasonably satisfied with this year's results. Now it is a question of my getting into *Golden Prague*,[12] *Lumír* and the *Bell*.[13] I'll certainly get in. Also I shall write something for

---

* There is some confusion here. Was Maryška the same as the gypsy? At the beginning of the letter Hašek refers to them as two different persons but at the end of it he seems to telescope them into one.

Švanda the Bagpiper[14] ... Today people know my name and I'm trying to ensure that one day people will point to you and say: "That is Mrs Jarmila Hašková" and say it with respect.'

And so, whatever may be said about his bohemian life, Hašek was making genuine efforts with his writings to prove to Jarmila's parents that he was capable of maintaining her. In 1909 he wrote sixty-four stories, most of which were published in *Caricatures*. He also contributed to *Young Currents*,[15] *Merry Prague* and the *Animal World*.[16] With all he was publishing Hašek ought not to have been so short of cash.

At home Jarmila suffered a lot of unpleasantness. Twice she ran away and stayed with friends. Anxious to protect her more securely from Hašek, her parents decided to send her even further afield—this time to her married sister, Milena, at Přerov in Moravia.

Left alone, Hašek struck out on quite another tack: he started making extempore speeches at election gatherings, where his witty sallies met with great success. In the bye-elections at Vinohrady in 1908 he apparently accepted the advice of the friendly Police Commissioner and took charge of the offices of the National Socialist Party in its campaign against the Young Czech Party, but the way he handled it showed that he regarded the electoral process in Austria as little short of a farce.

He and his supporters used to tear down or paint over the Young Czech Party's electioneering posters. Not content with that, he used his ingenuity to think up ways of discrediting Dr Kärner, the Young Czech candidate. Hašek—an avowed ex-Anarchist—arranged for a poster to appear on the street corners depicting Kärner with the traditional wide-brimmed hat and bomb of the Anarchist. Underneath was the caption: 'Elect me your deputy and I shall blow the whole of Vinohrady sky-high.' Under banner headlines in *Czech Word*, for which he was at that time writing, he published an unsigned report that a lunatic had barricaded himself in his house, and the fire-brigade and the sappers from the barracks had had to be called to force an entry for the police. When the lunatic was put into a strait-jacket and taken off in the police van, he shouted desperately: 'You must vote for Dr Kärner! He is one of the best people in "the party with clean hands".' The report went on to say that the poor man had been driven mad by a visit from the 'Czech Maid of Orleans' who had tried to force him to vote for the Young Czech Party and that the mournful procession passed through silent crowds on its way to the lunatic asylum. The 'Maid of Orleans' was Milada Sísová, editor of *Woman's World*,[17] a leading light in the Young Czech Party and close to the Škardas—the family who had always helped the Hašeks. She later published the speeches of Václav Škarda, the president of the Party. The joke was not likely to be appreciated by Hašek's family.

The copy of *Czech Word* carrying this report sold like hot cakes and before the Young Czechs could strike back Hašek had put up a huge placard outside his electoral office carrying the news: 'Vinohrady Young Czech electioneering committee murders two National Socialist voters!' The Young Czechs only found out about this at night and rushed off to take their vengeance on Hašek, whom they rightly identified as the culprit. But he had the good sense to slip outside and, while the bands of outraged Young Czech supporters set about destroying his office, he could be seen standing nearby and shouting: 'Help! Police! The Young Czech committee has come to murder us!'

One day, not long after the Vinohrady elections, Hájek found Hašek sitting alone at the Golden Litre.[18] It was wintry weather, his boots were gaping, he looked completely down at heel and said he had nowhere to sleep. Hájek generously gave him his own spare pair of boots and let him stay in his rooms.

Hájek was at that time editor of *Animal World*, a journal published by a Mr Fuchs, who owned a villa with kennels at Klamovka off the Pilsen highway. Hašek said he wanted to get away from the life he was leading and offered to come and help him. It was another attempt to find a stable job and break down the opposition of Jarmila's parents. Hájek promised that if Hašek wrote something he would show it to his chief. Fuchs looked at what he had written and agreed to employ him in his office, although he was not prepared to give him more than a pittance.

Hájek was in love with his chief's daughter and Fuchs exploited to the utmost the advantages this offered him. While Hájek would have much preferred to stay near the daughter at Klamovka, Fuchs forced him to accompany him on tiresome journeys to Prague. In the end Hájek became so irritated that he had a row with him and gave notice, the only result of which was that Fuchs handed him his last pay packet and told him that he must have nothing further to do with his daughter.

Hájek hoped that out of solidarity Hašek would give notice as well, and that Fuchs, having no one to replace them, would be forced to take him back. But, contrary to his expectations, Hašek, who was rarely inspired by feelings of loyalty to his friends, stayed on and was made editor in the place of his friend and helper, who had to find another job.

Hašek wrote to Jarmila's mother on August 9th, 1909, that he had at last got a permanent post at eighty guilders a month, apart from what he earned from his freelance contributions. He thanked her and Mr Mayer for 'having brought him back to orderly life'. He should rather have thanked Fuchs. It was he who gave him a room in his villa, on condition that he never went out and only drank the beer which was provided as part of his wages.

He got on so well with his new employer at first that he decided to confide in him and tell him about his love for Jarmila and the desperate situation he was in. Fuchs agreed to go on employing him and in March 1910 promised to pay him 180 crowns a month as soon as he married. When Hašek informed the parents of this, they felt they must give in; Jarmila had become more and more miserable and had several times run away; even sending her away from Prague had not helped. Soon Hašek was able to write to her at Přerov and tell her the glad news that his future was assured for the moment at least and that her father had given them permission to marry.

(6)

Married Life

Mr Mayer stipulated that the wedding must be a church one.
Hašek tried to 'fix' his return to the Catholic fold by attempting
to bribe the sexton at the church to give him a certificate of
attendance at confession. When the sexton would not play, he
wheedled it out of a priest at the church of St Ignatius.[1] The
wedding took place on May 23rd, 1910, at the Church of St
Ludmila in Vinohrady.[2] The priest who married the couple was
one of the Škarda family, and the bride's brother, Josef Mayer,
was a witness. No further accounts of the proceedings have been
preserved.

Before she allowed Hašek to take her to the church Jarmila
had had some six years to reflect on whether she really loved
him and whether they were suited to each other. His letters
prove that he was an affectionate and attentive lover, and she
must have been very happy with them during their long years of
separation, even if, with all her femininity, she often let him
think that she was not and accused him of infidelity (of which he
certainly was innocent). As for Hašek, he really seems to have
believed at that time that marriage with Jarmila would be the
fulfilment of his life's desire. In the summer of 1908, when she
was away in Libáň, he wrote: 'It's strange that we still go on
loving each other more and more, and I am convinced that
when we finally belong to each other we shall not cool off but
go on and on loving each other in the lovely way we do
now.'

It was indeed one of life's miracles that Hašek, who had never
before really warmed to anyone of the opposite sex and who
admitted to Jarmila that it would have been quite inconceiv-
able for him to have kissed a letter all over before he met her,
suddenly experienced this very real and powerful explosion of
love for her, a love which he never seems to have felt again for

anyone else throughout his life. There is no doubt that this was erotic love, as is apparent from his letters, given the limitations which the conventions of the time and Jarmila's bashfulness imposed on him. 'Just imagine what I would have done with you, if I had had you instead of your letter. I should have crumpled your blouse with all my huggings and half eaten you with kisses.' 'I kiss your eyes, your neck and hug you passionately.' After a visit to Libáň to see her, when the time came for him to leave, they 'were brave and parted from one another as quickly as a husband and wife who were about to separate after having agreed on the conditions of divorce . . . Then you were gone, there was no trace of you, my love, and I gave way to weakness, wiped away a tear or maybe more, and nearly rushed off to you again, to give you a hug.' 'And I shall make it up to you for all the pain you have suffered, my love, all the wrongs they have inflicted on you. I love you boundlessly and yearn for you . . . I send you billions of kisses. Through your picture I kiss you and hope that I shall kiss you for ever.'

It is hard to appraise Jarmila's character when she herself was so reserved. From what we know of her from her friends she was clever, quick and witty and her conversation had in it something of Hašek's irony. But again, as with Hašek, much of this was on the surface. Underneath she too was deeply sensitive. She was certainly very much in love with him and shared some of his ideas and principles—at any rate initially. But there were many potential points of friction. She had inherited a puritan streak, while he was always itching to do something really shocking. Further, not only was Jarmila more than a little prudish; she was nervy, timid and superstitious.

Outwardly she appeared so sensible, self-controlled, reliable, discreet and practical that those who knew her would probably never have suspected that she was in fact highly strung and neurotic. This comes out clearly in Hašek's correspondence with her. He is often alternately scolding or comforting her for being melancholy and timid. He found her superstitious to a degree unacceptable for an 'advanced' woman: when she heard that the place she was going to stay at in the country was near a graveyard, she could hardly bear it. Hašek wrote and comforted her, saying that it was stupid to be afraid of graveyards. If he were lying rotting in it, she might have grounds for being miserable, but as he was not, why on earth did she worry about it?

'My golden heroine! If Erben had been such a coward as you he would never have written "The Wedding Shirt".* Or if he had written it, he would have read it over to himself and died of fright. Poor little heroine! You cry with fright. Do you really think something is going to come and carry you off? She hears bells ringing, footsteps in the yard, a doleful sound of trumpets and God knows what else! She imagines there is someone in the kitchen! Darling, it is you who are making all this misery for yourself. You're as frightened as a spoilt little child, my golden kiss. You torture my heart with your lamentations and complaints, my little golden one . . . How I wish you wouldn't be so afraid when you're already twenty-two!'

But it was of no avail. She was so scared of the dark that she had to get up early in the morning to write to him instead of doing so at night. What a wife for an Anarchist! And she was prudish too in matters of sex. When she learned that one of his letters to her had gone astray, she was much more concerned about what he might have written in it and who might have read it than what she had missed by its loss. 'You see, my darling Míťa,' she wrote, 'even in letter-writing you should show some reserve.'

She was certainly reserved and unemotional as he could never be. Hašek tells how, when he taught her the Russian sentence: 'The teacher loves the pupil' and looked steadfastly into her eyes as he said it, expecting she would blush, she did nothing of the kind. She was anaemic of course, he explains, but her voice sounded terribly indifferent. (Incidentally this 'anaemia' is mentioned frequently in their correspondence: she is often unwell and he is continually prescribing tonics and pills for her.)

Although herself not beyond reproach as a correspondent, she at once suspected the worst when no letter arrived from him and immediately jumped to the conclusion that he was angry with her or had ceased to love her. She was perennially jealous,

* *Svatební košile*, a poem by the Czech poet K. Erben (1811–70) later made into a cantata by Dvořák for the Birmingham Festival of 1885 under the title 'The Spectre's Bride'.

although it is unlikely that Hašek gave her any cause for it. She later claimed to her friend Vilma that Hašek's admission after their marriage that he once had surrendered to an importunate chambermaid in a hotel 'did not affect her at all'; on the contrary, she said, she admired him for having twice resisted the girl's advances before he finally succumbed. But she never forgot the Slovak gypsy or Maryška. Was it perhaps that she envied the latter that romp in the hay and everything he 'already knew about but hadn't actually experienced'? His protestations that he was not interested in other women were simply not believed.

'My golden one, my dear darling,' he wrote, 'you are so sincere, you are so open with me and you write that you are almost sorry for Miss Strnadová. You mustn't be sorry for her: she isn't a person to be pitied at all. She didn't love me and I didn't love her. She only flirted with me and after that went around with a technician called Šimek, who was an acquaintance of mine, and now she's married to some teacher near Turnov whom she knew for three years, in other words just at the time when she was going around with me and also with Janota and afterwards with Šimek. It's almost the same thing as with Slávka Hajnišová. And in the end she'll probably take that wretched Háša. But that hasn't stopped her from saying that I loved her. My darling, I never loved her the tiniest bit, honestly I didn't. I went out with both of them only because friends went on teasing me with their stupid talk and because I didn't like men as companions on walks.'*

And again:

'You're angry, because I was in the Rieger Gardens.³ But that was some fourteen days before I came to Libáň. And I told you that I was with Klognerová. I didn't go to that rendezvous with her, because I thought that it would be strange for me to go out with another girl, when no one saw me going out with you, my dear, and it was you I wanted so much to go out with...

'Don't get angry about the Rieger Gardens. I've only been there twice while you've been away.

* Probably they teased Hašek for not being interested in girls.

'Write to me again a nice letter saying honestly that you know that I never think of any woman except you and that I've never loved any woman except you, my darling.'

She dreaded any kind of unpleasantness with her parents, confessed to being very frightened of her father, and was perhaps even a tiny bit afraid of Hašek too, and it is quite understandable that so unpredictable and explosive a young man might scare a sensitive girl, especially when he had been drinking. Finally, like most girls she wanted stability and a home—a place not just where they could 'kiss in a warm room' as he liked to put it, but where she could arrange things as she wanted them and be a little house-proud.

Like a true bourgeoise she was very concerned about how Hašek dressed. She would rather have him look smart, she wrote to him, than get a present from him. 'See to it, dear little Mít'a, that you have your linen in order. Don't spend money on anything except linen and clothes, so that you always have enough ... Don't forget to buy cuffs, collars and white shirt fronts; yours are always disgusting. Please get new ones when I come, and do wear braces, darling.'

And she certainly had her way with him over this: Hašek writes repeatedly to her about the new clothes he is buying and he never looked so smart as during the time of his courtship. The photograph of him in Charles Square with Jarmila in 1908 in his dark overcoat and black fur cap shows a Hašek who would be unrecognisable to those who had only seen the conventional pictures of him after his return from Russia, when he seems to have lost all interest in his personal appearance. He was penniless and in debt, both as a young man and an older one, but it was only under Jarmila's influence that he took any pride in his appearance. Otherwise he was happiest when he could go about dressed like a tramp. He was irresponsible, enjoyed creating minor public scandals (the sort of thing that must have made Jarmila blush in spite of her radical leanings) and was unable to summon up any interest in the home or how it should be furnished and decorated, and while Jarmila admired him for having the courage to challenge the existing order, she preferred him to keep that challenge 'within the bounds of the law'. And this was just what he would not and could not do.

If we can believe what Hašek wrote in an article which she herself copied for him before his marriage, he had had no success with his attempts to convert her and her school friends to Anarchism. He brought them copies of *Commune*, gave them Kropotkin's books, bought them Przybyszewski's *The Children of Satan* (which was popular in Anarchist circles), but soon found he was getting nowhere with Jarmila, because she defended the Young Czech Party and Máňa Masaryk's Realist Party. Jarmila joined him in singing the Anarchists' song, but also said to him: 'Do you know what, Grýša? I'm fed up with these Anarchists. Be a Social Democrat. Then afterwards you can become a National Socialist and finally a Young Czech and perhaps a deputy. How would it be if you were called Excellency?' . . . 'Would you marry me then?' 'Who wouldn't want to marry an Excellency?' Hašek commented: 'I left *Commune*, I'm still not an Excellency but Jarmila is now my wife. Yet she goes on hoping that what isn't could still be.'

When they had such different characters and were from such contrasting backgrounds it was evident that they would have quarrels, perhaps nothing more than one would expect between any lovers, but enough for Hašek to give her to understand that he did not like her nagging at him and hoped that she would not continue with this after they were married.

'You mustn't go for me at once. I'm very sad, my love, when you are away and in spite of it are cross with me . . . Again you've given me a good wigging, my darling. I shall obey you, be sure of that, but I won't be ruled by the petticoat. Do you understand, my darling?

'. . . You mustn't be so strict with me and immediately scold me. You know that I have promised you truthfully that I shall be good and do what you say . . .'

All the same, when she persisted in her nagging he firmly warned her off.

'My dearest darling,

'I wrote you last time how much I hate certain things you wrote in one part of your letter, and so I beg you once more, please $(+1)$ don't make allusions like that when you write, and don't hurt me . . .

'When you come, you really must not quarrel with me.'

Married life was certainly likely to be a problem for them but who would have thought it would be so short-lived?

Mr Mayer had promised that he would take a flat for the young couple in a new building near the Pilsen highway and not far from the villa at Klamovka where Hašek had been living as editor of *Animal World*. After a brief honeymoon in the suburb of Motol outside Prague (which was again not far from the editorial offices) they installed themselves in the new flat and Hašek returned to his work.

Copies of *Animal World* are still extant. It was quite an attractive family magazine, characteristic of the time, with many illustrations and articles of an interesting and entertaining kind. It should not be forgotten that at that time the popularly written family natural history book, Brehm's *Animal Life*, was in almost everybody's home. It must certainly have been Hašek's everyday reading.

Fuchs was at first well pleased with his new editor. He thought that he had ideas and was developing *Animal World* very well. Hašek not only ran the magazine and wrote most of the articles in it, but also supervised Fuchs's kennels. Not only did he display his great gift with dogs, he was also very successful in managing his chief's pet monkey, Julča, which he subsequently wrote about in 'My Dear Friend Julča',[4] a story which he published in the fashionable weekly *Golden Prague*.

As part of his 'sales drive' he would take some of the dogs out on walks or even use them to help him in his business negotiations. One of the editors of *Golden Prague* relates how Hašek once brought an enormous mastiff into his office and tried with its help to bully him into granting him an advance. Many of the experiences which he had while working with Fuchs went into his various stories and *The Good Soldier Švejk*.

At home he appeared to have become a reformed character. He stayed with Jarmila most of the time and sent to the pub for beer instead of going out to drink. He saw nothing of his former drinking companions. But unfortunately this hallowed period did not last very long. He felt himself to be a writer first and foremost, and the bohemian life to which he had become addicted was essential for his artistic self-expression.

Whether it was that he became bored with his work on *Animal World* and particularly with Fuchs, who was a tiresome man, or whether he found it impossible to bridle his mischievous imagination, he soon started to play the fool again. According to Lada, whose paper *Caricatures* he was contributing to, Hašek began to publish in the magazine poems of the order of 'Mary Had a Little Lamb' over the signature of 'Josef Lada'. Not content with that he made the unfortunate Lada into a translator of Hungarian. Once indeed Lada was accosted by a stranger who congratulated him on knowing Permak. 'I know Finnish and I am studying Tartar, but Permak! Why, it's fantastic. You must be the only person in Central Europe to know it.' Again the explanation lay in one of Hašek's 'false entries'. The truth was, as Lada said, that it did not suit Hašek to have to write articles about the disease of roup in poultry and how to treat it.

And so he later embarked on the more hazardous course of publishing imaginary facts about animals, which he supported with bogus quotations from learned authorities. One of these was that elephants liked gramophone music, while tigers did not. An apparently serious article of his began: 'Dangerous herds of wild Scottish collies have recently become the terror of the population in Patagonia.' It was grist to his mill when he heard a rumour that Princess Coloredo-Mansfeld of the beautiful palace at Dobříš outside Prague had imported a pair of musk rats and they had multiplied to such an extent as to become a threat to the park and the agriculture in the district. Seizing upon this, he published on the first page of *Animal World* a picture of the river Vltava with the rock of Vyšehrady in the background, showing how the whole river was flooded with musk rats from the Dobříš palace. Crowds of readers flocked to the river to see the sight, but were disappointed.

Perhaps his best hoax on the magazine was to advertise a couple of 'thoroughbred werewolves' for sale. When the office was drowned with applications Fuchs nearly went off his head. But Hašek was fully in command of the situation. 'It's quite simple, Mr Fuchs,' he said, 'I'll send them the following circular: "We are unfortunately out of stock of thoroughbred werewolves.

Be assured that as soon as a new consignment arrives we shall pick out a nice pair for you".'

His article on 'the newly discovered fossil of an antediluvian flea' was so convincing that it was translated and published abroad. He was certainly being autobiographical when he made Marek, the one-year volunteer,* boast how he had invented animals while working on the same magazine.

Very soon these wild statements roused the suspicions of other natural history journals. Alarmed at the possibility that his more serious subscribers might desert him, Fuchs secretly re-solved to get rid of his editor. He drove to Poděbrady,[5] where Hájek was now working, and presented him with an ultimatum: either he loved his daughter and would return to the journal or there would be an end to the attachment altogether. Hájek capitulated and came back. Hašek stayed on two months longer and then left for good. Not long afterwards Fuchs died, and Hájek took over the sole ownership of the paper. This was in the autumn of 1910.

It is hard to know what construction to put on Hašek's hoax-ing. Was it a mad obsession or was he merely indulging in a common human weakness? From time immemorial it has been an accepted form of enjoyment to fool people by telling them a yarn and afterwards laugh at them for having been taken in. April Fool's Day is still a well-observed tradition, especially in Europe. On this day newspapers stuff their columns with false reports. In 1953 one of the leading Brussels dailies announced that oil had been found in the Ardennes, and a member of the British Embassy staff, who had forgotten it was April 1st, would have reported it to the Foreign Office if he had not been stopped in time. David Attenborough gave a talk on the Third Pro-gramme of the BBC on April 1st, 1975, in which he described a totally unknown group called the Sheba Isles, the fauna of which included the 'night singing treemouse—one of several strange specimens called in Latin *mus dendrophilus*'. Only when he referred to one of the islands as Loo Flirpa, which when read backwards was April Fool, did some listeners become suspicious.

For Hašek hoaxing could be one of many things: a pleasant diversion, a way of getting out of a scrape, or an opportunity for exercising his qualities of imagination and satire. But not every

* *The Good Soldier Švejk*, p. 323.

one likes to be fooled, and Hašek made more and more enemies for himself. The news of his departure from *Animal World* must have come as a cold douche for Jarmila, and it certainly put Hašek himself in a dilemma. At first he could find no other employment. Then Hájek took pity on him and tried to get him the job of editor of the provincial paper at Poděbrady, but unfortunately Hašek 'stoked up' beforehand in a local hotel, where he regaled the company with a Hungarian song, and when he finally arrived at Hájek's flat, where the board was assembled, he just sat there like an old tramp chewing a cigar stump. When they asked him how he thought the paper should be conducted in future, he replied airily, regardless of Hájek's horrified nudges, that it should stop publishing stupid leaders about archaeology. Unfortunately the author of these articles was an influential citizen of Poděbrady who had many friends in the printers' union. As might have been foreseen, Hašek was not offered the job, and when Hájek reproached him afterwards for his tactlessness he reacted angrily and went back to the hotel.

At the end of 1910, in an attempt to keep his head above water he formed a business partnership with Jarmila and set up kennels of his own nearby in Švédská, to which he gave the pretentious title of the Cynological Institute.[6] Naturally it would be competing with Hájek's establishment. All that can be said for this new venture is that it again provided Hašek with useful themes for his literary work. He wrote an article 'My Trade with Dogs'[7] which he published in *Horizon*, and used his servant Čížek's experience in dyeing and trimming dogs in *The Good Soldier Švejk*.* An actual pedigree forged by Čížek is still preserved.

But there is a difference between hoaxing in literature and hoaxing in business. Hašek's methods as a kennel proprietor were regarded in the district as fraudulent. As a result of a number of suspicious purchases and manipulations with dogs carried out by Čížek, Hašek and Jarmila, in whose name the firm was registered, they were successfully prosecuted by the local court. The adventure ended happily, however, because thanks to a lawyer friend they were acquitted on appeal.

Clouds were settling on the horizon of their married life, which had had such a rosy dawn. Vilma tells us: 'When Grýša

* *The Good Soldier Švejk*, p. 173.

was again without a job and they had no money, the Mayers rented an apartment in a house where an aunt lived in the Prague suburb of Vršovice and took the furniture there. They brought Jarmila home to them.' Mr Mayer felt there was no point in continuing to pay the rent for the house near the editorial offices of *Animal World*, when there seemed little chance of his son-in-law getting another job in the neighbourhood. By trying to appeal to Jarmila's reason and by the use of pressure they hoped to get her to break with Jaroslav. The pressure came mainly from Mrs Mayerová, who disapproved of Hašek even more strongly than her husband and in whose opinion he was a rake, an incorrigible drunkard and now a bankrupt. 'Jarmila gave in for a time, but later they met again and began to go out in secret, just as they had done before they were married.'

Just about this time a mystifying incident occurred which has never been properly explained. It was reported as follows in the paper: 'In the small hours of this morning Jaroslav H. wanted to throw himself from the parapet of the Charles Bridge into the Vltava . . . The theatrical hairdresser, Mr Eduard Bräuer, pulled him back. The police doctor diagnosed a pronounced neurosis, and he was taken to a mental home.'

Naturally there was a police report too: 'Today on February 9th, 1911, at 1.45 a.m. Jaroslav Hašek, a reporter from *Czech Word**, domiciled at Smíchov No. 1125, climbed over the parapet of the Charles Bridge with the object of committing suicide by throwing himself into the Vltava. He was prevented from doing so by the hairdresser Eduard Bräuer, who firmly restrained him and handed him over to the Imperial and Royal security police sergeant František Melech. Hašek's behaviour at the police station was very agitated and he was accordingly examined by the Imperial and Royal police doctor, Dr Kalmus, and taken away as a mental patient for fear he might become dangerous. He was escorted by the Imperial and Royal security police sergeant Heinrich Hlinka to the Imperial and Royal Bohemian regional mental home. Hašek's wife was informed . . .'

In the archives of the *Kateřinky* there have been preserved not only the report of Hašek's medical examination at the police station but also his medical bulletins during his stay at the asylum. At the police station he is reported first to have said

* Hašek was not in fact on the paper's staff.

that he had intended to commit suicide: 'He confirms that he wanted to drown himself and claims that he hates the world. He ran away in a temper. He is sullen. He failed his examinations in his fourth class at school, was in the Commercial and also (as he claims) in the Export Academy in Vienna,* where he obtained excellent marks. Dangerous to himself.'

The next day, when he was brought to the asylum, he resolutely denied having had suicidal intentions: 'The patient remembers that he had been in very many bars and had drunk beer and wine in all of them. He recalls that he climbed up somewhere, perhaps on a lamp-post, but cannot remember clearly how he got there. He claims he wanted to produce an effect on the passers-by and see how they would react.' Afterwards Hašek said that he had been sent to the asylum because he had made fun of the police doctor. It should be noted that neither the police records nor the medical report of the police doctor refer to any signs of drunkenness.

The later entries in the bulletins at the asylum show Hašek acting calmly and normally. He asked for employment and was given the job of putting the medical bulletins in order. The day before he was discharged, he expressed a wish to stay on, to cure himself of alcoholism.

A curious aftermath of this was that a month later Hašek contributed to *Caricatures* a sketch called 'The Psychiatric Enigma',[8] a grotesque version of his own adventure on the Charles Bridge. According to this, Hurych, the president of the Temperance Society, while crossing the Charles Bridge on his way home from a meeting, thought he heard a shriek coming from below and leant over the parapet to investigate. Suddenly a 'noble rescuer' appeared in the person of a hairdresser, who, taking him for a would-be suicide, dragged him down from the parapet. In vain Hurych pleaded that he had no intention of taking his life. The rescuer could not be moved and Hurych's struggles were useless. A police car took him away to the police station, from where he was sent to the lunatic asylum. There he was kept for one and a half years, because the doctors would not discharge him as cured until they had found evidence of mental disturbance in him.

When he was arrested on February 9th Hašek had given

* Untrue

Jaroslav Hašek in 1887, aged four, looking much as he must have done when going for long walks with his grandfather in Prague, deliberately getting lost and joking with the soldiers outside the military hospital.

Josef Hašek, Hašek's father, who died in 1896 when Jaroslav was thirteen. Was alcoholism a family weakness? It certainly contributed to Josef's early death. His son Jaroslav could not give it up for long and his other son Bohuslav died of drink.

Kateřina, Hašek's mother. Her husband's death left her destitute with three children to bring up. Josef had no pension rights and Kateřina had to depend upon the kindness of relatives. Jaroslav's truancy disappointed her bitterly.

Jaroslav Hašek as a young man, over-fond of practical jokes
and alarming chemistry experiments.

Hašek the would-be Anarchist, who turned his literary talents
to the editing of Anarchist journals.

A photograph of Hašek 'as
known to the police' which
was circulated on one of the
warrants for his arrest
between 1905 and 1907.

Jaroslav and Jarmila in the park in 1908.
Jarmila's efforts to improve his appearance are successful—
if only for a little while.

Hašek with his friends at Poděbrady. On his left are Josef Lada, the illustrator of *The Good Soldier Švejk*, Longen's wife and Longen (half-hidden), prominent members of the Prague Bohème.

Hašek (right) perpetrating perhaps the greatest hoax of his life as a candidate for his 'Party of Moderate Progress within the Bounds of the Law' during the Austro-Hungarian parliamentary elections in June 1911.

Hašek and his bohemian friend Kuděj go bathing in ladies' swimming attire. Hašek is the one with the cigarette.

Outside the restaurant U Brejšků Hašek (fourth from the left) takes a job as an ice-breaker. The ice was used to preserve the carp which were part of the obligatory Christmas fare in Bohemia.

This photograph of Hašek (centre) among a group of soldiers in an army hospital appeared in *Horizon* on April 30th, 1915. His experiences of army medical practices reappear both in *The Good Soldier Švejk* and in some of his short stories.

The 11th Company of the 91st Regiment just before leaving for the front in the early summer of 1915. Hašek, thin and dispirited, is on the right.

his address as Smíchov 1125, which was his old apartment at Klamovka. But when Jarmila came to fetch him from the asylum on February 27th, she was living at 23 Komenského in Vinohrady, which was the family home of the Mayers. Possibly, before the adventure on the bridge, there had been some serious quarrel between them and Jarmila had moved to her family home in Vinohrady, where Hašek did not want or was perhaps not allowed to come. We know he left home for a short time and lived with his mother. But after the bridge incident there seems to have been some sort of reconciliation. Jarmila visited Hašek several times in the asylum and persuaded her father to come with her. Mr Mayer was moved by his apparent repentance and especially welcomed his idea of staying on in the asylum to try and cure himself of alcoholism. He is said to have paid for a first-class bed for him.

Was Hašek so upset by the evident failure of his marriage that he seriously contemplated suicide, was the Charles Bridge episode just another example of his inability to resist a hoax, or was it sheer exhibitionism? It seems most likely that it was one of those sudden mad ideas which came into his head without any particular motive or explanation—an excuse for drawing attention to himself which came to him on the spur of the moment. Although it could have been a gesture of truculence, it seems improbable that it was an act of despair, because there is no evidence, other than Jarmila's general observations of his character, that he was deeply shaken by his failure. If he had been, he would not have made a humorous article out of it. In fact the article suggests that the whole episode may have been misunderstood.

Jarmila herself looked at it in a different light, but that was long afterwards:

'Grýša no longer had much hope in the future. He was in despair because in spite of his energy, gifts and success, and the fine offers he had had from all sides, he could not make a living. A desperate man does all sorts of things which would make happy people shrug their shoulders or turn up their noses, especially if he is ambitious and proud and is able to turn his art into a trade just to earn a crust of bread. He suffered. You can imagine how much he suffered. And then he drank. You can imagine how he drank. This is no idle gossip, and I can write about it now because others have written about it before me, but they never said that he suffered, and that he stopped drinking as soon as fortune smiled on him.'

Of course Jarmila never saw Hašek when he seemed to others to be at his gayest, when he was the centre of attention among his bohemian friends in some Prague bar, where in the atmosphere of drink and merriment he grew inspired and told stories which were later to be worked into sketches and to appear in print. Jarmila thought she knew the real Hašek. But did she?

(7)

The Birth of Svejk

It is not clear where Hašek went to live when he left the lunatic asylum. He does not appear to have gone back to Jarmila, who was then staying with her parents. And yet, as Jarmila tells us, it was in May 1911 when Hašek first hit on the idea of creating the character which made him famous throughout the world, the Good Soldier Švejk, and it seems clear that they were then living together.

One evening he had returned home very exhausted. Hardly had he woken up next morning when Jarmila saw him feverishly searching for a scrap of paper which he had left about the night before. Before going to bed he had jotted down on it a 'brilliant idea' and to his horror had now completely forgotten it.

'In the meantime I had thrown it on to the rubbish heap.' (Jarmila had a fetish for tidiness.) Hašek rushed to search for it and was delighted when he found it. He carefully picked up the crumpled note-paper, read its contents, crumpled it up again and threw it away. 'Meanwhile, I rescued it again and preserved it. On it I saw clearly written and underlined the heading of a story, "The Booby in the Company". Underneath was a sentence which was just legible: "He had himself examined to prove that he was capable of serving as a regular soldier."* After that came some further words which were illegible.'[1]

Two world wars have made us familiar with the figure of the stupid conscript who does everything wrong, turning to the left when he should turn to the right, marching backwards when all the rest march forwards, enraging his superiors, especially the company sergeant-majors, by involuntarily throwing a spanner into the otherwise smoothly running military machine. The

---

* At a time when no Czech wanted to be classified as mentally or physically fit for service, the 'booby in the company' was actually asking for it!

pages of *Punch* during the First World War, after conscription
had been introduced for the first time, contained jokes of this
kind. Conscription brought into the army people from ordinary
life who could be totally unsuitable for its humdrum 'bull'. In
the Scandinavian press between the wars there was a popular
strip cartoon about a conscript who got into a scrape every day
but often triumphed over his superiors. The popularity of 'Dad's
Army' proves that this form of humour is still with us, and has
been since Shakespeare first brought it onto the stage in the
scene where Falstaff and Justice Shallow examine their recruits.

In 1911 this was far from being the case. The German and
French armies were serious institutions and even the Austrian
army was no subject for comedy. True, there were exceptions
and *Simplicissimus*, the famous Munich satirical journal, felt free
to mock young Prussian officers, products of a caste system, particularly as the North German, the *Pfiffke*, was a favourite butt
of the South German and Austrian press; but only very rarely
did the rank and file come under the cartoonists' spotlight. It
was dangerous to represent Austrian soldiers as anything but
heroes longing to lay down their lives for the Fatherland.

Exceptionally, a sketch called 'Military Honour' appeared
one day in *Simplicissimus* and was later published in translation
in the 'Workers' Column' of the Czech Social Democratic daily
the *People's Right* on March 16th, 1905. It told the story of a
peasant in uniform who looked like an idiot but who proved to
be quite shrewd and more than a match for the officers who had
to deal with him.

' "You know the younger men better than I do, Baron," said
the German Captain. "What do you think about Mayer? Is this
chap as idiotic as he looks, or is he only pretending?"

' "He's even more idiotic than he looks, sir, but I think someone must have told him that in the army a man can't make
himself appear too stupid. Nobody could possibly be as stupid
as he is. Look at the way he acts. When he was undergoing
training for the first time I asked him who was the highest
officer in the army and the fathead said: '*You* are, sir'.* I
couldn't help laughing and the men all roared too. Well, I
believe that this rogue has now got it into his head that it'll be

* Best translated into French: *C'est toi, mon lieutenant.*

to his advantage to go on acting like this. In the end people will just laugh at him and he'll get away with it. You know, sir, you can't believe what a lot of trouble it cost me to stop him saying 'You',* and I'm perfectly certain that the cunning bastard hadn't been here three days before he'd seen through it all, because those peasants of ours are a damned sight more shrewd than anyone could possibly suspect." '

Pytlík has suggested that this story may have contained the seeds of *The Good Soldier Švejk*. And it poses the question which has never yet been satisfactorily explained: How far is Švejk dim-witted and how far is his supposed dim-wittedness only assumed?

It is impossible to say whether Hašek actually read this story, but he was a voracious reader of papers in the public libraries—including *Simplicissimus*—and it might well have caught his eye and given him the idea.

Menger declares that Hašek was called up for military service in 1906 and that he served for a few weeks at Trient before being cashiered for incompetence. If this were true, it would of course have given him first-hand experience of a conscript's life, but like much that Menger writes there is not a scrap of evidence from other sources to support the statement. On the contrary, army records show that he was not called up until 1915.

Hašek had no doubt learned his anti-militarism from his earlier association with the Anarchists, who had spat on the Austrian uniform and refused to do military service for 'the enemies of the Czech people'. Here Anarchistic pacificism went hand in hand with national sentiment, because Czech conscripts were often ordered about by German officers and the language of command—and of vituperation—was German. As Hašek emphasised in many parts of the final version of *The Good Soldier Švejk*, the Slav personnel were often treated like dogs by German officers and under-officers.

The Austrian government were quick to clamp down on any signs of anti-militarism. On June 30th, 1909 there had been a trial of young people in the National Socialist Party connected with the journal *Young Currents*, led by the editors Špatný and Hatina, both of whom were friends of Hašek's. Forty-four of the

* *Tu.*

accused were convicted, the two editors receiving in 1911 two years' imprisonment each.

Other trials followed and Hašek, who still kept up contact with the group, as well as with Anarchists and Social Democrats, was brought before the police for interrogation in 1910. On December 11th, 1911 his apartment was searched, but no incriminating material found. Jarmila described this experience in her story 'The House Search':[2]

'Once in 1911, at the time of the trial of the anti-militarists, Miťa came home in the early hours of the morning.

' "Hasn't anyone been looking for me, darling?"

' "No, no one."

' "Listen, they took me to the barracks and confronted me with soldiers. Tomorrow we'll probably get a house search."

' "My God!"

' "My stupid angel, a house search, that's just fun, you'll see."

'The day was already beginning to break when we fell asleep. We were aroused by a loud ringing . . .'

According to the rest of the story the police officials dragged husband and wife from their beds but were helpless in the face of the ironical composure of Hašek, who behaved just as Švejk would have done.

' "I would go on looking," he advised them. "The Devil never sleeps and Christ said: 'Who seeks shall find.' "

'They looked in the various drawers in the bookcase and under the carpet, they stirred around in the stove; and finally when they couldn't find anything else they impounded some of Jarmila's old love letters.

' "When shall I get them back?" asked Jarmila, when she met one of them later in a tram. "They are all ready, but if you only knew what trouble we had with them! They had all to be translated into German and sent to Vienna."

' "But you forgot one packet." '

' "Then, please don't tell anyone, madam." '

It is not certain where Hašek got the name of Josef Švejk. Menger suggests he took it from a deputy of the Agrarian Party of that name who represented Kutná Hora. Pytlík thinks it more likely that it came from the Josef Švejk who was concierge in the house where the landlord of the Chalice* lived. He had a son of the same name and Hašek invited them to his home in 1911, because they had once lived in the same house as the Hašeks.

In the *feuilleton* 'How Much Does Someone Have Round his Neck?'[3] published in *Čechoslovan* in Russia on February 2nd, 1917 Hašek mentions another house search which was probably carried out soon after the outbreak of war by the well-known Prague police inspectors Slavíček and Klíma.† (Here they are called Slíva and Klabíček.) 'Commissar Slíva was black and Klabíček was blond. They always went about together and formed a sort of living black and yellow flag.'‡

Meanwhile, after his initial idea of the 'booby in the company', the concept of Švejk had germinated and ripened in Hašek's imagination. In a few days' time he had knocked out the first story in which Švejk appears, which has been christened by the Germans the *Urschwejk* (as the first version of Faust was the *Urfaust*).

Since the story of Švejk emerged altogether in three versions —the *The Good Soldier Švejk*[4] (before the war), *The Good Soldier Švejk in Captivity*[5] (in Russia during the war) and *The Good Soldier Švejk and His Adventures during the World War*[6] (in the Czechoslovak Republic after the war)—it is as well to be clear about the differences between them.

An essential feature of the first version is that it was written during the period when Austrian censorship was very strict. Consequently it presents a primitive and bowdlerised Švejk, a mild figure who lacks the complexity and refinement of the finished article. The second, written in Russia in the heat of anti-Austrian war propaganda, is a cruder and more drastic version of the final book. Hašek undeniably grew in status as a writer between 1911 and 1923; his daily practice of writing during these years, enriched by new experiences, brought him

---

* The Prague tavern often mentioned in *The Good Soldier Švejk* but not actually patronised by Hašek.

† Slavíček and Klíma are referred to in *The Good Soldier Švejk*. The Staff Warder in the Garrison Gaol is called Slavík. *The Good Soldier Švejk*, p. 80.

‡ The Austrian colours.

subtlety and maturity. The final version of *The Good Soldier Švejk* written towards the end of his life reflects this development.

The very first story about Švejk, 'Švejk Stands Against Italy',[7] was published in Lada's *Caricatures* on May 22nd, 1911.

'Švejk joined up with a happy heart. His object was to have fun in the army and he succeeded in astonishing the whole garrison in Trient including the garrison commander himself. Švejk always had a smile on his lips, was amiable in his behaviour and perhaps for that reason found himself continually in gaol . . .

'When he was let out of gaol he answered every question with a smile. And with complete equanimity he let himself be gaoled again, inwardly happy at the thought that all the officers of the whole garrison in Trient were frightened of him—not because of his rudeness, oh no, but because of his polite answers, his polite behaviour and his amiable and friendly smile, which anguished them.

'An inspecting officer came into the men's quarters. A smiling Švejk, sitting on his camp bed, greeted him politely: "Humbly report, praise be to Jesus Christ."

'Lieutenant Walk ground his teeth at the sight of Švejk's sincere friendly smile and would have relished knocking his cap straight on his head to make it conform with regulations. But Švejk's warm and fervent look restrained him from any such manifestation.

'Major Teller came into the room. Lieutenant Walk sternly eyed the men, who stood at their camp beds, and said: "You, Švejk, bring your *kver** here!"

'Švejk carried out the order conscientiously and, instead of bringing his rifle, brought in his pack. Major Teller looked furiously at his charming innocent countenance and flew at him in Czech: "You not know what *kver* is?"

' "Humbly report, I don't." And so they took him straight away to the office. They brought in a rifle and stuck it under his nose: "What this? What it called?"—"Humbly report, I don't know."

* The Lieutenant and the Major, when speaking to the Czechs, speak a kind of pidgin Austrian. *Kver* (*Gewehr*) is not a Czech word and Švejk, as an unfledged recruit, was fully justified in not understanding it.

' "It's a *kver*."—"Humbly report, I don't believe it."

'He was put in gaol and the prison warder considered it his duty to tell him that he was an ass. The rank and file marched out for heavy exercises in the mountains, but Švejk sat behind bars smiling placidly.

'As they could do nothing whatsoever with him they appointed him orderly to the one-year volunteers. He served at lunch and dinner in the club.

'He laid the knives and forks, brought in the food, beer and wine, sat down modestly by the door and uttered from time to time: "Humbly report, gentlemen, Lieutenant Walk is a nice gentleman, yes, a very nice gentleman, indeed." And he smiled and blew his cigarette smoke in the air.

'Another day there was an inspection at the officers' club. Švejk was standing modestly by the door and a new officer was unlucky enough to ask him which company he belonged to.

' "Humbly report, if you please, I don't know."—"Hell's bells, which regiment is stationed here, then?"—"Humbly report, if you please, I don't know."—"For Christ's sake, man, what's the name of the garrison town here?"—"Humbly report, if you please, I don't know."—"Then, man, how on earth did you get here?"

'With an amiable smile and looking at the officer in a sweet and extremely pleasant manner, Švejk said "Humbly report, I was born and after that I went to school. Then I learned to be a carpenter. After that they brought me to an inn, and there I had to strip naked. A few months later the gendarmes came for me and took me off to the barracks. At the barracks they examined me and said: 'Man, you're three weeks late in beginning your military service. We're going to put you in gaol.' I asked why, when I didn't want to join the army and didn't even know what a soldier was. All the same they clapped me in gaol, then put me on a train and took me all over the place until we reached here. I didn't ask anyone what regiment, company, town it was, so as not to offend anyone, but immediately during my first drill they gaoled me, because I lit a cigarette in the ranks, although I don't know why. Then they put me in gaol whenever I appeared, first because I lost my bayonet, then because I nearly shot the Colonel at the rifle butts until finally I'm serving the one-year volunteer gentlemen." . . .

'Christmas Eve was approaching. The one-year volunteers had decorated a Christmas tree in the club and after dinner the Colonel gave a moving address, saying that Christ was born, as all of them knew, and that he was delighted in having good soldiers and that every good soldier should be delighted with himself . . .

'And at that moment, in the midst of this solemn address, a fervent voice could be heard: "Oh yes, indeed! That's so."

'It came from the good soldier Švejk, who stood with a beaming face, unobserved among the one-year volunteers.

' "You, volunteers," roared the Colonel, "who was it who shouted?" Švejk stepped forward from the ranks of the one-year volunteers and looked smilingly at the Colonel: "Humbly report, sir, I serve the one-year volunteer gentlemen here and I was very happy to hear what you kindly said just now. You've got your heart and soul in your job."

'When the bells in Trient rang for the midnight Mass the good soldier Švejk had been sitting in clink for more than an hour.

'On that occasion he was locked up for a pretty long time. Later they hung a bayonet on him and assigned him to a machine gun section.

'There were grand manoeuvres on the Italian frontier and the good soldier Švejk marched after the army.

'Before the expedition he had listened to a cadet's speech: "Imagine that Italy has declared war on us and we are marching against the Italians."

' "Good, then, forward march!" Švejk exclaimed, for which he got six days.

'After having served this punishment he was sent after his machine gun section with three other prisoners and a corporal. First they marched along a valley, then they went on horseback up to the mountains and, as could have been expected, Švejk got lost in the dense forest on the Italian frontier. He squeezed his way through the undergrowth, searching vainly for his companions until he happily crossed the Italian frontier in full equipment.

'And it was there that the good soldier Švejk distinguished himself. An Italian machine gun section from Milan had just had manoeuvres on the Austrian frontier and a mule with a machine gun and eight men got up onto the plateau on which the good soldier Švejk was making his reconnaissance.

'The Italian soldiers, feeling confidently secure, had crawled quietly into a thicket and gone to sleep. The mule with the machine gun was busily pasturing and straying further and further away from its detachment, until finally it came to the spot where the good soldier Švejk was smilingly looking at the enemy.

'The good soldier Švejk took the mule by the bridle and went back to Austria together with the Italian machine gun on the back of the Italian mule.

'From the mountain slopes he got down again into the valley from which he had climbed up, wandered about with the mule in a forest for the whole day, until at last in the evening he caught sight of the Austrian camp.

'The guard did not want to let him in, because he did not know the password. An officer came up and Švejk smilingly assumed a military posture and saluted: "Humbly report, sir, I've captured a mule and a machine gun from the Italians."

'And so they led off the good soldier Švejk to the garrison gaol, but we now know what the latest Italian machine gun type looks like.'

This story was followed by four others about Švejk—'The Good Soldier Švejk Obtains Wine for the Mass',[8] 'The Good Soldier Švejk is Cashiered',[9] 'The Good Soldier Švejk Learns How to Deal with Gun-Cotton'[10] and finally 'The Good Soldier Švejk Operates in Aeroplanes'.[11]

The last of these brings Švejk up to date and is memorable for its opening sentence: 'Austria has three dirigible airships, eighteen non-dirigible ones and five aeroplanes.' Here the original Czech has for 'non-dirigible' *airships which cannot be steered*, which can also mean *airships which are unpilotable*. Appropriately enough Švejk, with his hands on the controls, flies over the Alps, southern Europe, the Mediterranean and gets carried away to Africa. He had received the order 'Fly to the devil' and, as always, he had done his best to obey.

Hašek played a dirty trick on the kindly editor Lada. Because he had to wait longer for his fee than he liked, he cheated him by publishing the third instalment of *The Good Soldier Švejk* not only in *Caricatures* but also in the *Good Joker*,[12] a rival magazine.

Lada at once resolved to pay Hašek back in his own coin. He said to himself: 'Rather than share Švejk with another paper, I'll have him executed at once.' And so he commissioned another humorous writer to prepare a plagiarised fourth story, in which Švejk met his death in a perilous adventure, and published it over the signature 'Jaroslav Ašek'. He relished the thought of Hašek's rage when he found that his hero had been killed, but his *Schadenfreude* did not last long. When the next edition of *Caricatures* returned from the censors, of the whole story only the headline had survived: 'Jaroslav Hašek: End of the Good Soldier Švejk'.

The collection of stories about Švejk was published in book form at the end of 1911 under the title *The Good Soldier Švejk and Other Strange Stories*.

(8)

A Most Peculiar Party

When Hašek found himself on his beam ends once more, he resolved to perpetrate his biggest hoax yet. This time it was to prove a highly organised one: he planned to found a new political party—the 'Party of Moderate Progress within the Bounds of the Law'[1]—and stand as its candidate for the Prague Vinohrady seat at the Imperial parliamentary elections in June 1911.

This crazy idea was suggested to him by Eduard Drobílek, an eccentric who worked in the accounts department of the Technical College and happened to be infatuated with the daughter of Zvěřina, the landlord of a café-bar which stood on a crossroad in Korunní třída and rejoiced in the bucolic name of V Kravíně.*

Zvěřina faced stiff competition, because the other three corners were occupied by old-established café-bars, each of which accommodated the electoral offices of one of the traditional parties—the Young Czechs, the National Socialists and the Social Democrats. Drobílek thought that a new and completely original party would boost Zvěřina's business and so improve his own chances of being accepted as his son-in-law.

Although the 'party' did not take on life until 1911, the idea of making fun of the whole parliamentary system in the Monarchy had already been a favoured topic in a bohemian group of artists, poets and intellectuals sympathetic to Anarchist ideas, who used to meet together at the Golden Litre, a café-bar in Vinohrady. As early as 1904 Hašek and the Anarchist Křížek had written a mock poem entitled 'The Meeting of the Political Club of the Constitutional Party of June 24th in the *Konvikt*',†[2] in which the expression 'moderate progress within the law' first

* In the Cowshed.
† *Konvikt* was the Czech for a student hostel, but the Prague *Konvikt* was a popular meeting hall.

appeared. Later Hašek performed at the 'Tortoise'[3] cabaret in a number called 'I'm a Member of a Country Deputation'.

Hašek's cynical and nonsensical attitude to politics had also been expressed earlier in a poem he had written and dedicated to 'The Tortoise' and to Karel the head waiter at the café-bar, which he happened to be patronising at the time:

> Education, gentlemen? The main thing's BEER!
> I like to go where there's plenty of cheer.
> Our nation's a church, where a candle flames.
> Velké Popovice* is one of its names.
> Long life to 'The Tortoise'. Let's get used to Karel.
> My politics, gentlemen, are—the barrel.

He had already been writing satires on the parties and their leaders in *Caricatures* and he saw in this mock election campaign a good opportunity for developing his talents as a parodist. It not only satisfied his pathological craving for exhibitionism but offered him the opportunity to have a really good dig at the despised old Monarchy.

The name of the 'party' had been Hašek's own inspiration. Accustomed from his Anarchist days to ridiculing the moderate or reformist tendencies of the orthodox Left (the Social Democrat Party), it gave him peculiar pleasure to pretend to be making propaganda for them. Masaryk and his Realist Party, who advocated gradualism, were further targets for his ridicule.

Since the original manuscript of the 'party' manifesto, issued in April 1911, is in Jarmila's handwriting, it is more than probable that Hašek himself drafted it. It has many features of his style. Explaining the importance of the concept 'Moderate Progress within the Bounds of the Law', he argues that just as an infant does not become a man by violent explosive growth but by the process of natural development from day to day and year to year, so the 'party' too has to evolve in the same way. 'Czech people! Before you came under the rule of the Habsburgs, the Přemysl, Jagellon and Luxemburg dynasties had to be born . . . and before the Bridge of Svatopluk Čech† could be built,

* A famous brand of Prague beer.

† Svatopluk Čech was a leading Czech poet of the time. The bridge in Prague bears the same name today. It crosses the Vltava from a spot near the Intercontinental Hotel.

Svatopluk Čech himself had first to be born, then become famous and finally die. After that they had to clean things up and only then could they build the bridge.'

In his electioneering speeches the 'candidate' made various points. Animals must at last be rehabilitated. There must be an end to the practice of maligning them at election meetings by calling human beings by their names. When a heckler shouted at the candidate of another party, 'Shut up, you ox', it was important to realise that an ox weighing 700 kilos was much more valuable than a candidate weighing about 80. For the one you got 400 guilders, whereas for the other you'd be lucky to get even a guilder. At the same time noble creatures like dogs must no longer be insulted by being given names of kings and emperors. The faithful dog on the milk-round was called Nero and the small terrier who had never injured or tyrannised anyone, Caesar.

The 'party' was not so 'progressive' as to support current demands of the day, like women's rights or funeral by cremation, but as Hašek explained, progress was a two-edged weapon. The newspaper *Time*[4] (Masaryk's party) had written that Yorkshire piggies were more 'progressive' than the Czech variety. This had induced a woman reader to buy a couple of Yorkshire piggies. Later she wrote to the paper that they could go to hell with their 'progressive' pigs. Her Czech sow had once produced sixteen piglets, whereas the 'progressive' one could hardly manage five.

Hašek was a clever speaker at that time and a good compère. His ripostes kept his audience in fits of laughter. When someone shouted out, 'Hašek, when are you going to pay me back the crown I lent you?' he swiftly retorted: 'Don't let's bring the Crown into this!' On another occasion he rebutted charges levelled against him by the other candidates. The Social Democrat accused him of having been twice in prison. Hašek's reply was that it was a base and vulgar invention. He had certainly not been in prison twice. He had been in prison three times. And to the candidate for the Young Czech–National Socialist coalition, who accused him of having stolen dogs while at Smíchov, he replied that it was not a case of theft at all but of cynological research into the question of which breeds of dogs were most widespread in the Smíchov district and what was the

influence on this of the long-haired terrier from the Count
Wittenberg litter which Čížek owned.

The 'party' had its platform, its executive committee and
even its hymn, which was sung at the beginning of each meeting. It was the work of Josef Mach,[5] parodied the Anarchist
hymn and ran as follows:

> A thousand candidates rose up
> To hoodwink honest people
> And take the electorate's votes.
> Let others call for rapid progress,
> By force world order overturn,
> Moderate progress is our aim
> And Hašek our candidate.
> Voters in this town,
> Bring your misery to the Cowshed!
> Only those of you who have the itch,
> Pray stay away!
> Down with immoderate progressives!
> Down with lay bankrupts too!
> To arms, to arms, to arms!
> Moderate progress is our aim.

The public were invited to put questions to the candidate
rather than shout him down. The first question was free, the
rest cost half a litre of beer each. All weapons had to be placed
on the chairman's table. It was no good shooting the speaker,
because it would be too late to find a replacement. Anyhow a
gun cost an unheard-of amount of money and what was the
price of a glass of beer in comparison?

Langer has given us a first-hand account of one of these election meetings:

'On Sunday evening the café was full. Lots of well-known personalities came—artists, journalists, bohemians,* as well as
respectable citizens from the neighbouring streets. They were
attracted by Hašek's name or by the news of a new and unknown political party. Hašek appeared clean and sober an hour

* Pytlík includes among them Max Brod and Franz Kafka, but the
evidence for this is sketchy.

before the start . . . As eight o'clock struck the solemn hymn was intoned by the committee . . .

'Then Hašek got going. He presented himself in the most favourable light as the most suitable candidate for the seat (and as particularly eligible for the daily subsistence allowance, which the elected deputy would draw). He expounded his programme, which consisted of innumerable promises of reform, abused the other parties, cast suspicion on the rival candidates —in fact did exactly what a normal candidate for such a distinguished position always does . . . He spoke for a good three hours . . .'

He appears to have improvised the whole time, sometimes keeping fairly closely to his subject, at other times jumping from one theme to another. Sometimes what he said was quite new; at other times he repeated a number he had had success with before, or borrowed an idea from one of his stories.

'. . . We listened to speeches about various saints, about the war on alcohol, the genuineness of the manuscripts,* the usefulness of missionaries and other phenomena of contemporary life. He pilloried nuisances supported or tolerated by the state, such as the obligatory charge of twenty hellers levied by houseporters for opening the outer doors at night and the entrance fees for public lavatories, which forced needy citizens, who cared for their health and could not afford the payment, to use more public places and be fined by the police for doing so. He thought up grandiose promises, likely to attract voters of the most varied occupations and the most contradictory interests, and with mysterious allusions to the next evening's performance, promised various revelations about rival candidates, hinting at crime and the murder of their grandmothers.'[6]

In the manifesto which he read out at one performance Hašek summed up the 'party' programme as follows:

* This referred to the notorious 'newly discovered' mediaeval manuscripts, which at that time were the centre of a heated controversy. Many had been taken in by them, including Goethe, but they were eventually proved by T. G. Masaryk to be an ingenious forgery.

1 Moderate progress within the bounds of the law.
2 Greater strictness with the poor.
3 Nationalisation of house-porters and sextons.
4 Down with lay creditors.
5 Credit banks to be placed in the hands of the clergy.

The argument for the 'nationalisation' of house-porters and sextons was that it was not right that a citizen should be able to go into a pub gratis at 2 a.m., but not be admitted to his own home after 10 p.m. without paying a fee. 'Nationalisation' of house-porters would mean that they would be on duty all the time, like the police, and consequently the need for payments would not arise. As for sextons, he argued with typically Hašek-ian absurdity and echoes of Gogol's *Dead Souls*, they had access to church offices and thus to lists of deceased voters, who could be of considerable importance on polling day, as had recently been shown by the great success of the Young Czech Party in winning their votes. If, with the cooperation of the sextons, an election campaign were well organised and of course generously financed, a dead voter in the Vinohrady district would know his duty and vote for the new 'party' even if he had difficulty in walking and had to be taken to the polling booth in a cab. After all, the candidate of the immoral Young Czech–National Socialist Bloc already had all cabs booked for polling day.

Hašek had not of course gone as far as to register his 'candi-dature' officially and those few ballot papers which bore crosses against his name were declared invalid. In his district there were eighteen spoiled and seventeen invalid. The National Socialist came first with 3,215 votes and the Social Democrat second with 917, but the well-known patriotic poet, Viktor Dyk, who was a candidate for the small Constitutional Progressive Party received only 205.

Hašek's escapades naturally did not escape the attention of the press. *Time* of June 15th, 1911, reported that on election day and the day preceding it a crowd of people collected in front of Zvěřina's. All the windows of the café-bar were pasted over with sensational notices which read:

'Vote as one man for our candidate, the candidate of the Party of Moderate Progress within the Bounds of the Law, the writer Jaroslav Hašek, who at numerous meetings has unfolded his resourceful programme for the nationalisation of house-porters. We still need fifteen votes . . . What you cannot get out of Vienna, you will get from us. Today there will be a memorial mass for the unsuccessful candidates. Everyone who votes for us will receive as a gift a small pocket aquarium.'

Hašek hoped to capitalise on the prevailing disillusionment with the existing political parties and their lack of principle—which was shared by his boon companions and probably by wider circles of the electorate. The National Socialist Party, for instance, after having sharply attacked in its press all 'immoral compromises' such as electoral pacts between parties, decided a fortnight later to make just such a deal themselves with the Young Czech Party, claiming that differences among nationalist parties could be more easily bridged than those among parties belonging to the 'red international'. Hašek pilloried the National Socialist candidate, inventing a story that, although his party was free-thinking, he had called on the nuns of the order of St Barnabas and tried to persuade them to pray for his victory. Hašek commented: 'We ourselves have an offer from the nuns of St Ursula and from the Rabbi of the Majzl Syna-gogue to pray for us for a modest fee, but, my friends, we do not intend to go so far in our 'moderate progress' as to rely on the help of God.'

The Social Democratic slogan of 'unity, equality and fratern-ity' was represented in Czech by the initial letters SRK. For Hašek they meant '*slivovice*, rum and *kontušovka*'.* He showed no respect for 'sacred cows', referring to a portrait of Jan Hus as 'fly-blown', and even mercilessly caricaturing Ziegloser, the patriot who had received the longest sentence at the Progressive Youth treason trial, whom he depicted as exploiting his martyr-dom in the interest of touting wines.

When the elections were over, Hašek started to write what he called the *Political and Social History of the Party of Moderate Progress within the Bounds of the Law*.[7] Completed in the autumn of 1911, it has never been traced in its entirety, but seems to have con-sisted of (1) the 'party' records; (2) the 'apostolic activity' of three of its members, as recorded in their letters to the executive

* A Polish brandy.

committee, 'apostolic activity' being a euphemism for the vagabond tours of Hungary made by Hašek and two of his bohemian
friends; (3) the 'party's' 'reconnoitring scandals' (such as
Hašek's attempt to infiltrate himself into *Czech Word* in order to
spy on the National Socialist Party), and finally (4) the 'party's'
activity in the elections. In effect the work consisted of no more
than a loose string of articles ridiculing the activities of the various political parties of the time, satirising their leaders and
parodying their speeches. To this gallimaufry Hašek added for
good measure humorous personal sketches of many of his friends
and companions, including even Jarmila's brothers. Since
some of them were highly libellous, if not scurrilous, they obviously could not be published when they were written or indeed
in the foreseeable future, and were lucky to survive at all in
view of Hašek's known carelessness in the handling of his
manuscripts.

In 1912 Hašek gave the completed manuscript to Karel
Ločák, the publisher of *Merry Prague* and other magazines.
When the latter realised how defamatory the contents were,
he felt it would be too risky to publish them and sold them
instead to Alois Hatina, another of Hašek's friends from his
Anarchist days, who in 1924 and 1925 published ten chapters
in *Trend*,[8] which he edited.

In 1936 Menger happened to see the manuscript in Hatina's
possession and asked to borrow it for study. Hatina agreed on
condition that he did not publish extracts in any journal, since
much of the satire in it was directed against the National
Socialist Party, of which he was a functionary.

However Menger, being short of funds, broke his word and
sold it to the young Communist literary critic, Julius Fučík, an
admirer of Hašek's work, who began to print twenty-three
chapters of it in *Red Right*[9] in 1937, including some which ridiculed functionaries of the National Socialist Party, by that time
a strong opponent of the Communist Party. Hatina then took
the manuscript back from Menger. A year later Menger begged
Hatina to let him have it back, swearing this time that he would
not let any more of it be published. It was fortunate that Hatina
consented, since, when the Nazis in 1939 seized his apartment
and destroyed his whole library, the manuscript was safe in
Menger's possession and survived the war untouched. After the

war it was placed in the Czechoslovak National Museum in Prague and only published as late as 1963. As it was obviously incomplete (chapters bearing the titles 'Electoral Activity'[10] and 'The Party Propagates its Principles at Cultural Evenings'[11] had disappeared and could not be traced), other of Hašek's relevant manuscripts were added, when the 'complete' version was published.[12]

The rest of the *History* consisted mainly of profiles of various 'party' members, or of Hašek's 'friends' and enemies, which would certainly not have pleased them if they had seen them in print. They took the form of mock eulogies, the subjects being treated as outstanding members of the 'party' or of society. The totally unimportant Drobílek for instance was described as one of the noblest of men, but, as was sometimes the case with noble men, always unlucky in love.

One day he fell in love with a seamstress and 'in his goodness and honesty, in all pureness of heart' invited her to go with him on an excursion. He arrived at the rendezvous with a large packet under his arm.

' "What are you carrying there?" asked the young girl with a charming smile, when they got on to the steamer to Závist. "Wait until we are in the wood, miss," Drobílek replied, looking at her devotedly in the eyes, "there are too many people here."

'When they were finally in the wood and sitting in a place concealed from all human gaze, he nestled up to her and said tenderly: "Heart of gold, I've got with me two pairs of pants, two shirts and a reel of cotton. The pants are torn in the fork and the shirts have holes in the elbow. Heart of gold, please mend them here and now." And turning round he cried out in enthusiasm: "See how beautifully the birds are singing!"

'And as he told us about this, Drobílek always sighed and added: "You know what she did? She called me a nasty brute! And before I could hand her the pants and shirts she was gone. Whatever did she think, when I suggested we should go into the thicket together?" '[13]

Then there was Miss Süss or Sísová, whose gruff voice contrasted astonishingly with her sweet-sounding name. Hašek described a visit made to her by Opočenský, when she was editor of *Vydra's Magazine*.[14] When he knocked at the door, a bass voice answered 'Come in'. Opočenský was so surprised that he suddenly took it into his head that Miss Sísová had perhaps asked her brother to take her place for a short time and that this devoted fellow had given himself a good shave, dressed himself up in women's clothes without padding his chest and was sitting there waiting for contributions. When Opočenský addressed her in the masculine and asked 'the brother' to take a message for the sister, Miss Sísová's reaction was terrifyingly fierce and he fled. Hašek's one-time guardian and benefactor would not have taken kindly to this absurd story about the good lady who had edited his political speeches—referred to by Hašek as 'the Czech Maid of Orleans'.[15]

Some of these sketches foreshadow episodes in *Švejk* or other of Hašek's writings The sketch 'Augustin Eugen Mužík'[16] (the editor of the *People's Magazine* and *Horizon*) describes for instance how Hašek called on him and hoped to persuade him to accept his contributions by pretending to know all his relatives in south Bohemia. He was nearly caught out several times. While they were talking about a certain Volešňák, the editor asked him how many children the man had.

' "Eighteen."

' "What, eighteen!"

' "No, Mr Editor, I mean that on the 18th he had his third child."

' "But I know myself of five children."

' "Of course, Mr Editor, but I mean three *live* children. The other five were still-born."

' "And so," [concluded Hašek] "thanks to that Volešňák from Kozovary I made my connection with the *People's Magazine* and *Horizon*. I thank him warmly for it." '

Švejk used the same trick on the Colonel's maid when he was trying to steal the dog she was taking out.*

Much of Hašek's satire was **directed** against the National Socialist Party. He devoted a whole sketch to Šefrna, the servant in the editorial offices of *Czech Word*, who apostrophised everyone as 'brother', whether he was a party member or not. He

---

* *The Good Soldier Švejk*, p. 193.

believed that Jesus Christ himself had been a National Socialist. Otherwise he did not much care for Jews, because he had never seen one wear red and white carnations (the National Socialist colours) except when the National Socialist Youth wanted to break his windows! Šefrna was an Old Catholic* as well as a National Socialist and so had two reasons for loving Jesus Christ. He had joined the Old Catholics, because unlike ortho-dox Catholics they took Communion in both kinds—in wine as well as bread.[17]

In another chapter Hašek amusingly analysed the difference between Hungarians and Czechs:

'Hungarians have a flair for politics. It is said that when we Czechs argue about politics, we do it over a tankard of beer, while Hungarians do it over a bottle of wine.

'Beer will never make a man as politically developed as wine will, because *in vino veritas*. And Hungarians go on searching for that truth until they fall under the table. When a Czech falls under the table, he stops talking. But even under the table Hungarians go on arguing about politics.'

In a chapter of the *History* called 'Election Day',[18] Hašek parodied the way the political parties tried to present their failures as successes. 'Our defeat . . . is only the harbinger of future victories,' he says and quotes the Realists as saying, 'It is true that we got a thrashing, but the moral victory is ours' or the Young Czechs 'We were beaten down like corn, but it augurs a happier future for us'. In the case of his own 'party' he blames failure on the fact that 'by an unhappy combination of circumstances they served Vinohrady beer in our electioneering offices, whereas in the others they served Velkopopovické or Smíchov (famous brands). As a result our electioneering agents had to keep on rushing to the WC and that was the sum total of their 'electoral agitation'. The combination of the WC, the 'cowshed', the 'party's' odd name and the pot-belliedness of the candidate (Hašek must already have been quite fat by this time) spelled disaster.

Hašek relates that to counteract the successful 'agitation' of

* Those Catholics who rejected the encyclical on papal infallibility.

the other parties, they had even advertised for a special assistant, posting up in the windows the notice: 'Vacancy for a moral
young man for the job of slandering the opposing candidates.'
They also offered a free lunch, with the menu on display, which
gave Hašek all the scope he desired for embroidering on his
Animal World hoaxes—elephant's trunk in aspic, roast camel tail
with crab, fried sea-horse with roast skua, stuffed kangaroo
stomach, whale liver, paté of nightingales' tongues, swiftlets'
nests and Tartar cheese made of mares' milk. Unfortunately
only one customer came along and ordered nothing more than
a piece of cheese, which was a bad sign. At six o'clock when the
results showed that they had lost by an enormous majority he
had to be carried away dead drunk in the 'municipal trunk'.*

Apart from these examples, which cannot fully convey the
flavour of what may be regarded as Hašek's second major work,
the *History* contains amusing sketches, musical scenes etc. They
have little to do with each other and still less to do with the
'party'. But we must remember that many of them were not
originally intended to be read, but to be recited or acted in
cabarets.

The *History* is significant in that it showed Hašek ceasing to
work in the one-dimensional framework of the average humorous writer. Here he not only writes and acts the products of his
comic muse, but actually lives some of them. Few writers before
him had ventured to break out of the pages of the written book
and make their literary fancies a living reality. Further, it is a
civil counterpart to *The Good Soldier Švejk*. The *History* mercilessly destroys political life in Bohemia and the Monarchy just
as the novel was to destroy the army and the spirit of militarism.

* A trunk in which drunks were laid and then carried off in a hand-cart
to be sobered up.

(9)

The Break-Up of a Marriage

After a short period of quiet life, Hašek returned once more to his bohemian and vagabond habits. He left Jarmila for a while and went to live with his mother.

He was once more in the black books of the police, having been summoned for disturbing the night peace, 'because on July 14th, 1911, at about 2.45 a.m. . . . in Vinohrady, he was firing a child's pistol fitted with a cork so that each shot made a powerful report like that of a revolver. The pistol was confiscated and is included as *corpus delicti*.'

By August he had left his mother's home and the police were looking for him in Choděra's and Brejšek's bars, but no one there knew anything about him. It was finally established that he had moved at the beginning of the year to the suburb of Vršovice, but was not yet registered there. Only at the end of 1911 did the police find his exact address.

By now Jarmila was expecting a child, and when the parents learned of it they were very upset. But after the first excitement, realising that there was nothing they could do to prevent it, they calmed down and allowed the couple to move back together into the Vršovice apartment.

Vilma Warausová has described her impressions of it:

'Jarmila led me into an old apartment house in a side street. The door opened directly from a passage into the kitchen. There was no hall, no bathroom, no comfort. In the kitchen there was some white furniture, a part of a bedroom suite of Canadian birch, every piece piled on top of the other, reaching up to the ceiling. Behind the kitchen there was a dark long room and in it lay higgledy-piggledy study furniture of polished oak and more bedroom furniture. It was not a flat at all but a furniture warehouse.'[1]

Hašek was there during part of Vilma's visit and when he went out he asked Jarmila to finish off a story for him. Vilma was surprised by this but Jarmila explained that she was now quite familiar with his literary techniques.

Again he had been making vain attempts to find a fixed job. At last in November he was appointed assistant local news editor in *Czech Word*, where he was to deal with what in English newspapers used to be called 'the seamy side' of life. His comment on his change of occupation was typically wry: 'From *Animal World* I slid smoothly into *Czech Word*. My friends said that I did not change my political thinking in any way. For bulldogs I simply substituted a new party. The only difference was that I had been feeding bulldogs and mastiffs, and now it was I who was being fed by the new party.' He also referred to it in his satire 'One Day in the Editorial Offices of *Czech Word*', which was included in *The History*. 'The best job for a man to have in a political newspaper office in order to follow as from a hiding place all the political moves and tricks is a local reporter's. You deal with murders and broken legs and other fine calamities, but while you're doing so you have a splendid chance of seeing what's going on around you.' (A reference to his 'intelligence mission' as a member of the 'party'.)

In Prague bars he used to sell his news stories to other correspondents at two glasses of beer apiece. The general opinion was, however, that he invented many of them and they were not worth a great deal. According to Hašek, if there were not enough suicides, accidents etc. one simply had to invent stories to entertain the readers. A report of his that a meteor had fallen in Bavaria aroused considerable interest and a professor from Moravia wrote a very long letter to the paper saying that when he returned home at two o'clock in the morning he had seen something on the horizon the size of a shooting star of the third order. Later he had second thoughts in case people in Bohemia might think he had been out on the tiles that night, and wrote again asking for his name and address not to be published. But it was too late. They were already in the paper. Another of Hašek's *canards* was that remnants of the historic sect of the Adamites, who went about naked on principle, had been observed in the forests round a certain southern Bohemian village. When the gendarmerie read about this they immediately went to investigate and a peasant who happened at that moment to have taken his trousers down for an urgent purpose was caused grave embarrassment.

The editorial offices of *Czech Word* were then in the building of the Golden Goose,[2] a hotel where he used to stay overnight, playing cards in its restaurant and attending balls and other entertainments, in his quest for topical items and oddities. He began to get drawn back into night life and alcoholism. In the end he even dropped his regular drinking companions and found other company, sinking lower and lower.

Jarmila was anguished at his behaviour. In one of the few letters of hers which have been preserved she wrote:

'Míťa, my darling, how can you torment me like this? How can you sit somewhere . . . in the company of people who have never known true love and fritter away their nights? You know that if they had promised to meet a fallen woman they would never give her up for your sake. But for their sakes you can desert and destroy your wife, who loves you and weeps at home . . .'

As usual Hašek's answer was to cover himself with reproaches, to beg to be forgiven, and swear that he would never do it again and really turn over a new leaf. But the next day he again found the call of the bohemian life irresistible.

Jarmila wrote him a letter after the death of his mother, two and a half months before the birth of their child. It was sent from the hospital at Vinohrady (where Mrs Hašek had presumably died) and bore the date January 24th, 1912:

'I am very worried that you did not come [to the hospital]. They looked for you in the office and could not find you. I know that you will suffer great pain because of it. At least see that you get to the funeral in time. And take care to be decently and suitably dressed. They will look at you very thoroughly, you know they will. Everyone knows that you did not go [to the hospital] although B.* told you that Mamma was seriously ill. Please don't miss the funeral. It would be shameful and unforgivable if you did. Get yourself a bowler hat.

* Possibly Bohuslav.

'Have you got your overcoat out of pawn? Come here in the morning. I'll give you the ticket for the black trousers.

'And come back to me in the evening or I'll think that you want to abandon me altogether. You know that you are the only person in the world I love, and you won't find anyone else. I am sorry for you. Telephone me whether you got the news in time.

'And weep for her, if you can, at home. I know that you loved her but it's your frightful carelessness in everything. Don't weep there. They would only think you were play-acting. But come back to me.'

She had every reason to be disillusioned about him. He had definitely failed her. In spite of her disapproval of his drinking companions and her entreaties to him not to join them, he went on wasting his nights with them. And then, to crown everything, he lost his job again.

There was a strike of tramway employees in Prague. As an assistant editor of the paper he attended a meeting in the Rieger Park in Vinohrady where some of the employees attacked the management and the general mood, which Hašek actively fomented, was for a strike. When the union leaders advised the men to give in, Hašek suddenly rose and spoke. He did not say very much, but what he said about them was quite enough. 'Don't listen to them. They have betrayed the strike because they are in the pay of management. I am the writer, Jaroslav Hašek, editor of *Czech Word*, and I declare that the strike is on!' The meeting broke up in uproar.

Hašek's energetic stand in favour of the strikers had its special background. *Czech Word* had for a long time been waging a campaign against the management of the tramways and inciting the employees to fight for higher wages, and Hašek had contributed some sharp polemics himself. Suddenly the politicians behind the paper changed their line and advocated a compromise. But the day after the Rieger Park incident *Czech Word* carried a report under the headline 'Stormy Evening Meeting' which stated that 'the Presidium had with difficulty held back an extreme explosion of discontent'. Once more the old Anarchist and radical in Hašek had been roused. Once more he had shown his utter irresponsibility in allowing himself to be carried away by his enthusiasm at the risk of losing his post and all hopes of a stable existence. It was not to be wondered at that the following day he was met by the sour-faced directors who told him that they had decided not to employ him any longer. He describes this whole adventure in the story 'How I Left the National Socialist Party'.[3]

After this he was once more out of stable employment and devoted himself exclusively to literary activity. He quickly finished the *History* of his 'party' and prepared his Švejk stories for publication in book form. He would soon finally sever his connections with his family.

Shortly after the birth of his son in April 1912 the final breach came. It seems that the Mayers came to the flat in Vršovice on a visit. Hašek welcomed them joyfully, although obviously in some embarrassment at having lost another job. He volunteered to go out and fetch some beer—and never returned. The parents waited for him in vain and then took Jarmila and the baby, first to their home in Vinohrady, and later to a villa they owned in Dejvice. Jarmila's explanation of the event was as follows: 'After leaving *Czech Word* Jaroslav was without a job. He felt that he could no longer maintain a family, especially after the birth of little Ríša [Richard]. He knew too that if he went away his father-in-law would look after his wife, and this is in fact what happened.' It was as terse as an official communique.

There were funnier legendary versions of this event. According to one of these the father-in-law gave Hašek the money to buy a perambulator, but he lost nearly all of it at cards. Then suddenly his luck turned and he won so much that he proudly returned with three perambulators. According to another version he was so delighted with his newly born son that he proudly showed him in all the café-bars but unfortunately forgot about him and left him behind in one of them. Although this story certainly fits well with his irresponsibility it is more likely to have been thought up by Hašek himself, as a similar motif appears in his story 'The Paternal Joys of Mr Motejzlík.'[4]

10

A Cabaret Star

As readers of *The Good Soldier Švejk* know only too well, Prague had in Hašek's day a wide assortment of hostelries varying from hotels, restaurants and taverns to beer halls, beer gardens, cafés, café-bars, night dives, *cafés-chantants* etc. This was remarkable for a city which just before the First World War had a population of only just over half a million as compared with Vienna's two and a quarter.

Competition between them all was very keen. As we have seen, at some Prague crossroads there could be one on every corner. Normally it was the quality of the beer which determined the public's choice, although other factors like the landlord's personality, the prices, the cuisine and the company played an important role too. One way for the proprietor to secure more custom was to attract a political party's electioneering headquarters to the premises or the neighbourhood, although it had the disadvantage that it might limit custom to adherents of that party only.

At the end of the nineteenth century, floor shows or cabarets had begun to catch on. This was a more important development than might appear, since from these often improvised and amateur performances there finally grew up the tradition of cabaret or small theatre which was to have a special place in the history of Prague.

The first genuine Prague cabaret was started in the Lucerna in 1910 by Emil Longen and Eduard Bass with Jaroslav Kvapil as artistic director and Karel Hašler[1] as his assistant. Considering that Bass became one of the leading Czech novelists of his day, Kvapil the director of the Prague National Theatre as well as the author of the libretto of Dvořák's opera *Rusalka*, and Hašler one of the most popular singers of Czech *chansons*, the standard of performance must have been high. Longen, whose real name was Pitterman, was an actor, producer, caricaturist, translator and film director, who specialised in Grand Guignol and grotesque scenes and had had considerable first-hand experience of cabaret work in Paris. His wife, Xena, was a talented actress who played the parts of prostitutes and 'down and outs' with zest because of her genuine sympathies for the proletariat. From the very beginning the Prague cabarets attracted the bohemian society of the Left.

The first faltering experiments in this genre were later to give birth to significant developments in the history of the Czech stage—the literary cabaret group the Red Seven[2] before and after the First World War, the political satires of Voskovec and Werich (known as V+W)[3] between the wars, and the less heady revues of Suchý and Šlitr[4] after the Second. The bureaucratisation of the State theatres in Central Europe and their control by ministries of education or culture favoured the growth of independent theatres. Bereft of subsidies, they had to be small and almost improvised. As they were 'free enterprise' they enjoyed greater immunity from censorship, so that political jokes and *double-entendre* flourished here as nowhere else. The police tended to turn a deaf ear to the words or to join in the laughter.[5]

In 1912 Hašek, finding himself unemployed, gravitated towards the cabaret. With his ready wit, active pen and penchant for parody there was obvious scope for his talents on the small stage, especially after the popularity and success he had achieved as a candidate for his Party of Moderate Progress within the Bounds of the Law. Moreover, the plentiful supply of beer, always at hand, and the society of boon companions provided as 'homely' an atmosphere as this inveterate bohemian could wish for. It was Drobílek who had the idea that the 'party' should continue its existence as a cabaret group to be called 'The Maccabean Brethren'. With Mach, Langer, Longen, Bass and Hašek all ready to give a hand in both writing and acting, there was no dearth of talent. The first sketch to be performed by the group was *A Glass of Black Coffee*[6] by Hašek himself. He had made a wager that he could write a one-acter with five characters, which could all be played by himself. It is believed to be the first dramatic piece he ever wrote. The five characters are a Capucin friar, a waiter, a country wench, Professor

Masaryk and Quido Maria Vyskočil, a writer of popular sentimental slush. They could all be played by the same actor because they never appear on the stage together. The scene is a
café-bar in Prague and each customer comes for a different
reason: the friar to enjoy the temptations of the city, the country
wench to recover from an attempt to seduce her, Professor
Masaryk to read a copy of *Time* (his party paper) and Vyskočil
to boast about his poetic talent. Each of them orders a black
coffee—the friar because he hates Kapuziners,* the wench to
recover from her ordeal. The waiter is always asleep and only
wakes up when the customers have already lost patience and
left. Masaryk is the exception. He is so absent-minded that,
after having steeped himself in *Time*, he thinks he has already
had his coffee. The play is written in light verse and is quite
amusing. It would obviously go down very well with a bohemian
audience.

A more ambitious revue, written by Hašek, Mach and Langer
was called *The Mount of Olives* or *The Czech Expedition to Jeru-
salem*.[7] Its premiere took place at Zvěřina's on March 27th, 1912
and was given on a low podium in the corner of the hall. The
public were either regular customers or members of Prague's
bohemian set. The victim of the piece was again the wretched
Vyskočil (played by Langer), whom Hašek had already ridiculed in one of his stories in the *History*. Hašek played a female
role. Other burlesques followed, taking off Alfons Mucha's Art
Nouveau paintings and the topical case of the theft of the 'Mona
Lisa'. Another character to appear was Professor František
Drtina, Masaryk's close supporter in the Realist Party, who
pontificated: 'Progress only takes place where there is no
violence'—a parody on the 'reformist' programme, which was
one of Hašek's favourite Aunt Sallies. The cabaret also included
a lecture by Hašek himself, who was described as 'editor of
Animal World'. The subject was 'The Saints from the Point of
View of the National Economy'. He also acted as compère and
talked about 'the training of police dogs' and his experience of
'police sleuths'. Questions, discussion and 'decent polemics'
were encouraged.

Langer recalls how they wanted to be in the fashion and produce a trilogy on one theme, the titles of which were to be

* Kapuziner—the term used in Austria for *café-au-lait*.

Firmness, *Flexibility* and *Expansibility*,[8] but they never got beyond the first one, the name of which also means in Czech 'fortress'. Consequently the scene was laid in a fortress on the frontier between the Austrian Tyrol and Italy. Guarding it was the Good Soldier Švejk, who was pursued there by his landlady from Prague, Mrs Blažek. This lady was in her turn being pursued by Vyskočil, who had fallen secretly in love with her. Various historical characters appeared as well including Prokop Diviš,[9] the Czech inventor of the lightning conductor, and the Emperor Charles IV. Langer remembers playing the part of Vyskočil and throwing himself in despair from the top of a cliff. Immediately afterwards a notice appeared on the cliff: 'From this cliff there jumped the Czech poet and assistant magistrate Vyskočil.' ('Vyskočil' is one of those Czech names which indicate an action and means 'He jumped out'.)

Švejk, who was already quite a well known and popular figure although he had not yet appeared in book form, was presented quite differently from the way we are used to him from Lada's drawings. He was played by a very elegant, young and handsome shop-assistant, who was chosen because he was wearing army uniform at the time, was a lance-corporal and happened to be on leave. He was apparently the only one of the group who knew how to act and was an excellent comedian. Hašek played the part of Švejk's landlady. It fell to Mach, who played Prokop Diviš, to speak the last lines of the play: 'It's lightning, it's raining, a lot of water is falling from the sky. Now I'm going home to invent the lightning conductor.'

Hašek also joined another cabaret group which appeared in popular café-bars like Kopmanka and Montmartre. Kopmanka was an old traditional tavern in the Old Town with a large garden and a glass veranda, renowned for its excellent *velkopopovické* beer (the finest in Prague) and its popular landlord, Karel Flašner. Montmartre was run by Josef Waltner, who started life as a type-setter, and went on to become a celebrated singer of *chansons* and *restaurateur*. It had a wine saloon with a guitar on the wall and a room in black with shaded lights called *Chat Noir* which had been decorated with cubist paintings and furniture by leading Prague artists. František Kysela[10] painted the ceiling and V. H. Brunner[11] a series of frescoes of the Seven Deadly

Sins for the dance hall. Both artists eventually became professors at the Prague School of Industrial Art.

One of the star turns of the show at Montmartre was an Apache dance performed by Waltner and a dancing girl called Emča or 'Revolution'. There were also performances by Longen and his wife, Xena, who sang Parisian songs and danced. Among the most frequent patrons were the faithful members of the Prague Bohème—the poet Opočenský, the writer and tramp Matěj Kuděj, and a mysterious character whom Hašek called 'my friend Hanuška'. Some of these Hašek took as companions on his wanderings and together they made up the 'Four-leaved Clover.'[12]

Hašek generally came to Montmartre at the end of his extensive night pilgrimages. After a few initial beers he set about telling his renowned funny stories and proved for a time a most agreeable companion. But later he became noisy and quarrelsome, splashed beer all over himself and made difficulties over the programme. Once, after having come back from a round of pub-crawling, he stood on the podium and, when the audience was looking forward expectantly to his jokes, sat down, slowly and deliberately took off his boots and undid his dirty ragged foot wraps. After this episode Waltner told Hašek that he did not want to see him there any more. Henceforth he could be seen late at night waiting pathetically outside Montmartre in rain and bad weather, in the hope of meeting an influential friend who would take him in with him.

When he was finally thrown out of Montmartre for good, he went to Kopmanka. The performances there consisted of comic scenes and speeches alternating with musical productions in which Karel Pospíšil[13]—a popular composer of marches for the patriotic gymnastic movement, the Sokol—accompanied at the piano. Hašek spoke during the intervals. Usually he recounted his 'travels in Central Europe', as he called the journeys in Bohemia he had recently made with Kuděj (who afterwards was to write a book about him), and as 'a well-known student of Balkan relations' he poked fun at Austrian foreign policy.

Hašek appears to have been inordinately vain about his performances. He was childishly pleased if applauded, and most unhappy if anyone criticised. But it was sometimes difficult to fit his highly individual type of turn into the programme. He lacked the training of a professional actor and could not unbend to the extent of making grimaces and mimicry. He had the limitations of a *feuilletonist* and was more at home when he was telling an aphorism or a joke than when acting.

After successful appearances in Montmartre and Kopmanka where there was a bohemian public that he knew, he acted with much less success as compère with Longen's cabaret company before a larger public and took part in its various performances in Prague and on tour. Longen described his performances here as a complete fiasco. He behaved so carelessly on the stage that at times he seemed to forget that the public was there at all. He would for instance start a lecture on cholera and its effects and go into such realistic detail that some members of the audience could not sit it out any longer and walked out. But he still clung to cabaret because it gave him the opportunity to show off his virtuosity in verbal improvisation.

On one occasion Vilma Warausová came to Montmartre with her husband and waited for Hašek's appearance, which for them at least was the main turn of the evening:

'Finally Hašek came to our table and said: "Lend me twenty hellers." He had very much run to seed since I had last seen him in the flat at Vršovice. His parting from Jarmila and his son was certainly not a matter of indifference to him. He sat down with us and asked after her. I told him that she was well and that the little boy was fine and looked just like him. He was obviously very agitated. He blamed the Mayers for having separated him from her and taken away his son. His father-in-law had let him down: he had promised that he would secure him financially and then not kept his word. I had difficulty in defending the old gentleman. As far as I knew, I said, he was anxious that the family property should not be split up until after the death of the parents. For this reason he had not given a dowry to any of his children. Hašek asked me to use my influence with Jarmila to persuade her to return to him.'

Hašek's downhill course excited pity among those who wanted to see him reformed, but no one who tried to help him had success or found the experiment rewarding. The well-known

naturalist and traveller A. V. Frič,[14] who offered him the hospitality of his villa for a short period, was one of several who
tried the experiment of shutting him up for the day, leaving him
some food and about five hundred blank sheets of paper so that
he could write. But when he returned home, his prisoner had
flown. The sheets of paper remained blank: some of them had
been made into paper boats and scattered all over the furniture.
Later Hašek became so disorderly that Frič threw him out of his
villa and consigned him to a summerhouse in the gardens.

During this time there are many stories of how Hašek sponged
on his friends in the country, protracting his stay so long that
they had finally to pay his fare back to Prague. Even then he
often cheated them and sat drinking in the station until next
morning, when he would come back and beg to be tolerated for
another week. On July 25th, 1912, an innkeeper in southern
Bohemia made a deposition 'that the editor Mr Hašek in the
company of one gentleman and one lady incurred a debt of
thirty-eight crowns for food, accommodation, beer and cigars
for three days and nights without having paid the bill, and that
they were all untraceable'. The landlord's complaints were taken
up at police headquarters and a description of Hašek was circulated, which gives us an idea of what he looked like at this time:
'The alleged Hašek is about twenty-eight to thirty years old,
five foot seven inches tall, slender with chestnut hair, no beard,
clean shaven, round face, grey eyes, fair eyebrows, well nourished, blunt straight nose, good teeth, dressed in a light green
woollen suit, boots with laces, grey cap, calls himself an editor.'

The police were particularly stupid in this case. They
searched for Hašek for a whole year and compiled a huge dossier
about him. But they appear to have overlooked the fact that
Hašek had paid the landlord five days afterwards and the summons had been withdrawn.

In the middle of 1912 Hašek stayed with friends in different
parts of Prague. One of them, Opočenský, recalls: 'First, Hašek
only came for a moment, but later, when luck seemed to be
slowly running against him, he often slept the night in my apartment . . . He was incredibly unpretentious: even in the winter
he slept on a couch with nothing more than an overcoat on top
of him and an old rug rolled under his head. He angrily refused
pillows or blankets.' But as the weather grew colder Opočenský

urged Hájek to take him to his place. 'We can't leave Jarda like this. If you approach him tactfully, he will respond. He can look after your paper and it would be a good idea if he could live and have his meals with you. But you must be strict with him and not let him go out at night.'

Hájek describes how he and his wife, who had liked Hašek from the time when he worked for her father, old Fuchs of *Animal World*, at once went off to Montmartre and found him sitting at a table making one of his incoherent speeches. Overjoyed at seeing them he said he would be delighted to come and stay. He would sleep 'somewhere on the floor'. He was given the maid's room, as they were without a servant who slept in. They found that he was badly affected by rheumatism (probably contracted on his many wanderings). When he heard that he could also have a modest job on *Animal World* again and stay with them over the winter he was very happy. 'But shan't I disturb your honeymoon?' he asked. Warned by Opočenský, the hosts laid down firm conditions. Hašek must promise to give up his night life. He could write or do what he liked, but if he once started to go out on the tiles, he would have to leave.

Hašek promised faithfully to abide by all this. How easy it was for him to give such assurances and how often he had done so! This time he managed to stick to his promise, helped by the Hájeks' kindness in taking him out to many café-bars themselves. This did not keep him out of scrapes however. At Christmas he came back loaded with presents for everybody, including the charwoman. He had bought them out of an advance he had wheedled out of some editor. When the Hájeks wanted to light the Christmas tree, Hašek begged them to leave it to him. 'I've prepared some special effects,' he said. The result was a gigantic explosion and total darkness. He had used a combination of gun-cotton and flares—more suitable for an Anarchist celebration than a family Christmas.

A frequent guest at the house was Hájek's young brother-in-law, who became very thick with Hašek and got into mischief with him. In the daytime the pair could be seen going around Prague together, Hašek ostentatiously sporting a monocle. But to make a more dashing impression he needed better clothes and looked covetously at Hájek's riding outfit, especially his boots. When the Hájeks went away for a week-end and left the two alone together, Hašek borrowed the boots and strutted about Prague in them. Unfortunately they were too small and he had to stretch them to get into them. When Hájek came back and tried them on, they were like Wellingtons.

There is a Russian proverb—'an uninvited guest is worse than a Tartar', and a Czech one that 'a guest and a fish begin to stink after three days'. Hašek, whether invited or uninvited, certainly bore both these sayings out. The Hájeks had taken him to the tavern called King Wenceslas IV, where the landlord told them of the king's visits there and pointed with great pride to the royal portrait (which presumably some artist had done to pay his debts). Once, when Hašek was in a difficult mood, he quarrelled with the landlord in front of the Hájeks, insulted him, seized his precious portrait and tore it in two.

Hájek was understandably relieved when the spring came and he knew that Hašek would move out and go back to his bohemian way of life. By this time Hašek was bored both at Hájek's home and in the offices of *Animal World*, where he spent most of the time trying unsuccessfully to teach flies how to perform tricks. When Hájek decided he could not afford to keep him on the paper any longer, he began to come home less and less, until one day he finally disappeared altogether. One frosty night he returned to ask forgiveness and beg a bed for the night. He stayed two nights more, after which Hájek never saw him again until the war.[15]

Opočenský felt he must rally to Hašek's support once more and took him to stay with Josef Lada, who put him up in the little kitchen in his small apartment. Lada afterwards gave a typically humorous account of his experiences of him:

'Hašek's stay with me was interrupted at various times for different reasons. Either he was employed as an editor somewhere for a short time, where he was provided with board and lodging, or he went away on some journey with Kuděj, or he took shelter with another friend just for a change of scene. I always greeted him on his return like the prodigal son and enjoyed his stay, until he suddenly vanished again without giving any reason or notice.

'When he eventually came back it was usually like this: he rang the bell and, when I opened the door, he held it back so that there was only a little chink through which he stuck his stick and called out: "Here I am. Now flog me, flog me unmercifully!" Of course I would not have struck him. In any case he held the door firmly in the way so that I could never have done it.

'. . . To begin with I had only one room and Hašek came only occasionally: either just on a visit or to bring a contribution to *Caricatures*, of which I was then the responsible editor. Later he became my sub-tenant simply because he had nowhere else to sleep.'

At that time Lada's room was also his editorial office and many other contributors used to come and see him.

'For some of these visitors I always had ready a liqueur, cognac or rum, and the bottle stood on the cupboard at their disposal. Many of them poured out a drink for themselves uninvited, regarding the bottle as an institutional part of the office, while Hašek, who always despised any kind of ceremony, drank straight from the bottle. His knowledge of alcoholic products was truly amazing: he could drink from an opened rum bottle and tell me at once approximately how much it had cost. One day I played a little joke on him. I poured some water into an empty rum bottle and put it in the usual place. Hašek came in, reached for the bottle, and, all unsuspecting, took a big swig at it. I expected that at the very least he would want my head for this, but the poor boy didn't have the strength for it. He turned pale and his hands shook. Then he put the bottle on the floor, which in his opinion was the only place fit for it, and went towards the door. Before he shut it behind him, he turned round, his face pale and sweating with the martyrdom he had undergone, and said sadly: "You ought not to have done that to me." At the time I thought he wouldn't survive the blow, but his healthy nature got over even that treachery and a week afterwards he was just as active as ever . . .

'We once gathered a little party, where we concentrated on intellectual rather than physical enjoyment. He and I were to compose an opera from scratch . . . without waiting to see whether the libretto was suitable or not. It was, or so he claimed, intended as an item in a programme arranged in honour of

Ružena Nasková, an actress of the National Theatre, and it was very important that it should be a success. Hašek recited the libretto and I played impromptu music on the mouth-organ for every sentence of it. The plot, which was suggested by one of the guests, was the discovery of America by Christopher Columbus. When we consider that Hašek could dictate such a difficult libretto without previous preparation . . . we really have to take off our hats to him. But if we take into account too that I had immediately to compose music to sentences dictated by Hašek, who hadn't the remotest trace of a musical ear and could sing four hundred Czech, German, Russian and Hungarian songs all with the same tune, well, I think you could not only take off your hat to me, but go further and take off your hair as well.

'The opera began as Hašek dictated it: "Columbus intends to discover America, but Ferdinand and Isabella don't care a damn about it and won't give him a sou. Columbus goes on trying to persuade them until he finally succeeds in getting three leaky caravels out of them. Then he sets out on the wide seas." That was the first act. As he dictated each sentence I had immediately, without any kind of inspiration provided normally by the murmuring of a mountain brook or the rhythmic rattling of a train . . . to play them on the mouth-organ, and do it in such a way that the music always expressed exactly what was required, to a hair. It's a pity, a great pity that it didn't occur to either of us to write the opera down. I still firmly believe today that it could be broadcast, and in my imagination I hear the voice of a well-known commentator analysing the composition in the smallest detail and exclaiming enthusiastically over one passage: "Yes, this intentionally discordant screeching expresses with magnificent accuracy the moment when Isabella screams out that she won't give a damned sou towards the discovery of America."

'The second act was no less dramatic. It is discovered that there is not a drop of rum on the ships. The sailors mutiny and some of them are thrown overboard. Columbus is bad-tempered because there is no land in sight and refuses to change his linen. There is another mutiny and more sailors are hurled overboard. Someone calls out: "Land, land," but it turns out to be a hoax. Columbus's faith in God is shattered and he becomes an atheist . . . And at that point I really came unstuck in the music. I managed to play the passage "Land, land" with such verve that I nearly swallowed the mouth-organ, but the theme "Columbus's faith in God is shattered and he becomes an atheist" was the last straw which broke the camel's back.

'Hašek was in fact paying me back for the water in the rum bottle. He took his revenge when I least expected it and made me ridiculous in front of the whole company. He showed that even my wonderful musical gifts had their limits and weak points. But even that was obviously not enough to satisfy his thirst for vengeance. The very same evening, before he went out with some guests to a café, under the pretext that he wanted to burn some grease paper in which delicatessen goods had been packed, he crammed the stove with fireworks and squibs. In the morning the maid could easily have had a stroke, for when the stove was lit there was a thunderous bang, followed by devilish fireworks, explosions and spluttering squibs with light effects. It was with difficulty that I could revive the old woman.'

Hašek seems to have been Lada's guest or sub-tenant for most of 1913. During this time he was quite productive as a writer and published many satires, sketches and short stories, as well as many short and witty pieces for a book of nursery rhymes for children by Lada.

Lada never forgot the wonderful meals Hašek cooked while he was staying with him. He well deserved the reputation he had acquired for being as talented a cook as he was a writer, and the culinary details in *The Good Soldier Švejk* merit serious professional study.[16]

Before Hašek left, he handed Lada a bill.

December 2nd, 1913

ACCOUNT

for Mr Josef Lada, for nursing him in his illness.

1	Journey home from the Balkan Bar and accompanying Mr Josef Lada there	*Kr.*	1.20
2	Applying a small compress		.50
3	Applying to the head larger compresses to the number of 26 @ 70 hellers		18.20

4 Six journeys downstairs for tea and
  black coffee @ 30 hellers   1.80
5 Six journeys upstairs @ 40 hellers   2.40
6 Transport of Mr Lada to the lavatory
  @ 50 hellers   4.00
7 Execution of various commissions   5.00
8 Putting on one pair of socks   .40
9 Journey to the doctor—travel expenses   5.00

                                        Kr.   38.50
                   Received in advance   *Kr.*   2.50

                   Balance outstanding   *Kr.*   36.00

               Received 2/12/1913 with thanks
                       Jaroslav Hašek[17]

11

On the Way to the Front

Although the fateful assassination of the Archduke Francis
Ferdinand and his wife at Sarajevo on June 28th, 1914, is the
opening theme of *The Good Soldier Švejk*, the event itself does not
appear to have made any deep impression on the author at the
time. He was staying with Lada, which meant spending a few
nights with him and then going off on long tramps with Kuděj.
On the actual day of the assassination he was on an outing with
Lada in the country not far from Prague.

The World War which broke out a month later was bound to
have an effect on his life. He shared with most of his countrymen their detestation of it. It would be waged mainly against
two Slav peoples, Serbs and Russians, with whom they had
strong ties of kinship and sympathy. Moreover the alliance with
Germany was disliked and distrusted as likely to strengthen the
position of the hostile German minority at home. The Czech
political leaders, who up to that time had not worked for or
wished to see a break-up of the Monarchy, saw the war as a
decisive milestone pointing the way to independence. 'We were
here before Austria. We shall be here after her,' the great Czech
leader and historian, Palacký, had written nearly half a century
before. Yet Bohemia had for centuries been part of a large community of peoples, of whom the Austrian lands formed the
nucleus, first under the Holy Roman Empire, later under the
Austrian Empire and finally under the Dual Monarchy, and the
Czechs had been ruled over by the Habsburgs ever since 1526,
when they had themselves freely chosen the future Emperor
Ferdinand I as their king out of many other candidates. Many
of them therefore still felt traditional loyalty to the Monarchy.

This and the ruthless measures adopted by the Austrian
government in war-time was why, when hostilities broke out,

there were only isolated pro-Russian or anti-war demonstrations. Indeed the impression created in *The Good Soldier Švejk*
that the whole Czech population to a man were against the war
is much exaggerated. Relatively few Czech officers deserted.
Even Švejk himself never speaks of deserting, although the
author may have intended to make him do so at a later stage of
the unfinished book.

Hašek certainly felt no obligation at all to defend Austria and
did his best not to let the war interfere with his life. Censorship
may have put an end to his satirical writings about politics, but
it could not dry up the rich springs of his humour or curb his
irresponsible pranks.

In the late summer he went to see some friends in north-east
Bohemia and reached Náchod, a town not far from the Russian
front and in the direct line of the Russian advance. When he
heard a retired captain from a German-speaking part boast that
he would massacre the Serbs, he could not resist sitting down at
his taale and saying to him in Russian: 'I suppose you understand Russian?' The captain turned crimson and groped for his
sabre. The waiters and guests sprang to intervene and led Hašek
out by a side exit. As he went out, he turned and shouted: 'You
bastard, you'd better remember that you'll soon *have* to learn
Russian and like it.'

On another occasion he started an argument as to whether
the night porter at Hotel Valšu in Prague was in the pay of the
police, and on his return to the capital immediately tried to find
out for himself. Taking a room in the hotel, he coolly registered
under the name of 'Ivan Fyodorovich Kuznetsov, merchant,
born in Kiev and coming from Moscow', giving as the reason
for his visit: 'Checking up on the General Staff.' In an instant
the hotel was ringed with uniformed and plain-clothed police
and he was taken to the police station. Like the gendarmerie
sergeant in *The Good Soldier Švejk*,* the police at first rejoiced in
the delusion that they had caught a Russian master spy, and
Inspector Klíma had a great shock when he turned out to be
nothing more than the by now notorious 'artful dodger'. 'What
on earth made you cause us all this trouble at such a critical
time?' he asked. Hašek said nothing and looked about him in

* *The Good Soldier Švejk*, p. 252.

feigned amazement. At last he replied: '*Nye ponimayu.*'* It took hours before Klíma could get a Czech word out of him. At length with an innocent expression in his eyes Hašek explained how as a conscientious Austrian citizen and tax-payer he had wanted to find out whether police measures for checking up on foreigners in wartime were really effective. After this piece of cheek he was lucky to get off with nothing worse than a serious warning and five days' confinement from December 7th–12th. Once again the authorities showed themselves surprisingly lenient to him. They seemed to have acquired a sort of perverse affection for him.

After his release he continued his extravaganzas. He went into a wine-cellar and again started speaking Russian ostentatiously. When one of the customers asked: 'Why do you speak Russian, Mr Hašek?', he replied: 'Is that Russian? I've recently been in Náchod and that's how they talk there.'

Meanwhile, within three weeks of the outbreak of the war, the Austrian army had found itself hard pressed on the Eastern front in Galicia. The Russians advanced into Galicia, occupied Lemberg and encircled the major Austrian fortress of Przemysl. There was panic in Austria, the alarm was sounded and German units were brought up to reinforce and stiffen the Austrian lines. As a result the Russians were pushed back to the river Vistula and Przemysl was relieved. Hindenburg was made supreme commander on the Eastern front and a German counter-offensive under Mackensen was launched in November. It broke through the Russian lines and stabilised the front. By the end of the year Cracow was saved, Silesia protected and, although Austria was not cleared of Russian troops, the Carpathian mountain barrier still held. In the south the Austrians were driven out of Serbia but they managed to stabilise the front there also.

One wintry night in Prague, when the Hájeks returned to their home, they found the light on in the kitchen. The maid rushed out to meet them. 'Madam, we have a visitor. He's wounded, poor wretch, and has a bandaged arm. He came to Prague from a military hospital and says he is your best friend. It's pitiful . . . You should have seen how hungry he was. He ate everything.'

* Russian for 'I don't understand'.

When the maid said he was asleep on the sofa and had covered himself with a carpet 'because he was used to sleeping like that at the front,' Hájek said: 'Hašek.'

When Hájek came into the room, the visitor got off the sofa, went down on his knees and begged forgiveness. He had nowhere to sleep, he pleaded, and it was so cold outside.

When they came down to breakfast next morning Hašek was already up and having a nice conversation with the maid in the kitchen. She laughed when he confided to her that he had no injured arm: it was only a joke, a trick to get himself let in.

Then he casually invited himself to lunch, offering to help Mrs Hájková with the cooking. When she had no pepper, he dashed out to buy it and startled the wife of the house porter out of her wits as he came down the steps.

'Good morning,' he said with an innocent smile. 'I'm better again.'

He stayed for three days and then said: 'Well, now I think I'll go and look somewhere else. This damned war! In the end I'll have no alternative but to join up too and have a peep at the other side—go to Russia once more.'[1] And so it appeared that he looked at it only as an excuse for another one of his wanderings.

At the end of January in the following year, when preparations were being made for a renewed Austro–German counter offensive on the Galician front, Hašek was summoned to appear before a recruiting commission. To quote *The Good Soldier Švejk*: 'At the time when the forests beside the river Raab in Galicia saw the Austrian armies fleeing across the river, and when down in Serbia the Austrian divisions were caught one by one with their pants down and got the walloping they long deserved, the Austrian Ministry of War suddenly remembered Švejk. Why, even he might help to get the Monarchy out of the mess.'* So it was with Švejk's creator too.

When he presented himself before the call-up board he behaved flippantly and gave inaccurate or incomplete information about himself. On the form which he had to fill up—which is still preserved—he wrote that the only language he knew was Czech, although his biographers claim that he could speak Russian, German, Hungarian, Polish and French. He also put

* *The Good Soldier Švejk*, p. 55.

himself down as 'unmarried', although he had a wife and son and had never been divorced. He was passed fit and ordered to report for duty with the 1st Reserve Company of the 91st Regiment at České Budějovice, the chief town of southern Bohemia, and a military base, where the regiments which had been badly mauled in Serbia were reformed and re-equipped.

Hašek's false entries are commonly interpreted as proof of his contempt for officialdom but there could be other explanations. Faced with the choice of only two alternatives—to state either that he was married or was unmarried—he may well have felt that, having abandoned his wife and small boy, he could not in all honesty say he was married. And with the trauma of guilt still haunting him after the ghastly failure of his marriage, he may have been afraid that if he entered himself as married he would later be exposed to questioning on a very sensitive subject. Further, since there had been no divorce or legal separation, he was still under an obligation to support his wife and son, which he could barely do. As for his failure to mention his knowledge of languages, he had not studied Russian since the time he had courted Jarmila—some ten years ago—and had never been in Russia. Some Russian lines of verse with which he ended a Czech poem to Jarmila contain elementary errors. The simple Hungarian, German and Serbo-Croat expressions which he uses in *The Good Soldier Švejk* often needed correction. Probably he preferred to boast his knowledge of languages rather than risk letting them be put to the test.

When he received his call-up he was back again with Lada, who has described his return from the recruiting office:

'He came home to supper in the mood of a typical recruit and barely acknowledged my greeting when I opened the door for him. He just walked straight past me to his room and ignored me completely. When I kept on asking him how he had got on, he finally replied rather rudely that he was not going to talk to any dirty civilian and then went and shut himself up in the kitchen, where he began to sing army songs with his drolly unmusical voice. From that moment on he treated me like an inferior being, not as his landlord. Soon he moved out of my home altogether and was no longer staying with me at the time of his actual departure for his regiment.'[2]

Lada's version of this event is described with his usual humour, but it is difficult to explain this cavalier treatment of a friend who had been so helpful to him—not that it was by any means the only occasion when Hašek showed ingratitude. If he was being serious, the simple explanation probably was that he had long ago got tired of living with Lada and wanted a change. Anyone who tried to discipline him, even in the most gentle way, was likely to receive this treatment.

After leaving Lada, Hašek disappeared, putting in an occasional appearance at the Longens. One night in particular they were woken up by a banging on the door. It was Hašek begging to be let in. He had frightened the house-porter out of his wits by telling him that he had cholera. He had already reported at the surgery because of Švejk's complaint—rheumatism. Now he was suffering from a violent attack of nose-bleeding, so severe that he had to be taken off to Vinohrady hospital, where he stayed from January 31st to February 9th, 1915. According to the medical report he suffered from headaches also and there was a danger that his kidneys were affected. His weight was eleven stone four pounds, which was not excessive considering that he drank thirty-five or more glasses of beer a day! The doctors in the hospital tried to keep him longer but he ran away, allegedly because of the non-alcoholic diet. His stay there postponed for fourteen days his departure for the regiment.

According to Menger's colourful story Hašek celebrated one of his last days in Prague by standing on the ramp which leads up to the National Museum in the Wenceslas Square dressed in the costume of a Macedonian *comitadji* with a Turkish scimitar hanging from his belt and an enormous leather medallion on his chest containing the portrait of the Tsar. He had scarcely time to shout more than a few patriotic greetings of '*Nazdar*' than the police seized him and took him off. 'Goodbye, chaps,' he called out to the crowd which had collected. On the way the police had to protect him from some of the chauvinist German elements, who took him for a Russian spy. More echoes from *The Good Soldier Švejk*!

According to more reliable sources he spent his last nights in a melancholy mood among his friends at a Prague café-bar drinking only water. Towards midnight he began to brighten up and sing army songs. Indeed at one period he grew extremely 'exalted' and even threatened to shoot his companions and march off to Budějovice on foot. His sudden change of mood was apparently due to the ingenuity of the waiter, who prepared successive glasses of slivovice for him in the passage to the lavatory, which he had to visit rather often that evening. The following morning he left for České Budějovice. On April 30th, 1915, his photograph appeared in *Horizon* among a group of soldiers in an army hospital. He had grown a small moustache and looked miserable and forlorn.

While staying in Budějovice, he changed into mufti, walked about the town like Marek with a *Krankenbuch** under his arm and visited numerous café-bars. In one inn he is said to have dictated two stories, 'The Affair with the Thermometer'[3] and 'The Affair with the Hamster',[4] both of which he sent to Prague to be printed.

The former, which could not be published at the time because of censorship and appeared only after his death, tells of a patient in an army hospital named Binksenhuber who gets furious with his thermometer because it refuses to show any temperature. Finally he squeezes it so powerfully under his armpit that he smashes it to smithereens. Now the only thermometer in the ward is broken. The doctor will soon be making his round and for the want of any temperature reading the male nurse has to invent them. To please Binksenhuber he chalks up 109.8 on the board. The doctor expresses considerable surprise; the patient should have been dead long since at 109, let alone 109.8 he says. The story ends with the male nurse being sent to gaol for a fortnight and the ward getting three thermometers in his place. Binksenhuber decides to volunteer for the front on the next march battalion.

Hašek had enrolled as a one-year volunteer. This was preferable to a normal call-up, because it offered the chance of becoming an officer. Recruits who had passed through the middle school, like the Commercial Academy, had this privilege. Later, again like Marek,† he was found guilty of breaches of discipline, expelled from the volunteer school, gaoled and transferred to

---

* Book recording the illnesses of the patients. See *The Good Soldier Švejk*, p. 288.

† *The Good Soldier Švejk*, p. 288.

work in the kitchens. The exact reasons for his demotion are not known. According to one story he turned up completely drunk at an army medical board and was insolent to the medical officer; according to another he wrote on the doors of the military hut: 'There ain't no fun in this stinking shack.'

He has given a fictional account of his expulsion from the school in his story 'God Punish England'.[5] According to this the commandant of the school, Captain Adamička, wanted it decorated with patriotic slogans and ordered Hašek to compose some appropriate verses. When he came to the school that evening the commandant was met with the following inscription:

> On the wall by command
> 'God punish Engeland!'
> Now we've mobilised the Lord
> Who with His mighty name
> Puts Albion to shame.

Hašek commented: 'I got thirty days' imprisonment for this. They even had me up for blasphemy and finally sent me to the front with that pleasant "next march battalion".'

According to other accounts Hašek disappeared before the battalion left Budějovice and was found again only after a long search. His company commander, Lieutenant Lukas, persuaded him to reform and stop drinking and Hašek promised to do so, but before leaving for the front ran away once more.

Hašek described his treatment in one of his 'Bugulma' stories, 'In Strategical Difficulties'.[6]

'They threw me out of the volunteer school of the 91st Infantry Regiment at the beginning of the war. They tore off my one-year stripes and, while my friends and former colleagues were given the rank of cadets and ensigns and fell like flies on all fronts, I sat locked up in the barracks at the base in Budějovice or in Bruck an der Leitha. When they finally let me go and wanted to send me with a company to the front, I hid in a haystack and so outlasted three companies which were drafted for front duty. Then I pretended I had epilepsy. By that time they would almost have shot me if I had not then voluntarily volunteered for the front.'

146

The army were in no doubt about Hašek's character. On his personal file were inscribed the words: 'A swindler and deceiver.' Perhaps it was on these grounds that he was considered suitable for the 11th Company which included men from Czech penal units. Captain Wimmer, his company commander, was replaced shortly before they left for the front by Lieutenant Lukas, who was later to take over the command of one of the battalions of the regiment. He was a man of principle and a good disciplinarian, which tallies fairly well with the portrait Hašek drew of Lieutenant Lukáš in the novel, except that his affairs with women as described there are exaggerated, if not sheer invention.

Lukáš was a Czech from Prague. In *The Good Soldier Švejk* Hašek portrayed him as 'a kind of amphibian'. He spoke German in society, wrote German, read Czech books and told the Czech one-year volunteers: 'Let's be Czechs, but no one need know about it. I'm a Czech too.'* His stubbornness was an obstacle to his promotion and he had been several times passed over. Otherwise he was a decent man who was not afraid of his superiors and looked after his company at manoeuvres, as was seemly and proper. He always found them comfortable quarters in barns and often let the men tap a barrel of beer at the expense of his own modest salary.

The commander of the battalion, Captain Sagner, who also figures in the book under his own name, favoured Czechs too, but only if he could do so without risk to himself. He was not only a very shrewd customer but a very ruthless officer too, judged by one of his battalion orders which read: 'Russian detachments which go on fighting until the very last and then refuse to let themselves be captured should on no account be spared. This only gives the other detachments time to retreat. The enemy should be destroyed with carefully aimed fire, and as soon as the civil population shows the slightest sign of resistance it should be liquidated. The remainder should be arrested . . .'

The mad Major Wenzel—the 'Czech-eater'—was drawn from life too, as well as the officious and idiotic Cadet Jan Biegler who in real life was commander of a platoon in Lukas's company and the brother of his fiancée. Perhaps the most notorious character in the novel, the blockhead ex-school teacher

* *The Good Soldier Švejk*, p. 166.

Lieutenant Dub, was probably modelled on the reserve Lieutenant Mechálek, who like Dub, kept on saying: 'You don't know
me yet, but when you get to know me, you'll howl.'

According to Pytlík the chaplain Eybl (in the novel Ibl) was
still living in 1971 and before he died gave an interview in which
he recalled how Lukas had wanted to transfer Hašek so as not
to have to punish him for having refused to do rifle practice in
the mud. He had planned to send him on leave to Prague, but
two days before his intended departure Hašek was taken prisoner
by the Russians.

One of Hašek's closest friends was Accountant Sergeant-
Major Vaněk, formerly a chemist from Kralupy. Hašek helped
him in the office and soon became indispensable to him. He in
his turn got to know the documents in Vaněk's office, which
proved useful to him as material for the novel, as did the character of Vaněk himself.

In the company office he got to know Lukas's batman,
František Strašlipka, who was the prototype of Švejk. He was a
young man aged twenty-six with blue eyes who was always
cheery company. Hašek, Strašlipka and another soldier made
up a gay trio who helped to raise the spirits of the soldiers. Like
Švejk, Strašlipka loved to tell all kinds of stories about his life,
which generally began with the words 'I knew a man called
. . .' Hašek wrote a poem on the way to the front called 'In the
Reserve',[7] which, after retailing the horrors of the war, concluded: 'But the most frightful tribulations of all were Strašlipka's
hoary old stories.' Strašlipka's photograph fits much better with
the figure of Švejk as described in the book than do Lada's
famous drawings.

On June 30th, 1915, the 11th Company left for the Galician
front. They very nearly went without Hašek. Although three
days before entrainment an order had been issued prohibiting
men from leaving the camp, he was found to be missing at the
time of departure, but eventually turned up none the less. The
company was despatched by train through Hungary and followed the route described in the novel until it reached Sanok.

One of Hašek's poems written at this time has survived, because Vaněk made a copy of it. It shows that Jarmila still
remained in his thoughts, but unfortunately she never received
it until after his death.

All the more precious is every scrap of news
From places dear to me; and if my dreams came true,
I would, when I renounced all other hopes,
Content myself with one more line from you.

From the railway junction at Sanok the 12th Reserve battalion marched to the front on foot. Hašek was given the job of 'cattle-drover', having been passed by a medical commission on August 25th, 1915, as fit to undertake guard and light duties. He apparently reported sick every day and did his light duties, but, when the marches were particularly strenuous, always infiltrated to the rear. In Sambor he was appointed billeting orderly, a job he was well suited for, because he could speak some Russian and had acquired a good knowledge of Galicia as a result of his journeys there in his youth. The battalion then marched forward from Sambor until it met up with the main part of the regiment. Meanwhile Hašek had been appointed liaison orderly for the company.

The battalion reached the district of Gologór on July 11th, 1915. It quickly filled up the gaps in the ranks of the 91st Regiment, helped to complete the active battalions and moved to the north to the railway station of Zółtańce and from there to the important railway junction of Sokal. This formed a vital Austrian bridgehead on the eastern bank of the river Bug. The 3rd Battalion, into which Hašek's company had been incorporated, found itself right in the middle of the fire and emerged from it badly mauled. Towards the end of July it had lost more than half its men in the course of a week's fighting. On August 1st the regiment was again sent into the reserve and enjoyed a brief respite. After these engagements Hašek was promoted lance-corporal and wrote more verses: 'A War Poem About Lice',[8] 'In the Reserve' and 'The Corporal's Lament'.[9] In the last he bewailed the fact that the lance-corporal was the one man in the army whom everyone blamed and cursed. Even such a low degree of authority was unattractive to him. These 'occasional' verses were apparently written for Lieutenant Lukas and were treasured by him. After his death many of them disappeared.

Readers of *The Good Soldier Švejk* will already have been struck by the similarities between Hašek's experiences and those of the batman Švejk and the one-year volunteer Marek. Like Švejk, Hašek suffered from rheumatism and sang army songs just before he reported for duty, and like Marek he joined up as a one-year volunteer, walked about Budějovice in mufti with the hospital *Krankenbuch*, was expelled from the volunteers' school and transferred to less responsible duties. Hašek's poem about the trials of a lance-corporal recall the merciless way Švejk and Marek teased their lance-corporal in the prison van.* It is difficult to know whether all these things happened to Hašek and were later incorporated into his book, or whether his friends presented some of them as his experiences because he had written about them. From time to time Hašek's biography becomes cluttered up with mythical detail which one finds difficult to accept but has no good grounds for rejecting.

According to Lukas and Vaněk, Hašek was actually proposed for the Silver Medal for Bravery for having, with Lukas, taken a large number of Russian soldiers prisoner. He came to an understanding with the commander of the Russian detachment, a professor from Petrograd, who brought over three hundred of his men voluntarily to the headquarters of the regiment. This seems a somewhat curious episode, since although Czechs deserted to the Russian side, Russians did not normally want to be taken prisoner by the Austrians. His sudden appearance at the head of the detachment of prisoners caused something of a stir, not to say confusion. Major Wenzel thought that the Russians had broken through the front and ran off, dragging the whole of the brigade command with him!

Hašek certainly showed courage when, during the retreat, he guided the whole battalion to safety across the river Igla, having learned from local inhabitants where there was a ford. For this act he was let off three years' imprisonment he was due to serve for desertion at Bruck an der Leitha. But things turned out otherwise.

On September 17th Vaněk, Hašek and another man were sent out on a night patrol near the enemy positions. Hašek lost his way and reported to the unit only the following night. There has been some speculation whether this was an early attempt to desert which did not come off. But according to Vaněk he had made no previous plans to get himself taken prisoner. He had

---

* *The Good Soldier Švejk*, p. 311 ff.

been on telephone duty and listened carefully to the conversations between the regiment and the brigade. He lived in the same trench as Strašlipka and was helping him to look after a dog they had 'taken prisoner' in a village and which now belonged to Lukas.

Early in the morning of September 24th the Russians unexpectedly appeared. The alarm was immediately sounded. Hašek, who contrary to general instructions slept undressed, said sleepily: 'Well, well, perhaps it won't be so bad.' Lukas excitedly shouted at Section No. 4 to secure the company's flanks and gave the order for a retreat.

According to Lukas the Russian armies broke through the front in the sector defended by the 91st Regiment. The situation looked grim and he wanted to inform battalion command about the attack. As the men were running away in confusion he caught a glimpse of Hašek climbing laboriously out of the trench with Strašlipka, slowly doing up his puttees and putting on his boots. He told both of them impatiently to hurry up, but Hašek only replied that he had a swollen foot and would have to tighten his puttees to run better. After that Lukas lost sight of them both.

On September 24th in the morning Hašek and Strašlipka took final leave of the Austrian army. On the battlefield 135 of the 91st Regiment were left dead, 285 wounded and 509 missing. A few days later Lukas's dog crossed the lines to rejoin his master. He brought no message from Hašek.

[II]
RUSSIA

(12)

In Russia

Bitter disillusionment lay in store for all those Czechs and Slovaks who had sighed with relief when they found themselves in Russian captivity and hoped that their tribulations were at an end. The fate which awaited them was far worse than anything they had yet experienced. First, their expectations of a warm and brotherly welcome were sadly disappointed: the Russians received them coldly and eyed them with suspicion and jealousy. As fellow Slavs they had hoped to enjoy most favoured treatment: in the event it was no better than that accorded to Germans, Austrians and Hungarians, in some respects indeed even worse, because the Russians deliberately burdened them with the hardest labour in the confident belief that they would be too loyal to complain. But their crowning grievance was the reluctance of the Russians to allow them to fight for the Allied cause. There were soon to be two hundred thousand Czechs and Slovaks languishing in camps and longing to help the war effort, and only a trickle of them were being freed.

This is not merely an English judgement on Russian conduct of a half century ago. It is a contemporary Russian view, based on an official letter written by the former Russian Commander-in-Chief, General Brusilov, on January 5th, 1917 when the Tsar was still on the throne. On July 8th, 1916 General Shuvayev had submitted a proposal to the Tsar for the liberation of all Slav prisoners. It was approved and signed by him but never implemented, reportedly because the Russian Premier Stürmer deliberately pigeon-holed it. On the eve of the February Revolution, General Brusilov brought the matter up again. 'There is no organisation on our side to look after these prisoners,' he wrote. 'Those who had the responsibility of doing so treat them in a most unbrotherly way . . . Germans and Hungarians are accommodated in comfortable camps in Siberia [!] while Slavs are sent to Europe starving, bare-footed, half-naked and ill, to work like slaves.' Life for prisoners was indeed cheaper, easier and more peaceful in Siberia than in European Russia.

Although the harvest was by that time over, the prisoners were still not set at liberty, on the alleged ground that they were needed on the land. Some were even sent to the mines. Their camp commandants were often Russians of Baltic German origin who despised the Czechs and Slovaks as traitors to their Emperor and took it out on them. Slav prisoners were not separated from Germans, and Austrian spies were thus enabled to collect information on the Czechs and Slovaks and denounce them at home, ensuring that their families were persecuted.

Hygiene in the camps was beyond description. Prisoners suffering from spotted typhus were sent into camps which had so far been immune and those who had not been infected were placed in camps where disease was rife. In Totskoye camp out of sixteen thousand inmates more than six thousand perished. At Troitski more than half of the four and a half thousand Slav prisoners died. Many of the Slav prisoners were sent to help construct the Murmansk railway in northern Russia or to do the work of sappers at the most exposed points of the front. The Tsarist authorities did not bother to enquire whether any of them had technical or other training and could be used more suitably elsewhere. In Brusilov's view it was understandable that the survivors' loyalty to Russia was turning to distrust and revulsion.

Shortage of railway trucks meant that Hašek and his unfortunate fellow-prisoners had to march to their camp on foot, goaded by guards with whips. After a trek of over one hundred kilometres through cholera infested districts, where the villages had been gutted and wells poisoned, they at last reached the main transit camp of Darnitse near Kiev.

This particular spot had a shocking reputation. Thousands of prisoners who had died during their long detention lay buried there. The first batch, which arrived in the winter of 1914–15, had had the hardest fate. At that time the so-called camp consisted of nothing more than a clearing surrounded by barbed wire and thick clusters of overgrown trees. The prisoners were given primitive tools and made to build their own dugouts in unbearable frosts and on very meagre rations. Until their primitive shelter was ready they had to sleep in the open air. Meanwhile dysentery and typhus were rife, overcrowding was terrible and the basic hygienic arrangements totally lacking. Hundreds more died of starvation, frostbite and disease.

Luckily for him Hašek was soon transferred to another camp at Totskoye which lay about nineteen kilometres south-east of Buzuluk on the river Samara. It is true that it was situated in marshy malarial country, but it was better than Troitski. Here he was to spend more than half a year. This time he travelled part of the way by train and managed to get into the vans in which tobacco leaves were packed and barter them for bread. An epidemic of typhus broke out in the camp that winter, Hašek caught it and only escaped death by a miracle. In one wooden hut there were up to six hundred people heaped together, some of them writhing in fever and delirium. Fortunately in the spring the camp came under the control of the Russian Red Cross just in time to save the lives of those who had survived.

It was about this time that the inmates of Totskoye were visited by emissaries from the *Družina*.*

Immediately after the outbreak of the war the Czechoslovak colonies in Russia—loosely joined in an organisation called the Council of Czechs in Russia—had sent a delegation to the Tsar to ask permission for Czech units to be formed within the Russian army. The Tsar granted their request and the *Družina*, which formed the nucleus of the subsequent Czech Legion,† came into existence, thanks to the initiative of Alois Tuček, one of the engineers of the Moscow branch of the Austro–Czech motor engineering firm, Laurin and Klement (afterwards to produce the famous Tatra car in the Czechoslovak Republic).

By September 1914 it already comprised four infantry companies, which were attached to the Russian Third Army on the Galician front. The Russian General Staff planned to use them for reconnaissance purposes and not as combat troops. They were sent across the lines dressed in Austrian uniform and

---

* An old Czech word meaning 'an escort of knights'.

† The Russian authorities only permitted the name 'Czech Legion' after the February Revolution in 1917.

exposed to great personal danger, since if they chanced to be caught, as was indeed the fate of some of them, they were summarily hanged or shot. The Russians' ultimate aim was to use them as agents to stir up revolt when they advanced into Bohemia. At first the command in the *Družina* was Russian, but later some Czech officers were appointed, although none more senior than second lieutenant. For a long time all former Czech and Slovak officers had to serve as privates and many of them preferred to enlist in the Serbian army in Russia, where they were able to keep their former rank.

The Russians were now capturing an increasing number of prisoners-of-war of Czech and Slovak origin—too many to go on ignoring. Many of these men, hearing of the existence of the *Družina*, asked to be allowed to join it, and the Fifth Army Command of the Russian army agreed that those who immediately volunteered for service should be considered. However the numbers were intentionally confined to those who applied for Russian citizenship, because the Russians regarded them and their leaders abroad as politically untrustworthy. Moreover there were some doubts about the legality of using prisoners-of-war at the front, and factory owners, especially those who were Czech, were lobbying to get them for industrial work. Later the *Družina* was augmented by the intake of large numbers of Czechs and Slovaks settled in Volhynia in north-western Ukraine, who were Russian subjects and not affected by international conventions.

At this stage of the war most Czechs and Slovaks in the Austrian army were not deserting. Those who deliberately crossed the lines had done so out of war-weariness and not in order to fight against Austria, but when they learned of the terrible conditions in the prison camps or experienced them first-hand they were easily persuaded by the recruiting officers to do so. The members of the Czech colony in Russia were inclined to follow their example. Many of them were still Austrian and therefore enemy subjects and were in danger of being sent to internment camps too. They were glad to serve in the Russian army to save themselves from this fate and to preserve their property from confiscation. At the beginning of the war there was little conscious feeling of Czechoslovak patriotism among the prisoners-of-war, but with the gradual organisation within Russia and outside of a movement for independence a definite national movement began to crystallise.

Hašek, who was as anxious as any of them to get out of the camp and at the same time genuinely eager to work against Austria–Hungary, immediately volunteered to join the *Družina*. With other volunteers he was drafted to the Fourth Prisoner-of-War Battalion. He was said to have shown great zeal and not flinched from doing his recruiting propaganda even among typhus victims. His initiative was appreciated and he was appointed assistant to the Russian commander of his battalion. He soon found himself in a reasonably cushy job, working in an office with a glass veranda. He divided his time between routine office chores and drafting recruiting propaganda, and it can easily be imagined which of the two occupations he entered into with the more zest. Like Marek* he told everyone that he was writing a history of the regiment, but there is no trace of such a work having been undertaken. It is more likely that he was spending his time roughing out episodes for his new book on Švejk which he had long planned to write.

The Czech emigré community in Russia was at this time deeply divided. On the one side was the League of Czech Clubs, which had grown out of the Council of Czechs in Russia and had fallen under the reactionary influence of Václav Vondrák† and the numerous and powerful old Czech colony in Kiev. They were hand-in-glove with the Tsarist government and planned a future Czech or Czechoslovak state united with Russia in personal union under a member of the Romanov dynasty. Their newspaper, published in Kiev, was the *Čechoslovan* and Hašek had already begun to contribute to it. On the other side was the colony in Petrograd who looked outside Russia to Paris, where the National Council[1] had been set up under Masaryk as an embryo Czechoslovak government in exile. Their paper was the *Čechoslovák*, published in Petrograd. While Kiev was conservative, Slavophil and monarchist, Petrograd was liberal, Western

---

* *The Good Soldier Švejk*, pp. 580 and 612.

† Václav Vondrák, a rich Czech magnate who was born in Volhynia in the Ukraine and became a deputy for it. Anxious that the League of Czech Clubs should be recognised by the Tsarist government as the only legitimate representative of the 'free Czechs', he opposed the National Council in Paris and eventually joined the Russian army.

and friendly with some of those who would make up the future Provisional Government of Russia. A third important group were the members of the Czech armed forces already serving in the Russian army and the prisoners-of-war in the camps waiting to do so. They were represented by the so-called Club of the Associates of the League,[2] who supported Petrograd.

Rather more needs to be said about the last named organisation. The leaders of the League in Kiev had ambitious plans for becoming the main body directing the affairs of all Czechs and Slovaks outside Austria. They realised that they would need a large organisation for it. In any case an immense task would face them when all the prisoners were freed. And so they looked about for suitable members of the intelligentsia in the camps who could work for them. They selected a number of men, mostly former Austro–Hungarian officers of Czechoslovak origin, and drafted them into the various departments of the League, such as war-prisoners' affairs, legal questions, finance etc. Soon these so-called 'Associates' were involved in every branch of the League and acquired a wide knowledge of its affairs. Later, when they organised themselves into the Club of the Associates of the League, they emerged as an influential political force, critical of the League and siding with Petrograd rather than with Kiev.

It was not long before Hašek was himself drafted to Kiev, but he was not immediately picked to work as an Associate. On arrival at the headquarters of the Czechoslovak Reserve Unit he had to go before a medical commission, where he was pronounced unfit for regular fighting service. This suggests that his health had been really undermined at the beginning of the war and his illness just prior to his call-up had not been only a pretence. Nor did he appeal against the verdict, which indicates that he was himself conscious of his poor physical condition. He was sent to the Regimental Staff at Berezhno in the Pinsk marshes in what is now Byelo-Russia—again not exactly the most healthy of locations—where he was assigned as a clerk in the Regimental Office.

He had already made contact with the influential Kiev industrialist, Tuček, when he was at Totskoye, and had started to write for the *Čechoslovan*. It was not long therefore before the leading officials of the League got to know of his presence in Berezhno and, aware of his journalistic talents, asked for him to

ašlipka, Lieutenant Lukas's
lerly. Was he the real
ejk?

Švejk according to the artist Josef Lada. Hašek never saw
or approved Lada's interpretation.

Lieutenant Lukas, Hašek's
company commander, who
attempted to persuade Hašek
to reform and stop drinking.

The artist Josef Lada's
interpretation of Lieutenant
Lukáš as he appears in *The
Good Soldier Švejk*.

šek in Tsarist days,
ppy as an editor in
ev. The change in his
ysical appearance as the
ult of abstinence makes
n almost unrecognisable
the drunken clown of
ague café society.

ura's commissar, the
ormed Hašek, who was
vays 'good and gallant'
l won her mother's
urt. He told them that
was unmarried and had
children, keeping his
t a secret.

On an excursion in 1921
after returning to Prague.

'It's a lovely fairy
tale of the heart—the
month of May in my
declining years.'

Jaroslav Hašek with his son Richard, who saw him only a few times before his death and was the only member of Hašek's family at his funeral.

Lilac time at Lipnice. Hašek is at the extreme right with Shura seated next to him. He is still wearing some of the Russian clothing he wore in

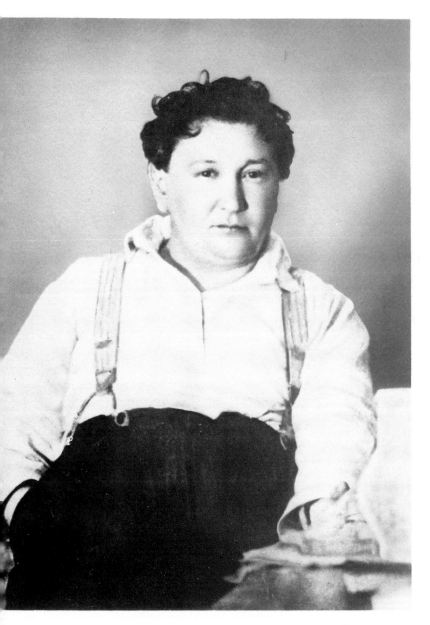

The last photograph of the creator of the Good Soldier Švejk, taken at Lipnice in 1922.

Jaroslav Hašek. An unkind sketch by his friend,
the artist Panuška.

be transferred to Kiev to work for them. And so he left the regiment, although his name still remained formally on its books, and began to work with the Associates of the League. Part of his duties was to act as a recruiting commissioner and go round the camps and trains, trying to persuade prisoners-of-war to join the *Družina*. At the same time he became a member of the staff of the *Čechoslovan*. Under the reactionary influence of the Kiev colony he worked whole-heartedly for the Tsarist regime—an unexpected development in a former anarchist and lampooner of crowned heads.

Hašek was one of the few members of the Club of Associates who supported the Kiev group and defended their dominant position in the League. He stood by them, because he thought they were in a better position to win the trust of the Russian General Staff and organise resistance against the Austrians. Later he was to explain his views in an article in *Čechoslovan*, 'What we owe to the Russian Czechs'.[3] 'Those of us who came to Russia in whole battalions as prisoners-of-war felt utterly lost when the war broke out, just as those did who stayed at home. We threw away our arms but did nothing else whatever. Numbed by the wall of artillery fire, we let ourselves become pusillanimous slaves.' It was the Russian Czechs, he argued, who had opened their eyes to the political struggle and showed it to them in a new light. No one could deny that they had only one idea and that was to organise armed resistance against Austria.

But working among these Russian Czechs was not to be so easy for Hašek. They were suspicious of any new recruit to the cause, and particularly so of him, whose reputation as a bohemian and clown had preceded him. Indeed, when he wrote his first leading article for *Čechoslovan*, the editor was privately warned to publish it as a *feuilleton* rather than a leader.

However it was not long before he had become the most successful *feuilletonist* and humorist of the Czech movement for independence. His first comic story, 'The Fortunes of Mr Hurt',[4] published in July 1916, enjoyed great popularity. His writings even came to the attention of Prague itself, where his satirical 'Story of the Portrait of Francis Joseph I',[5] published in the same month, was picked up and reported by the Austrian censor. As a result he was accused of insulting the Emperor, and the authorities were soon trying to find his whereabouts once more. Police proceedings against him for treason were continued throughout the war, eventually finding their way to the Austrian Ministry of Justice.

From the summer of 1916, when he was appointed to the staff of *Čechoslovan*, to the spring of 1918, when he deserted from the Legion, Hašek wrote very few humorous sketches and those he published, however popular they may have been, do not have the spontaneity and originality which were so characteristic of his peacetime writing. Most of them either pillory unpatriotic Czechs who are more interested in the comforts of life at home than the struggle for independence on the battlefield ('The Fortunes of Mr Hurt' or 'The Story of a Guarantee'[6]) or ridicule the Habsburgs ('The Story of the Portrait of Francis Joseph I' or 'A Ruler who Seats Himself on Czech Bayonets'*[7]). In the latter he wrote: 'We don't want to have a Habsburg on the Czech throne. We made the revolution for the very purpose of toppling the Habsburg dynasty and calling to the throne a member of the great Slav family of the Romanovs.' At this point of the war he was still a reactionary.

František Langer relates how when travelling in a convoy from Darnitse to a camp on the Volga in the summer of 1916 he saw Hašek in full activity as a recruiting commissioner. Just as his train stopped at a junction, another train coming from the opposite direction drew up alongside. Suddenly he heard someone shout from a window 'Are there any Czechs and Slovaks there?' When the answer came that there were, a lot of people 'hallooing in Czech' jumped out of the other train, and the first person Langer saw was Hašek himself, happily smiling at him. He obviously occupied an important position among them.

Langer was even more surprised when Hašek came up and kissed him on both cheeks in the Russian fashion. He had read of this practice in Russian novels but not yet personally experienced it. Hašek was dressed in Austrian trousers but wore a light Russian shirt instead of a tunic, a military cap with a red and white cockade and a pair of very fine top boots. The rest of the volunteers were also dressed in a patchwork of uniform and mufti.

* The new Austrian Emperor Charles I, who succeeded to the throne on the death of Francis Joseph in 1916.

'Hašek was slimmer and more agile than I had ever seen him in his life. His face had a real healthy ruddiness. And one of the first things he told me was that during his whole journey he had not tasted a drop of alcohol. This was confirmed by one of his companions, who had formerly been a waiter at the Union. Hašek was evidently in command of this small detachment . . .

'When the news broke in our train that Hašek was here, almost all the prisoners jumped out and took a look at this rare personality . . . Hašek stood on the step of the railway carriage and began to speak.

'It was the first public speech I had heard on the struggle against Austro–Hungary for Czechoslovak national independence which was not broken up by the police. And I couldn't help marvelling at the irony of fate in putting it into the mouth of Hašek of all people, from whom I had been accustomed to hear political orations only in the Party of Moderate Progress. He delivered this speech with unaffected solemnity. It contained all the stock historical references from the Battle of the White Mountain* onwards and like all such recruiting addresses was designed to appeal to patriot feelings . . . But in contrast to most such speeches, his did not sound like a tirade or a schoolmaster's lecture. He observed the required moderation and controlled himself so as not to be guilty of what he once used to parody in others. Moreover, he seemed to have unlearned all the tricks by which he had tried to beguile his listeners in the old days; there were no little jokes, no clowning, no covert grins . . .

'Altogether it was an entirely different Hašek from the one I had known. He, who had always been against militarism and patriotism, in fact always against something, was now for the first time speaking *for* something. And this something was nothing less than honest and consistent patriotism, the volunteer army and its fight for national independence. I listened to him and had the feeling that, although he had probably repeated them God knows how many times, these were not just empty phrases, but came direct from his heart.'

When the train moved on, Langer's prison guard could not

---

* In 1620 the forces of the Bohemian estates were defeated by the Imperial armies and Bohemia lost her independence.

help giving the men his opinion of the 'mad Austrians', who instead of sitting happily with safe skins in a prison camp wanted to go back to the front to help the Russian Tsar against their own Tsar.[8]

Hašek did not stay settled in Kiev, but from time to time visited the army, which was operating in the region of the Pinsk marshes to secure the rear of the Russian lines. There he wrote 'Letters from the Front' which were published in *Čechoslovan* in November and December 1916. In one of them he described how in a tumbledown hovel belonging to a man 'poorer than himself' he shared a room with a huge black boar. It grunted terribly and its bristles stood on end whenever it looked at him. Neither of them could sleep, the boar in case he should eat it and he in case it should eat him. Beyond the hovel were the Pinsk marshes which stretched to the North Sea [sic.] He had no idea how far they stretched southwards, but if it went on raining as it had done, in a week's time it would be as far as the Black Sea. 'Oysters are very dear here,' he added, '120 roubles a dozen!'[9]

Hašek spent most of his time with the members of the First Regiment, who were stationed not far away from the railway station at Sarny. He was interested in finding out how the other volunteers lived and enjoyed taking part in their discussions. He was already becoming known among the members of the *Družina* (since April 1916 the 'Czechoslovak Brigade') as a witty and popular speaker.

He still thought affectionately of Jarmila and was very happy when one day in January 1917 he received a visit from her brother, Sláva, by now an officer in the Russian army, who brought him one or two family photographs and a small picture of his son, Richard, which he wore throughout his stay in Russia. He was deeply moved by news of his family and started to weep, but later regained his composure and went on a regular bohemian spree with Sláva to the best café in Kiev, where the élite of the officers used to meet. He was soon the worse for liquor and uncontrollable (so much for his not taking a drop of alcohol!). Sláva was told by a Russian general, who happened to be sitting in the café, to take Hašek out. Hašek refused to obey and had eventually to be arrested.

In February there was a more serious incident. Entering

another café in Kiev and finding a table, at which a Russian reserve ensign was sitting, Hašek, who was an ordinary volunteer, sat down without asking the ensign's permission. The officer politely asked him to leave. As a 'Czech revolutionary' Hašek found this insulting and refused to go, asking 'whether Mr Ensign knows who Jan Žižka was?'* When finally the Russian officer drew his sabre, Hašek threw a bottle of wine at him, which struck him on the head.

As a consequence of his rash behaviour Hašek was arrested and imprisoned in the penal camp of Borispol, and only released when the League intervened.

Josef Mayer, another of Jarmila's brothers who had also deserted to the Russians, says that having learnt at Kiev station that Hašek had insulted Jindřich Jindříšek,† a leading figure in the Czech colony, he went to the hotel Praga to see Vondrák, by that time president of the League, who received him in a very friendly way as Hašek's brother-in-law. He reassured Josef:

'Look, the people who miss Hašek most are ourselves, because he kept up morale here. He is not in Borispol because of Jindříšek. That was quite an unimportant matter. We are used to his little jokes. Something worse occurred. Jarda walked about Kiev and attracted a lot of sympathy everywhere, but he was extremely indiscreet in his talk. Now, when our army is not advancing, everybody who wears a uniform is nervy, and Jaroslav has been going around saying to the officers—I am quoting you his words—that if he put a finger up his arse he could direct the front better than the whole Russian staff. Perhaps he is right —I don't know much about military affairs—but the officers saw in this a gross insult to the army and had him put away. You don't know how difficult it was for us to arrange for him to be handed over to us for punishment. When we finally succeeded, we sent him to Borispol so that he could have the chance of seeing things from another angle. He's not at all badly off, and yesterday he sent me a letter. Here it is. "Thank the Kiev ladies for their kind attention and especially for the bottles of

* The famous Czech Hussite general.

† Jindřich Jindříšek, an industrialist who had helped to found the *Družina*, also inaugurated 'Czech Roadway' (*Česká vozovka*), a scheme to find employment for Czech prisoners-of-war.

wine they sent me. I am sitting here in the dry and am writing *The Good Soldier Švejk*. That'll make the boys wake up. I am suffering in the cause of truth. Jarda." '

Thus, as well as enjoying the bottles of wine sent by the good ladies of Kiev, Hašek reportedly used his time profitably by working further on the novel's second version, eventually to be called *The Good Soldier Švejk in Captivity*.

In his articles he continued to defend the reactionary League and to criticise the more progressive Petrograd colony. He published a comic *feuilleton* under the title 'How Mr Potužník's Blood Flowed from the Parish Pump'[10] on January 15th, 1917, in which he mentioned no names but said in a footnote: 'If anybody thinks that he is referred to in this article, I ask his pardon.' In another 'When the Broom Sweeps',[11] he accused (anonymously of course) Bohdan Pavlů, the leader of the Petrograd group and editor of the Petrograd *Čechoslovák*, of specialising in 'slandering decent people'. 'Our editor wanted to get into history, just like Herostratos when he set fire to the temple of the goddess Diana'.* (A favourite simile of Hašek's which constantly recurs in his works.)

At one of the editorial meetings of *Čechoslovan*, which was held on February 16th, Hašek read out the initial extracts of an extensive *feuilleton* which he had written on *The Good Soldier Švejk*. It appeared in book form, published by *Čechoslovan*, that same spring. The object of this, the second version of the famous novel, was to serve the propaganda purposes of the Czechoslovak cause: to ridicule Austria and to attract recruits to the Legion. It has some of the characteristics of Hašek's other polemic writings in the Legion's journals. Conditioned by the period in which it is written and by the requirements of his assignment as a war journalist it is a much more limited and cruder version of the final book as most of us know it today.

In it Švejk appears as a shoemaker with an apprentice of his own, instead of as a dog-seller and falsifier of pedigrees with a charwoman, Mrs Müller. Although the beginning has many similarities with that of the final version—Švejk's resolve to serve his Emperor to the last drop of blood in his body, which only leads him to prison and the lunatic asylum, the theft of the

* See *The Good Soldier Švejk*, Preface.

Colonel's (General's) dog and the affair with Mrs Kákony—the emphasis is on the grotesqueness of the situation, with Švejk reiterating *ad absurdum* his patriotic intentions and the authorities obstinately refusing to see in this anything but a mark of treason or insanity. The humanity and epic sweep of the final version are nowhere to be found. The place of the kindly Lukáš is taken by Dauerling, who is a grotesque caricature, and the story ends with Švejk shooting him and going over to the Russian side—a quite un-Švejk-like act, although admittedly, as Dauerling has asked Švejk to shoot to wound not to kill him (so that he can get invalided out), Švejk can be seen as only carrying out orders rather too conscientiously, which is just what he does in the final version. But it is hard to imagine the mature Švejk with his tolerant philosophy of life ever firing a revolver at anyone, least of all his superior officer to whom he has been assigned as batman.[12]

Not only did Hašek write in the press, but he also took part in political meetings. One evening a delegate of the League, who had just returned from one of its meetings in Petrograd, told the Club of Associates: 'Either we give up Professor Masaryk, and the Russian government allows us to go on having an army, or else we don't, and the responsibility for what follows will fall on you'. A member of the Club rose and said: 'The honour and unity of our movement, with Professor Masaryk at its head, are dearer to us than the army.' Hašek, still a fervent supporter of the League, spoke in favour of keeping in the good books of the Tsarist government and so preserving the Czech army, even at the cost of having to disavow Masaryk. However, the dilemma was resolved by a totally unexpected development—the outbreak of the February Revolution. According to Křížek, the news of it came in a very dramatic manner. There was suddenly a sound of knocking on the door. Jindříšek, their host, went out and rushed back in great agitation: 'Gentlemen,' he cried, 'there's been a revolution in Petrograd! The Tsar and his government have been overthrown!'

(13)

The Russian February Revolution

The seizure of power by the new Russian Provisional government on March 12th, 1917 (February 27th old style), which was followed by the abdication of the Tsar three days later, was the first of the two revolutions in Russia in that year. Known as the 'bourgeois' revolution, it installed a Liberal régime of the Left. Some of the new ministers were Masaryk's friends, notably the Foreign Minister, Milyukov, and at first the new government gave him full support and invited him to come to Russia to help mediate with the Western Allies. However, behind them other more radical forces were gathering strength, such as the Petrograd Soviet and the All-Russian Union of Soviets, to which it had to defer in many questions. There was in fact dual control under which the Provisional Government was constantly undermined by the rival power of the Soviets. Meanwhile a momentous, though at the time little published event occurred in Petrograd: Lenin arrived at the Finland station on April 16th (April 3rd) to be met by leading Bolsheviks, and on the next day read out his famous *'April' Thesis*, which included the exhortation to defy the Provisional Government and oppose the war.

With the fall of the Tsarist government the League automatically lost its main support and the situation changed overnight in favour of the Petrograd opposition and the Club of Associates. It was indeed the end of the League's dominant role, if not of the League itself.

At a congress held by the League in the last days of April (new style) the Czechoslovak colonies in Russia—the 'old settlers'—found themselves for the first time in an absolute minority. They had only 55 delegates against 141 from the groups of prisoners-of-war and 86 from the army. It was decided to set up at Petrograd a Russian branch of the Czechoslovak

National Council (henceforth to be called the Branch)[1] under the presidency of Masaryk and the local direction of three vice-presidents: Bohumil Čermák,[2] Prokop Maxa[3] (both close supporters of Masaryk) and the Slovak Ján Országh.[4] The military and prisoners-of-war commissions were the only authorities to remain in Kiev.

This was a severe blow for Hašek, because the Kiev *Čechoslovan*, to which he had been contributing and in which he had conducted some intemperate polemics against the Petrograd *Čechoslovák*, would now lose its leading status, if not its whole existence. And so for the time being he gave up satirical and polemical articles and stopped proclaiming the desirability of a personal union between Bohemia and Tsarist Russia and offering the Czechoslovak throne to a member of the Romanov family.

By April 8th (March 15th) however, he had shifted ground sufficiently to express exultation over the fall of Tsarism and denounce the occult influences of Rasputin and the Russian court in the article 'The Dark Force'.[5] Always too impulsive to be consistent, he would throw himself passionately into what he believed in at the moment, only to change course with equal zest. In this case it was not difficult for him to hark back to the views he held in his Anarchist days and proclaim radical revolution as the only hope for his country.

His bohemian habits had begun to change. During his frequent visits to Kiev he was seen with his companions in many bars, but some of his friends observed that he consumed very little vodka, and then only in an emergency. Apart from tea he preferred Ukrainian beer and was not even drinking very much of that. He used to sleep overnight in the editorial offices of the *Čechoslovan*, putting a parcel of old newspapers under his head and throwing a military greatcoat over himself.

His taste for the subversive prompted him to join an opposition group within the Legion called the Black Hand[6] after the notorious Serbian conspiratorial society of that name. He also contributed to its journal *Revolution*,[7] publishing in one number a sharp article against the Club of Associates, which he offensively nicknamed the 'Czech Pickwick Club'.[8] He chose to do this on the day of the Third Congress of Czechs and Slovaks in Russia, April 23rd, 1917.

Hašek was hitting chiefly at Bohdan Pavlu,[9] whom he had referred to as 'the friend of the well-known German–Austrian spy Baron von Schelking'. But he attacked almost as violently Pavlu's supporters in Kiev—the 'new-baked, self-styled leaders from the Cable Company in the café at Podvalská', who with their refined cunning had 'conned' the leadership of the League.

He characterised the President of the Club of Associates, Chalupa, as a typical judge from the minor Bohemian provincial courts, one of those men who 'in the morning pass sentences on paupers and in the afternoon immerse themselves in their hobbies. They photograph, paint, play-act, go on shoots, drink their few glasses of beer a day, tell their usual stories, but remain mere dilettantes all their lives. For them everything is just a game. The only thing they really care about is that they should be mentioned in society, if only as attending a funeral. There was a time when their name never carried further than across the boundaries of a couple of districts, but now that they have no one above them they try to spread it as far as possible . . . All they want is that the bill stickers from the Club—I mean the Czech Pickwick Club—should post up their names on their placards.'

In addition to attacking Pavlu and Chalupa in person, Hašek pilloried various leaders of the Branch, some of whom were destined to occupy influential positions in the Czechoslovak Republic. Such an article, if published in the West today, would have involved him in a multiple libel suit. As it was, it did not expose him to legal proceedings, but it certainly increased the number of his enemies in Russia and later in Czechoslovakia. A curious aspect of the case was that Hašek was launching his attack not from a position on the Left, but on the extreme Right. At heart he was still clinging to his old conservative, Slavophil, Tsarist sympathies.

As a result of the offensive article Hašek was surprised one day by a visit from a delegation of the Third Regiment led by Captain Gajda,[10] who had him deprived of his functions on *Čechoslovan* and in the Club of Associates, and immediately sent to the front to join the Seventh Battalion of the First Regiment. But he was brazen enough to bring with him there a bundle of copies of *Revolution* with the offending article in it. As a result he soon found himself in gaol and required to attend a 'court of honour', records of the proceedings of which are interesting for the light they throw on the way Hašek was regarded by the officers of his Brigade. He is referred to in the official report as 'the *notorious* editor and volunteer Hašek'! The journal of the Seventh Company commented: 'If they hadn't put a guard over him, he would probably have been beaten up as well.'

The President of the Court asked Hašek what his intentions had been in writing the article. He replied: 'Purely propaganda.' The President invited him to read the article aloud. Hašek scratched his ears and said that that would be a punishment for him. This caused great amusement. Then to the accompaniment of general gaiety he did so.

The President asked him how he could accuse Pavlu so monstrously. Hašek replied that Pavlu was a fine and honourable man; he attributed the whole misunderstanding to his 'clumsiness in expressing himself'. Telling him forthrightly he had committed 'a moral crime', the President proposed that he should send letters to *Čechoslovan*, *Čechoslovák* and the *Slav Herald* retracting what he had written about the members of the Club. Hašek readily agreed to do so. The author of the official record commented: 'Mr Hašek would of course be perfectly ready to do this, for, as I know him, he is very susceptible to financial reward and is a man of no character whatsoever, writing one thing today and another tomorrow.' In addition Hašek promised to give up all political activity and be a good soldier. After signing a humiliating recantation he left the court 'with a happy expression on his face'—once more an enigma to everyone.

The consequences were severe. Pavlu refused to print his apology in the Petrograd *Čechoslovák*, and *Revolution*, in which he had originally published his offending article, would have nothing more to do with him on the grounds that he had 'betrayed' them. His recantation left them quite cold; they considered that with his article he committed political suicide.

Hašek was stripped of all his positions and sent from pillar to post: from the Seventh Company of the First Artillery Regiment, Jan Hus, to the machine-gun detachment of the Reserve Battalion and from there to the machine-gun detachment of the Regiment, and so on. And for four months he was forbidden to publish anything.

Under pressure from the Allied governments the Russian Foreign Minister Milyukov sent them a note on April 5th promising loyalty to the pledges to continue the war given them by the Tsarist government. This raised a storm of protest in the capital and led to his enforced resignation. At about the same time the so-called 'April Conference'—the All-Russian Social Democratic Party Conference—met and adopted the slogan 'All Power to the Soviets'. The following month a new government was formed with Prince Lvov still as premier, but containing six Socialists. At about the same time Trotsky returned to Petrograd from the USA.

Kerensky now took over the ministries of Foreign Affairs and War and showed himself almost as obstructive as the Tsarist government had been. 'I can't feel any enthusiasm for the way your countrymen carry on resistance against their [sic] government,' he said to Vondrák, President of the League. 'After all they had a constitution and the possibility finally of proclaiming a revolution, and of overthrowing a detested government, but to go to the front and then betray their [sic] state and surrender to the enemy! Excuse me, but I really cannot have any sympathy with such unchivalrous conduct.' However as he was preparing a new offensive against the Germans and Austrians and the Czech units were anxious to join it, he raised no objection to their participation. Indeed, with demoralisation swiftly developing among the Russian troops, he was lucky to be able to count on them.

Meanwhile the Czechoslovak National Council in Paris had been recognised by the Allies as the representative body of the Czechs and Slovaks and had ordered a general mobilisation of its citizens abroad. From being volunteers the Czechoslovak troops in Russia had now become conscripts. Masaryk had succeeded in bringing unity to the movement. He had won over the troops by his decisive anti-Austrian stand and his convincing arguments. At first the military training of the Czechoslovak troops had been very primitive, consisting of Sokol* exercises without arms, i.e. gymnastic training; now the Legion was a comparatively well-developed military formation, buttressed by discipline and inspired by a national ideology. On May 16th

* The national and patriotic movement for gymnastic training.

Masaryk himself arrived in Moscow to take personal direction of the whole movement in Russia.

In the middle of June 1917 various companies of what was now the Second Czechoslovak Brigade were withdrawn from certain sectors of the front and concentrated at Yezerno, north-west of Tarnopol, as part of the Forty-ninth Army Corps of the Eleventh Russian Army. The First Czechoslovak Regiment, in which Hašek was serving, was ordered to attack and occupy a sector of the front near Zborów, because the so-called 'Finnish Regiments', which consisted not of Finns but of Russians stationed in Finland, had refused to obey Kerensky's orders to continue the war and had had to be withdrawn from the line. They left their positions in a disgraceful state of disorder and, instead of handing their ammunition over to the Czechoslovak troops, buried it in the ground. On the eve of the attack the Siberian Infantry Regiment had to be disarmed. On all sides of the Legion the Russian troops were refusing to fight. Some of them crossed into the German trenches and fraternised with the enemy, others tried to persuade the Czechs not to move up to the front line. There were cries of: 'The Czechs want war. Put them behind bars!' which were greeted with applause by other Russian troops.

The only Czechoslovak troops who were affected by this demoralisation were those in the Second Battalion of the Second Regiment, who refused to march. They were not ex-prisoners-of-war but Czechs and Slovaks long established in Volhynia, and were Russian subjects.

During the morning of July 2nd the Second Czechoslovak Brigade captured three Austrian fortified positions at Zborów, broke the enemy front for a length of about two kilometres and took over four thousand prisoners. This great victory and the Russian generals' glowing report of it made Kerensky change his opinion of the Czechs. In the West the Legion's successes caused a sensation and proved of enormous help to Masaryk and the National Council.

Although it could not prevent the rapidly approaching break-up of the Russian front, Zborów was a milestone in the development of the Legion. It stiffened its backbone and raised its morale; in fact it founded a national legend. But there were troubles in store. Early in August Kerensky became Prime

Minister and in the following September after General Korni-lov's unsuccessful coup a republic was proclaimed with Kerensky as dictator.

In July Hašek was allowed to return to the Regimental Office and work there as a clerk. In August he was elected a member of the Regimental Committee and soon became its secretary. He was proposed by Lieutenant (later Colonel) Švec, one of the heroes of Zborów, who was later to achieve notoriety by shoot-ing himself when the Legionaries he commanded refused to obey his orders to halt the Red Army's advance. Still unable to par-ticipate in the political direction of the Legion, Hašek tried to help in minor organisational and cultural work. He became chairman of the Entertainments Committee, organised military festivals and acted as *compère*. No doubt Menger, who as a former actor was in charge of these activities, roped him in.

He also took up his literary work again. When the regiment was sent to recuperate at Berezhno, he resumed his connections with *Čechoslovan*. He continued to write despatches from the front, in which he praised the heroism of the Czechs and shared their faith in their 'revolutionary' future. By order of the First Rifle Regiment 'Jan Hus' he was awarded the Medal of St George, fourth class, for his deserving conduct at the Battle of Zborów and during the retreat from Tarnopol.

But the Ukrainian front was fast crumbling. The Russian soldiers were abandoning their trenches *en masse* and running home to their wives and *izbas*, a demoralisation which could easily prove infectious. Masaryk urged the legionaries to re-member that their hopes of freedom depended on the military victories of the Allies. With the Russian collapse the Legion found themselves in a desperate situation. They could only re-turn home if Austria were liquidated, and this would never happen if the Allies made peace with Germany. Feelings against the Bolsheviks ran high. They were looked on as capitulators and traitors to the Entente's struggle against Germany and Austria, who refused to help bring the war to a victorious conclusion. They were held responsible for the breach in the front and for the anti-war demonstrations in Petrograd. From here it was a short step to the conclusion that an attack on the Soviet govern-ment was a blow struck against Germany. Hašek, like others, blamed the collapse on the Bolsheviks. He saw the German offensive which followed the Provisional government's unsuccessful one as 'the war plan of the Austro–German General Staff, prepared in collusion with Lenin's people'.

Meanwhile he was promoted lance-corporal and appointed assessor in the Regimental Court. He even began to make a 'come-back' as a speaker. His reputation had grown thanks to the publication of his second version of Švejk—*The Good Soldier Švejk in Captivity*.

On October 10th he gave an address at a regimental manifestation: 'Our one thought must be the destruction of the old Monarchy. We must concentrate our minds every hour and minute of the day on revolutionary action, devote all our efforts to our cherished historical act of vengeance, to giving the cursed Monarchy its final *coup de grâce*.' The occasion ended with the singing of 'The Red Flag'. At the beginning of November he sat on the Brigade Committee as regimental delegate.

On November 7th came another dramatic chapter in the saga of the Czechs in Russia. The Bolshevik revolution (called the October Revolution because the Russians were then still using the old calendar) broke out. A week later Hašek was reinstated as a member of the editorial staff of *Čechoslovan*.

(14)

The October Revolution

With the outbreak of the October Revolution the Branch found itself in something of a dilemma, because the Legion were stationed in the Ukraine where the political and military situation was unusually delicate and complicated. But fortunately Masaryk was at hand to give directives.

The Ukrainians were fellow-Slavs and their language was very close to Czech and Slovak. There were Ukrainian minorities in Austria–Hungary, mainly in Ruthenia and Galicia. As fellow-sufferers the Czechs sympathised with their struggle against the oppressive rule of the Habsburgs. But when they began to press for independence from Russia and finally proclaimed an autonomous republic of their own it became embarrassing. Moreover the Ukrainian *Rada*,* or Soviet, was Menshevik and anti-Bolshevik and led by intellectuals who included a representative of the Ruthenians from Austria–Hungary. Masaryk knew these leaders well and was on friendly terms with them.

Moreover, important Russian strategic interests were involved. To the south-east of the Ukraine lay the southern territories, where the White generals Kornilov, Alekseev and Denikin (together with the Cossacks who had also proclaimed their own independent government) were organising the Volunteer Army against the Bolsheviks. The Soviet Government could not afford to let the whole of this vital area, especially the rich granary of the Ukraine, slip out of its control.

Masaryk had firmly maintained all along that the Legion must at all costs avoid involvement in Russian internal politics, Red versus White or Ukrainian versus Russian. Immediately after the Bolshevik *coup* in Petrograd, he had telephoned to Prokop Maxa in Kiev emphatically enjoining him to ensure that the Legion observed the strictest neutrality. Only in case of

* Council.

anarchy might Czech troops be used for restoring order. Yet on November 8th some detachments of the Legion had been ordered by their Russian commander to help the Whites in Kiev against the Bolsheviks and two legionaries had lost their lives in the engagement.

This untimely incident was due to the interference of Josef Dürich,[1] a Deputy President of the National Council in Paris, who had been sent to Russia to coordinate Czech affairs. Instead he had intrigued with the Russian government and the reactionary Czech landowners in Kiev to get himself recognised as Czech leader in preference to Masaryk. One of the reasons why Masaryk came to Russia was to restore his authority after Dürich's mischief had undermined the position of the National Council and caused confusion in the Legion.

Thanks to Masaryk the situation was quickly redressed, in spite of intrigues on the part of oppositional elements, and the policy of neutrality was restored. But when later a group of legionaries, who wanted to fight the Bolsheviks, deserted to join the Cossacks in the south and subsequently fought for Kornilov and Denikin, the Soviet government began to suspect that the Legion and their Tsarist officers were in league with the Whites.

Masaryk was faced with two unsatisfied elements—those who wanted to fight against the Bolsheviks and those who wanted to fight with them. His policy of non-intervention and disengagement was not trusted by the Soviet authorities nor was it immediately popular among the legionaries, but so great was his prestige and authority that the bulk of them fell into line behind him. Like him they were anti-Bolshevik but saw how important it was that they should not get involved in the Russian revolutionary struggle.

But this was not the view of the reactionary and radical Czech colony in Kiev. Dědina, the rich co-owner of a factory for farming implements, and Zíval, a wealthy owner of bakeries, had founded in 1916 a body called the Society for Czechoslovak Unity. Its pro-Tsarist, panslavist and Orthodox leaders continually intrigued against Masaryk and the leaders of the Branch. In order to propagate their views they started their own journal, the *Slav Herald*,[2] which they published in Russian, Czech and Serbian.

After the February Revolution, within this very conservative society and under its protection, a strong Social Democratic movement sprang up, nurtured by the reactionaries in the hope that it would turn against Masaryk and look to Russia. Two opposing factions now emerged—a conservative one, led by its original right-wing founders, and another more radical one, consisting of workers and prisoners-of-war, the vast majority of whom were supporters of the Social Democratic Party. This latter group tried unsuccessfully to secure control of the *Slav Herald*, which remained the preserve of the former. If this reactionary journal now ceased to lament the end of the Russian monarchy, it continued to be nationalist and anti-Socialist.

Just before the October Revolution a splinter group of left-wing extremists, who called themselves Social Democrats but were probably in Soviet pay, started a journal called *Freedom*,[3] which soon fell under the control of a slippery tailor named Alois Muna,* later to become the leader of the Czechoslovak Communist Party in Russia.

In *The Making of a State* Masaryk has described how at the beginning of November 1917 Muna and two or three of his comrades came to see him, bringing with them the first number of their journal. According to Masaryk the bulk of Muna's followers were prisoners-of-war employed in the Kiev Russian or Czech factories who were drawing bumper wages from their reactionary employers and had no wish either to join the Legion or pay a contribution to it. 'They hid behind the convenient slogan that we in the National Council were "bourgeois", and that the Legion served the aims of the "bourgeoisie" and capitalism. But in fact it was they who were serving the capitalists, and as for Muna, he was playing off not one side against the other, but all against all.' In his talk with Masaryk, Muna took a typically crafty line. He maintained that his attacks on the Legion were only a pretence. He had to please the Kiev workers, but in time he would bring the 'Kiev dodgers' over to Masaryk's camp.[4]

At first *Freedom* attacked the Bolsheviks, calling them 'fanatics and people from another world', who with their 'bandit terror'

* After the war he was sentenced to gaol for his part in the plot to set up a Bolshevik republic in Czechoslovakia. Much later, in 1929, he took part in a *coup* against the Gottwald faction and was expelled from the Communist Party. He is seldom mentioned in Czechoslovak official publications today.

were driving Russia to ruin and destruction. But after the October Revolution (November 7th) it changed its tone, took their side and attacked the Branch and its officials. Muna himself distributed subversive leaflets among the legionaries and entered into treasonable negotiations with the Kiev Soviet, which the Bolsheviks had installed after having deposed the *Rada*.

Meanwhile in all the chaos the German and Austrian troops were able to advance on Russia almost unopposed. Immediately after seizing power the Bolshevik régime had put out feelers to the Central Powers in the hope of securing an armistice. The legionaries were understandably worried what would become of them if the Soviet government accepted the German terms. An even graver and more immediate threat was that in spite of the fall of Kiev to the Bolsheviks, a separatist Ukraine might eventually go over to the Germans. In Kiev the Czechoslovak officers were desperately talking of trying to break out by crossing the Caucasus and linking up with the British in Persia, who would, they hoped, find means of transporting them to France and the Western front.

Hašek was at first attracted by this plan, but later had other ideas which he developed in an article, 'Past and Present',[5] published in *Čechoslovák*. Writing under a pseudonym he argued that terror was an essential part of a national rising, and advocated the training of terrorist groups to penetrate into Austria and carry out individual acts of terror: they should assassinate ministers and members of the Imperial family, destroy railways, blow up bridges and tunnels, foment social unrest and encourage anti-Austrian feeling in preparation for a general rising. These ideas, which were those of the Tsarist General Staff and had been probably suggested to him by the Kiev industrialist Tuček, ran counter to Masaryk's plans, which were that the Legion should make their way to Vladivostok and there embark for France, where they would fight on the Western front under the overall command of the French. *Freedom* now started an agitation to keep the Legion in Russia and let them fight side by side with the Bolsheviks. In its December number it wrote, 'There are a number of Socialist and good comrades who look on armed action against Austria (i.e. from France) as a piece of private enterprise on the part of Professor Masaryk.'

Meanwhile a reorganisation took place in the Legion. Their

commanding officers had been up to this time Russian and, since their sympathies would be strongly engaged on the side of the Whites, most of them, though not all, were now retired and replaced by Czech and Slovak officers, who had been promoted colonels and generals overnight. At the same time a tough drive was begun against left wing elements.

During these months Hašek's views were moving further and further to the Left. It was now the social rather than the national question which dominated his thinking. He argued in his writings that the only force capable of realising the social revolution back home was the working class. They alone had the revolutionary spirit indispensable for winning independence. Since he was not by nature a political animal, it seemed likely that he was being strongly influenced by someone who was. This was in all probability Břetislav Hula,* a Communist on the staff of the *Čechoslovan* who initiated him into Marxist revolutionary theory.

In two *feuilletons* published in January and February 1918 Hašek set out his nebulous and romantic ideas for a popular rising at home.[6] In a third he wrote: 'Socialism is no longer a romantic dream . . . Only the oppressed classes can bring to the world of today the great qualities of iron resolution, passionate resentment and energy stretched taut for final victory.'[7] The Anarchist enthusiasm of his youth blazed up once more and with it came crowding into his mind lurid visions of the wretched life of the poor in Prague—highly exaggerated because Prague was at that time socially more progressive than many other large European cities, as can be seen from the photographs of street scenes published in the illustrated weeklies to which he himself had contributed before the war.

The force of events was too strong for Hašek and those who were influencing him. Because of the danger threatening them from the invading German forces, the Legion had begun to withdraw from the Ukrainian front. Hašek denounced this rational and indeed inescapable decision as 'treason against the national cause' and pointed an accusing finger at the 'bourgeois' leadership of the Branch. Making common cause for the

* Later one of the leading workers in the Czechoslovak Communist Party in Moscow. On his return home he became editor of the Communist paper *Freedom* in Kladno. He was expelled from the Party in 1925.

moment with Muna and the *Freedom* group he called for the arrest of the Legion's leaders and tried to rally the rank and file to help the Soviet troops resist the advancing German armies. But the Czech Bolsheviks were not enthusiastic about his sudden support for their cause. Until quite recently Muna and his group had been the chief target for some of his most virulent onslaughts because of their lukewarm support for the Legion. If Hašek had found it convenient to forget all this, they certainly had not.

Nothing daunted, he eagerly took a hand in an attempted Bolshevik *putsch* organised by Muna against the Branch. The left wing had managed to win over to their side some of the members of the Club of Associates, two of whom were in the leadership of the Branch. They plotted to overthrow the Branch and put the Legion under a new organisation to be called 'The Czechoslovak Revolutionary Soviet of Workers and Soldiers'.[8] To deceive and confuse the troops and prisoners-of-war Muna did not scruple to invoke Masaryk's name. He announced that Masaryk would be president of the new 'Soviet' and that they would submit to him their proposals for changes in the personnel and organisation of the Legion.

The claim that Masaryk was behind them (which the Czech leader quickly repudiated) certainly did not imply any loyalty to him on their part. It was nothing more than a shady attempt to win over the right wing Social Democrats, some of whom had been so incautious as to let themselves be associated with the so-called 'Soviet'. But as a result of Masaryk's firm support for the Branch, they withdrew from the 'Soviet', leaving it to Communists like Muna and Hais and the 'former Anarchist Jaroslav Hašek', whom no one at all regarded as a trustworthy ally, least of all the Czech Communist leaders themselves.

The leaders of the Branch had no difficulty in disarming the 'Soviet' and restoring the authority of the National Council. The *putsch* was liquidated in twenty-four hours and its instigators quickly made off to avoid capture by the rapidly advancing Germans, who were hanging any 'ex-Austrians' who fell into their hands. It should be noted that they did not take up arms themselves or actively resist the invaders.

The National Council's decision to evacuate the Legion to France was not motivated by any change in its attitude to the

Germans, as the Czech Bolsheviks were insinuating, or by reluctance to fight against them, but by the fact that an anti-German front no longer existed in Russia and there was no hope at all of one being reconstituted. The Soviet government was in fact at the time making a peace treaty with the enemy and any effective resistance on its part could be discounted, owing to lack of troops, arms and ammunition. Moreover the base was utterly disorganised and demoralised, and there was no will to fight. The hollowness of the Czech Bolshevik pro-war propaganda was exposed when one day, February 23rd, the Muna group were loudly proclaiming that the 'revolutionary proletariat' would never let the Germans into the Ukraine and the next, February 24th, the Bolshevik government approved a proposal for the conclusion of peace with the Germans and the evacuation of the Ukraine.

In March, after lengthy negotiations, Stalin, who was then People's Commissar for Nationalities, agreed that the Legion might travel to Siberia, provided they surrendered all their weapons and ammunition, except for a specified minimum to be retained for their security. But, secretly afraid that as the Legion still had a few White Russian generals they might give help to the White forces in Siberia, the Soviet government encouraged the local Soviets in the towns the Legion passed through to insist on the surrender of even this minimum and to do all they could to delay their progress. This inevitably led to friction between the Legion and the Bolshevik authorities. Exasperated by these hindrances, the Legion were prepared if necessary to fight their way to Vladivostok.

Masaryk was scheduled to leave Russia on March 7th, his birthday. Up to the last moment he could not decide whether to go or not. He hated leaving the Legion in the lurch, surrounded as they were by German troops of far greater strength. They could not rely on help from the Bolsheviks: their detachments were few and far between and they were incapable of supplying food and ammunition owing to the chaos behind the lines. There was indeed a serious danger that the Legion might be completely engulfed. Only when they had successfully extricated themselves from the German advance columns did Masaryk breathe again and decide he could go.

The Legion had had to move really fast in order to escape

capture by the German armies, which were rapidly advancing on Kiev, supported by the Ukrainian nationalist Skoropadsky. At points the Germans made contact with the Czech troops, but by means of proposing a cease-fire and postponing replies to the German conditions the Legion bought time, which enabled them to leave Kiev with the last Bolsheviks and to take most of the city's supplies with them. The German advance units reached the city on March 1st. Later, near Bakhmach, the Legion were in danger of being caught in a pincer movement between two German columns advancing from the south and the north. They skilfully beat off a concentrated German attack on March 13th and succeeded in reaching the railway line, where they were able to entrain and move via Bakhmach to safe positions on the line and thence embark on their 'anabasis' to Siberia. From now on they faithfully followed the instructions of Masaryk, who had said: 'Our policy is the railway line.' The skill and courage of the Czechs in this fierce rearguard action were highly praised by the Germans: Ludendorff wrote afterwards in his memoirs that they fought considerably better than the Bolshevik troops.

Meanwhile Hašek was left isolated and vulnerable. He was practically outlawed in the Legion, although no disciplinary steps were taken against him. At the same time Muna and the *Freedom* group had gone off and abandoned him. Together with Hula he decided to desert to Moscow, where the Czech left-wing Social Democrats from Petrograd had moved now that Moscow was the new capital of the Soviet Republic. It was characteristic of the bad relations between Kiev and Petrograd that even Czech Bolsheviks from these two cities could not agree. Although it was not a final burning of boats for Hašek it was a step towards it.

On his way to Moscow he stopped at Kharkov, the industrial centre of the Ukraine, where he was happy to meet up with two of his brothers-in-law, Sláva and Josef Mayer, who had also fallen into Russian hands and were now staying in the town. Josef Mayer recalled: 'In the middle of the terrible chaos after the Peace of Brest Litovsk, Jaroslav suddenly turned up. "I'm so glad I've managed to catch you at Kharkov," he said. "I have two railway vans at my disposal . . . I'll take you with me. Get hold of Sláva as well and let's go." ' But Sláva was wounded and unfit to be moved and Josef persuaded Hašek to leave on his own. He was very optimistic and believed he could still stop the Legion going to France and force it to fight against the Germans in Russia.

In Moscow the Petrograd Social Democratic Left, now re-christened 'The Czechoslovak Section of the Russian Communist Party', had started a new journal *Pioneer*.[9] The editors, Beneš and Knoflíček, who had had no contact with the Legion or Kiev and were unprejudiced against Hašek, welcomed him with open arms. He now joined their new party and contributed an article to the first number of *Pioneer* on March 27th under the title 'Why are we going to France?',[10] calling for the Legion to stay in Russia, take part in the 'regeneration' of the Russian army and help the Russian nation to consolidate the Republic. Although critical of the Branch and condemning its attitude to developments in Soviet Russia, he gave it credit for the role it had played in the defeat of the old League. He still retained his sympathies and respect for Masaryk and refrained from attacking him for a long time. He was even charitable towards the Legion's great literary champion, Medek.

Not long afterwards Muna and Hais arrived in Moscow from Penza, where they had been busy agitating. On finding Hašek there they quickly took steps to expose and remove him. They had him sent to Samara as leader of a group assigned to carry out propaganda among legionaries and Czechoslovak prisoners-of-war.

Samara (today Kuibyshev), which lies on the middle Volga, was important as a point through which all the Legion's trains must pass on their way to Siberia. Hašek and his team arrived there in the first days of April and set up a recruiting office for the Czechoslovak Red Army at a hotel in the main street. They immediately started their work in the railway carriages standing at the junction, using as propaganda material the first two numbers of *Pioneer* containing leaders by Hašek.

In the face of strong opposition from the officers, Masaryk had allowed what he regarded as misguided Czech agitators to put their case before the legionaries. For one thing, good relations with local Bolshevik commanders required it. But he could in any case well afford to do so, because the Legion were proud of themselves and their morale was high, whereas the Bolshevik

armies had had little success in the field and were in a poor
state. Moreover there was much bickering going on between the
Communists of Petrograd and Kiev. His confidence was justified
when an insignificant number of men, whom the Legion could
well be quit of, chose to go over to the Red Army. But it was
believed in the Legion that these agitators abused their positions
by spying out how many of their weapons the units were taking
with them in the trains and then communicating the information to local Soviet leaders, who then held up the trains.

By his own decision or perhaps at the instigation of Hula,
Hašek now decided upon a final breach with the Legion. At a
meeting of the Branch on April 14th they read out a letter they
had received from him:

'I hereby declare that I am opposed to the policy of the
Branch and our army's departure for France. I accordingly proclaim that I am leaving the Legion, until other views prevail
both in it and throughout the whole leadership of the National
Council. I request that my decision be placed on record. I shall
continue to work for the Revolution in Austria and for the
liberation of our nation.'

When the contents of this letter became public knowledge the
loyal legionaries gave Hašek no quarter and launched a campaign of 'character assassination' against him. The writer Josef
Kopta[11] in his novel *The Third Company* wrote afterwards: 'It's
as though I saw him before me—his cowardly, guilty eyes;
every word of his a sophistry; his face bloated with booze. He is
moving into another house away from us, because he hated it
here, and there he is just about to start some new piece of
tomfoolery.'

Soon after this, according to both Communist and anti-
Communist sources, Hašek appeared to be experiencing some
doubts. One of his colleagues recalled afterwards that he looked
care-worn, his writings became for a time less vehement, and he
gave the impression that he was not completely confident of the
correctness of his stand. At a meeting in Samara on April 12th
he had wished the Legion a happy journey to France and promised he would not work against the army. Legionaries who con-
tacted him reported that he had 'quietened down'. They spoke

too of friction between the Communists of different nationalities and reported that Hašek had formed a separate section and proposed that the name 'Communist' should not be used. He even proposed making contact with the National Council over the head of the Branch, invoking the name of Masaryk and calling themselves the 'Second Czechoslovak Revolutionary Corps'. Some Communists were said to have attacked the Moscow leadership and stated that they would not obstruct the passage of the Legion, because they would spread the ideas of democracy all over the world. These accounts come mostly from legionary sources, but Communists admit that Hašek was suffering from second thoughts at this time and attribute it to the fact that he had not yet properly grasped the ideas of Lenin and was still imbued with nationalistic misconceptions.

None the less his recruiting activities met with some success. He managed to bring over to the Red Army all those in Samara who were working for the Branch. According to *Pioneer*, 'A few days before May 1st there was a revolution in the local branch of the National Council . . . Comrade Hašek spoke on the theme: "World Revolution and the Czech Emigration." He ended his speech with a call for the Branch to be transformed into a Communist organisation. A local revolution was thereupon carried out and the Czech Communist Party founded, which new members are joining daily.'[12]

The Legion was in a very difficult position. Their road to the east was blocked, not only by chaos and disruption in the railway system but by the policy of the Soviet government to get all the arms and ammunition they could out of them and to delay their withdrawal as long as possible. Distrusting the Soviet authorities and confused by reports that some of them might be required by the National Council to change direction and travel to the northern ports of Archangel and Murmansk (which they feared might be used as a means to divide them and make it easier for the Red Army to mop them up), they were growing more and more convinced that they would have to abandon the neutrality imposed on them by the National Council in Paris and fight their way to Vladivostok. They knew that many of the towns which they had had to pass through were thinly held by the Red Army and that reinforcements could be quickly overcome as long as they themselves held the strategic positions on the railway. The experience they had gained fighting alongside Russian troops had inspired them with a spirit of self-confidence, and the idea of 'going it alone' had an appeal for all of them from the officers downwards. They had indeed many of the characteristics of an independent entity already. They could continue to provision themselves by making requisitions on the countryside and their position would be strengthened if they could seize what had already been requisitioned by the Soviet authorities themselves. In their railway vans they had not only considerable supplies of frozen meat but also livestock as well, so that they did not have to rely exclusively on foraging parties. Photographs of the time document their amazing resourcefulness in constructing their 'travelling city'. In their trains they had carpenters' and cobblers' workshops, tailors' cutting rooms, bakeries, butchers, barbers' saloons and bath installations. And for entertainment they had their bands, their theatrical and ballet groups and their sports teams. In this atmosphere of isolation, autarky and nervous tension, it only needed a small spark to set off an explosion. And this happened when the Third and Sixth Regiments reached Chelyabinsk.

At this point on the railway line the legionaries were watching from their stationary carriages large numbers of trains passing in the opposite direction, bringing back German, Austrian and Hungarian prisoners-of-war due to be repatriated by the terms of the Soviet–German peace treaty. Not unnaturally they looked with hostility at men who immediately on their return would be mobilised again to fight against the Allies. Feelings were suddenly inflamed on May 14th when a prisoner-of-war, thought by the legionaries to be a Hungarian, hurled a piece of iron out of the window of one of the carriages and hit and wounded one of the legionaries. It is not known whether the act was intentional or not, but at once a detachment of legionaries pursued the train, stopped it, dragged the man they thought was the assailant out of it and beat him to death. Three days later the local Soviet intervened and arrested ten of the legionaries who had taken part in the incident. This provoked a tremendous uproar in the Czech trains and, when the legionaries failed to persuade the Soviet to release the men, they occupied the town in the space of half an hour and freed them. On May 18th the Legion left the town.

When the news of the Legion's action reached Moscow, the Cheka (the Secret Police and forerunner of the KGB) arrested the leaders of the Branch there, Čermák and Maxa, and threatened to hold them as hostages until the incident was satisfactorily cleared up and all the Czech units had surrendered their arms. Under pressure from Trotsky himself the Czech hostages sent a telegram to the Legion, ordering them to honour the agreement and hand over all their arms to the local Soviet authorities. The security of the convoys should be entrusted to the Soviets and anyone disobeying the order would be declared guilty of treason. Assuming rightly that the telegram had been drafted by the Bolsheviks, the Legion sent a defiant reply. Drafted on May 23rd, the anniversary of the Defenestration of Prague in 1618 which preceded the Czech Rising against the Habsburgs, it announced that the Legion were resolved not to give up their weapons, because they had no guarantee that their passage would be unmolested by 'the counter-revolutionaries'. In response to this, the Soviet government sent instructions to the authorities all along the line to stop the further progress of the Legion. Trotsky himself gave orders that 'every Czechoslovak found on the railway with weapons will be shot on the spot'. Any Russian failing to stop and disarm the Czechs would be severely punished. With this drastic order the conflict between the Legion and the Bolsheviks came out into the open and Masaryk's policy of neutrality and non-intervention was brought to a sudden and stormy end.

In the *Pioneer* of May 17th, 1918 Hašek published 'An Open Letter to Professor Masaryk,' [13] in which he attacked the 'bourgeois' policy of the Branch, gave a last warning against the departure of the Legion and demanded full support for the Bolshevik Revolution from the Czechoslovak troops. 'The leadership of the Branch has made an idol of you,' he wrote to Masaryk, 'and under the rays of your shining halo the Czech revolution has been enslaved ... When there is a desperate need for every single organised military revolutionary unit to be here in Russia, the departure of our troops to France is nothing less than a betrayal of the World Revolution ... When Austria and Germany dance with joy over the departure of the Czech troops, your duty, Mr Professor, is to say: "Turn back, boys! I was wrong. It is here where you are needed! ..." Stop the trains, Professor, stop them before it is too late!' The article was signed 'A Soldier of the Czech Army', but an article in the next number of the journal indicated that it must have been written by Hašek.

But the Branch was not slow to reply. After the setting up of the Czech revolutionary organisation in Samara, it sent out instructions on how to deal with Bolshevik propaganda. Hašek became the target of a vehement campaign on the part of the legionary press. Medek, who was cultural editor of the *Czechoslovak Soldier*,[14] heaped insults on his head:

'I see now that this is your fate, the unhappy fate of your amorphous soul and your mean indifference to all humanity. You with your jester's cap and bells have found in this war a sorry target for your shafts. The foulest of all your jokes is to try to damage our movement and disgrace it inside and out. I know that you will blush with the last remnants of your shame, when you read these lines, because you are sentimental as old prostitutes are, and because you know that I've already warned you several times about your lies and villainy. But you won't improve. You'll recant, it is true. You'll certainly recant. You'll do some penitence for a time. But afterwards you'll go on with your trade—which is dishonour.'

Medek was to be the antithesis of Hašek in the literature of the Legion—the 'angel' to his 'devil'. Originally like Hašek an Anarchist, he had, unlike him, remained unshakably loyal to the Legion throughout the war. After the war, as a romantic novelist, he helped to create and develop the heroic legend surrounding the Legion. His most controversial work was his play *Colonel Švec*[15] in which he presented as a moral hero one of the most loyal and able officers in the Legion, who shot himself when his men refused to obey his order to advance.

The most important centre of activity for the Czech Communists from Moscow was the town of Penza, where Muna had been working for a time. A Party organisation had been set up there too and from May 12th it began to publish its own radical journal *Czechoslovak Red Army*.[16] Under Muna's influence it carried attacks on Hašek. 'Counter revolution, the Soviet struggle to attain power and the general demoralisation . . . have made it possible for people like Beneš,* Hašek and others to speak in the name of the Czech proletarian movement . . . Because of their former conduct they do not enjoy the confidence of the proletariat, nor ours, and even today they do not appreciate the vital importance of the movement.'

The Branch not unnaturally gloated over this abuse of their former fellow-legionary. 'Poor old Hašek! And so he's already dropped!', commented its official organ, the *Czechoslovak Daily*, recalling the sharp articles he had formerly written against Muna and his group while he was in Kiev. 'When the Communist diplomat Jaroslav Hašek, writing in *Čechoslovan*, recently characterised his colleagues as "revolutionaries who went and had a look at the barricades and then went to bed," *Freedom* [Muna's paper] got very angry. What is Jaroslav Hašek going to write *now*?'

At the Congress of Czech Social Democrats and Communists held in Moscow on May 25th and 26th Hašek was again attacked and threatened with expulsion. One speaker protested: 'People like him should not be allowed to speak in the name of Social Democrats and Communists.' Although the delegates from Samara stood up firmly in his defence, opinion at the Congress went against him. Doubts were cast on his Communist allegiance and Beneš was forced to apologise for taking him on without verifying his party credentials. Muna summed up the feeling of the meeting when he said: 'Whoever has sullied himself must not be spared. Out with people of this kind!'

Meanwhile the Legion had gone resolutely to work. It had been divided into three groups—the eastern group of about 4,500 men under Gajda, the central group of about 8,000 under Vojcechovský, and the western group of the same strength under Čeček. Orders were given to all three groups to seize the important stations along their route, the post offices serving them and, where possible, the towns themselves. Gajda and his group were able to take under their control most of the stations in the East, including Tomsk and Irkutsk in western Siberia. Soon some echelons had got as far as Vladivostok.

The central group under Vojcechovský occupied the important stations at Chelyabinsk, Kurgan and Omsk. Čeček's western group, which was operating in the Penza region, had

* Not the later President, but the editor of *Pioneer*.

greater difficulties, because the Red Army was present there in considerable force and many branch lines were available to them for troop transport. On May 28th his forces stormed Penza. Some 5,000 Czech legionaries overwhelmed the city's garrison of 1,900 Red Army men. Here for the first time they found themselves fighting against Czech Communists—members of the Czechoslovak Red Army. It was rumoured in Samara that after capturing four they settled accounts with them. According to Communist sources they dragged them out of their carriages at night and hanged them.

The Legion would soon be approaching Samara. Hašek took an active part in the defence of the town. He penned a proclamation to be handed to members of the advance guard of the Legion, calling upon them to give their support to the Soviet. He gave Kuibyshev, the President of the Samara Soviet, after whom the town was later to be renamed, a report of the fighting capability of his unit. But as the Legion came nearer he began to fear seriously for his life. He had been warned that the legionaries had him on their black list and were out for his blood. When he was asked by Soviet officials to take over negotiations with the advance party of the Legion, he declined. Seized by panic he started to destroy his written material and to disguise himself in women's clothes. Did he remember the time when Hájek's old uncle had mistaken him for a young girl, when he had acted female parts in cabaret or when he and Kuděj were photographed together in Victorian women's bathing dresses? But he soon pulled himself together again. Samara fell on June 8th and he escaped just in time, this time disguised not as a woman but as the son of a German colonist.

The Legion searched everywhere for him but without success. On July 25th they put out an arrest warrant for him in which he was charged with 'the repeated crime of treason against the Czechoslovak nation'. All members of the Czechoslovak revolutionary movement were strictly enjoined to arrest him whenever and wherever he was to be found and to send him under a powerful escort to a drumhead court martial by the Czechoslovak army.

(15)

The Commissar

In August 1918 the Legion's campaign against the Red Army reached a culminating point. Then the Bolshevik forces began to recover ground. In October they won back Kazan, Simbirsk and Samara. After living for two months between the lines Hašek found his way to Simbirsk just after it had fallen to the Red Army on September 12th.

Simbirsk, which lay on the Volga about sixty kilometres north of Samara, was the birthplace of Lenin and is now rechristened Ulyanovsk after Ulyanov, the name he was born with. On re-porting to the Political Department of the Revolutionary Army Soviet of the Eastern Front, Hašek was arrested and detained on suspicion of being a spy. No one seemed to know him or have heard of his earlier activity in Samara. He was later released on the recommendation of some Czech Red Army men, who went bail for him. After the representative of the local Soviet had interrogated him, he was sent on October 16th as 'organiser' to Bugulma and placed at the disposal of its commandant. The little town lay some ninety kilometres to the east of Simbirsk. It was not known at the time whether Bugulma had in fact yet been liberated from the Whites or was still in their hands. It was only on the day of his departure from Simbirsk that Hašek learned that it was clear of hostile troops.

His experiences in this little corner of Russia far beyond the Volga—the unique 'Bugulma stories'—were published on his return to Czechoslovakia in the Prague weekly the *Tribune*. They show that he was just as capable of making fun of Soviet Russian authority as of Imperial Austrian, and they offer an amusing lesson in how to deal with irrational bureaucracy. According to the no doubt partly fictional account which he gave in two stories of the series, 'The Commandant of the Town of Bugulma'[1] and 'The Adjutant of the Commandant of the Town of Bugulma',[2] he had no sooner arrived and established his authority in Bugulma than the commander of the so-called Tver Revolutionary Regiment, Comrade Yerokhymov, appeared, claiming that he was the rightful commandant because he had captured the town.

'Drunk with victory he pointed a revolver at my head and said: "Hands up."

'I calmly put my hands above my head.

' "And who are you?" he asked.

' "I am the commandant of the town."

' "Of the Whites or of the Soviet Army?"

' "The Soviet. May I put my hands down now?"

' "You can but I demand that in accordance with the rules of war you at once hand over to me the command of the town, because I have conquered it."

' "But I was appointed Commandant," I objected.

' "To hell with your being appointed. You have to conquer it first. Very well," he said magnanimously after a short while: "I appoint you my adjutant. If you don't agree I'll have you shot in five minutes . . ."

'The next morning he took great pains to prepare his first proclamation to the population of Bugulma.

' "Comrade Adjutant," he said to me, "do you think it will be all right like this? *To the whole population of Bugulma! Today, with the fall of Bugulma I have assumed command of the town. I am dismissing the former commandant from his post on grounds of incompetence and cowardice and am appointing him my adjutant.—Commandant of the Town: Yerokhymov.*"

' "That seems to cover everything," I said approvingly. "And what are you intending to do next?"

' "To begin with," he answered solemnly, "I shall order a mobilisation of horses, next I shall have the mayor shot. Then I shall take ten hostages from the bourgeoisie and send them to prison until the end of the civil war. After that I shall carry out a general house-search and prohibit free trading. That'll do for the first day. Tomorrow I shall think up something else."

' "Let me point out," I said, "that I have nothing at all against a mobilisation of horses, but I definitely protest against shooting the mayor, who welcomed me here with bread and salt."

'Yerokhymov jumped in the air. "Do you mean to say that he welcomed you, but hasn't yet come to see me . . ."

' "That can easily be put right," I said. "We'll send for him." And I sat down at the table and wrote:

> '*To the Mayor of the Town of Bugulma*
> *I order you to come at once to the new Commandant of*
> *the town and bring with you bread and salt according*
> *to the old Slav custom.*
> COMMANDANT OF THE TOWN: YEROKHYMOV
> ADJUTANT: GASHEK

'When Yerokhymov signed it, he added the words: "*If not, you will be shot and your house burnt down.*"

' "Nothing like that can be added to official documents," I said. "It makes them invalid."

'I copied it out again in its original version and had it signed and sent off by my orderly officer.

' "Next," I said to Yerokhymov, "I am definitely opposed to ten members of the bourgeoisie being sent to prison until the end of the civil war, because that can only be decided by the Revolutionary Tribunal."

' "Revolutionary Tribunal?" said Yerokhymov gravely, "But that's exactly what we are. The town is in our hands."

' "There you're mistaken, Comrade Yerokhymov. What are we? Just a couple of ordinary people—the commandant of the town and his adjutant. The Revolutionary Tribunal is appointed by the Revolutionary Army Soviet of the Eastern Front.[3] Do you want them to put you up against the wall?"

' "All right, then," Yerokhymov heaved a sigh. "But surely no one can stop us carrying out a general house-search?"

' "According to the decree of the 18th June of this year," I answered, "a general house-search can only be carried out with the consent of the local Soviet.* Since nothing like that exists yet, let's leave that until later."

' "You're an angel," said Yerokhymov tenderly. "Without you I would have been completely sunk. But surely we have to stop the free trading?"

---

* The local Soviet referred to here is the (non-military) Soviet of the town of Bugulma.

' "Most of those who trade and go to the bazaars are from the country," I explained. "They are *muzhiks*, who can't read or write. First they'll have to learn to read and write before they'll be able to understand what our orders are all about."

' "You're right again, Comrade Gashek," said Yerokhymov with a sigh. "What am I to do?"

' "Teach the people of the Bugulma region to read and write," I answered. "And as for me, I'll go and see whether your chaps aren't up to some mischief, and how they're billeted."

'I returned late in the evening and at the corner of the square saw a freshly posted placard which read:

'TO THE WHOLE POPULATION OF BUGULMA
AND ITS REGION!
I order everyone in the whole town and region who can-
not read and write to learn to do so within three days.
Anyone found to be illiterate after this period will be
shot.
COMMANDANT OF THE TOWN: YEROKHYMOV

'When I found Yerokhymov he was sitting with the mayor, who had brought a few bottles of old Lithuanian vodka as well as bread and salt. Everything was carefully laid out on the table. Yerokhymov, who was in a good mood and was embracing the mayor, shouted at me as I came in: "Have you seen how I've followed your advice? I went to the printing works myself and drew my revolver on the director: 'Print this at once, my little love-bird, or else I'll shoot you on the spot, you son of a bitch.' He started to shake, the vermin. He shook all over. He read it and shook even more. And then—I went *bang! bang!* at the ceiling . . . And he printed it. He printed it beautifully. To know how to read and write, that's the main thing! After that you issue the order, they all read, they understand and they're happy. That's right, isn't it, Mayor? Come and have a drink, Comrade Gashek!" . . .

'I drew my revolver and shot at all the bottles of Lithuanian vodka. Then, aiming at my superior, I said to him emphatically: "Get to bed at once, or . . ."

'Yerokhymov slept till two o'clock in the afternoon. When he woke up he sent for me and, looking at me in some uncertainty said: "I've got the impression that you wanted to shoot me yesterday."

' "Yes, I did," I answered. "I wanted to forestall what the Revolutionary Army Tribunal would have done to you when they learnt that as commandant of the town you got drunk."

' "But, my little love-bird, you won't tell anybody, will you? I won't do it again. I'll teach people to read and write . . ."

'In the evening the first deputation of *muzhiks* arrived . . . There were six old grandmas between sixty and eighty years old and five old grandpas of the same age.

'They threw themselves at my feet. "Don't destroy our souls, *batyushka*.* We can't learn to read and write in three days. Our heads can't manage it. Saviour, have mercy on the district."

' "The order is invalid," I said. "It was all the fault of that idiot the Commandant of the Town, Yerokhymov."

'In the night a few more deputations arrived, but by morning new placards had already been posted up and distributed to the villages around. The text was as follows:

'TO THE WHOLE POPULATION OF BUGULMA
AND THE REGION!
I proclaim that I have dismissed the Commandant of the Town, Comrade Yerokhymov, and have again resumed my office. His order Number 1, as well as his order Number 2 concerning the liquidation of illiteracy within three days, is hereby invalid.
COMMANDANT OF THE TOWN: GASHEK

'I could afford to do this, because during the night the Petrograd Cavalry Regiment had arrived in the town . . .

'I assured Yerokhymov that if he and his regiment tried to make further unpleasantness I could disarm them and have him up before the Revolutionary Army Tribunal . . .

'Comrade Yerokhymov on his part assured me with great frankness that as soon as the Petrograd Cavalry Regiment left the town he would have me hanged on the hill overlooking

---

* 'Little father'—an expression used by Russian *muzhiks* to persons in authority.

Little Bugulma,* so that I could be seen from all directions. We shook hands and parted the best of friends.'

All the available documents tell us is that on December 26th Hašek was appointed Deputy Commandant of Bugulma by the Political Department of the Fifth Army. There is no trace in the records of a commander of the Tver Regiment named Yerokhymov, but at the beginning of 1919 the newspaper *Our Path*[4] printed a report that the Revolutionary Army Tribunal of the Fifth Army, at its meeting on January 1st, 1919, judged the case of Yerokhim, a Communist in the Moscow organisation, who as a member of the special commission of the Bugulma district had misappropriated items during house searches. Yerokhim, who had been sent from Moscow headquarters to the front at a difficult time, was found to have brought dishonour on the Soviet régime and was sentenced to death by a firing squad. No doubt this stark example of Soviet justice captured Hašek's imagination. But in spite of his zeal for the Soviet cause he could see the ridiculous side of Commissars because, fundamentally, nothing could be sacrosanct to him for long; he would satirise all authorities, secular or religious, Catholic or Orthodox. And when he became an authority in his own right he was quite capable of laughing at himself too.

Hašek relates how after Yerokhymov's departure he had to billet the Petrograd Cavalry Regiment in the local barracks. But how could he find someone to clean and tidy up the neglected building? All the local inhabitants seemed otherwise engaged. He described this in another short story 'The Procession of the Cross'.[5]

'. . . I remembered that near the town there was a convent, the Convent of the Most Holy Virgin, where the nuns had nothing else to do but pray and gossip about each other. And so I wrote the following official letter to the Abbess:

> '*To Citizen Abbess of the Convent of the Most*
> *Holy Virgin.*
> *Send at once fifty maidens from your convent to be at*

---

* A small town outside Bugulma. The whole district is called Bugulminsko.

the disposal of the Petrograd Cavalry Regiment. Send
them straight to the barracks.
SUPREME COMMANDANT OF THE TOWN: GASHEK

'The letter was despatched and about half an hour later an extraordinarily beautiful and powerful peal of bells could be heard. All the bells of the Convent of the Most Holy Virgin groaned and wailed and in response those of the town joined in.

'My orderly officer informed me that the head priest of the main church together with the local clergy were asking if I would receive them. I nodded amiably and a number of bearded priests filled my office. Their spokesman said: "Mr Comrade Commandant, I come to you on behalf not only of the local clergy but also of the whole Orthodox Church. Do not ruin the innocent convent maidens. We have just had news from the convent that you want fifty nuns for the Petrograd Cavalry Regiment. Remember that the Lord God is above us."

' "At the moment only the ceiling is above us," I answered cynically, "and as for the nuns it must be as I said. I need fifty of them for the barracks. If thirty prove enough for the job, the remaining twenty will be sent back. If fifty are not enough, then I shall take a hundred, two hundred or three hundred. It doesn't matter a rap to me. And as for you, gentlemen, I warn you that you are interfering in official matters and so I am constrained to fine you. Every one of you will bring me three pounds of wax candles, a score of eggs and a pound of butter. I authorise you, Citizen Head Priest, to arrange with the Abbess the time at which she sends me those fifty nuns of hers. Tell her that I need them really urgently, and that I shall return them. None of them will get lost."

'The Orthodox clergy left my office very downcast indeed.

'In the doorway the oldest of them with the longest beard and hair turned round to me and said: "Remember that the Lord God is above us."

' "I beg your pardon," I said. "You will bring me not just three but five pounds of candles."

'It was a glorious October afternoon. There had been a severe frost and the cursed mud of Bugulma had become crusted . . . The bells rang gravely, solemnly, in the town and in the convent. This time they were not merely sounding the alarm, but calling Orthodox Bugulma to "A Procession of the Cross".

'It was only at the most critical times in Bugulma's history that a Procession of the Cross took place—when the Tartars besieged the town, when pestilence and smallpox raged, when war broke out, when they shot the Tsar. And now. The bells rang meltingly as though they were going to burst into tears.

'The gates of the convent opened and out they came with icons and banners. Four of the eldest nuns, with the Abbess at the head, were carrying a large heavy icon.

'The image of the Most Holy Virgin stared aghast from the icon. And following it walked a number of nuns, old and young, all dressed in black, singing psalms such as: "And they led Him away to crucify Him. They crucified Him and two others with Him, one on the right hand and the other on the left."

'And at that moment the Orthodox priesthood came out from the town church in gold embroidered chasubles, followed by the Orthodox community in a long procession carrying icons . . .

'They progressed round the church and then turned towards the offices of the Commandant of the Town, where I had already made fitting preparations.

'Before the building stood a table covered with a white cloth, on which there was a loaf of bread and salt in a salt cellar. In the right hand corner stood an icon and around it there were lighted candles . . .

'I came out in a dignified manner and asked the Abbess to accept bread and salt as proof that I did not harbour any hostile intentions. I also asked the Orthodox priesthood to cut off a slice of bread. They came, one after the other, and kissed the icon.

' "Orthodox men and women," I said solemnly, "I thank you for your beautiful and very fascinating Procession of the Cross. It is the first time in my life I have seen it and it has left me an impression which I shall remember to my dying day. I can see here a crowd of nuns singing, which reminds me of the processions of the early Christians in the days of Nero. It may be that some of you have read *Quo Vadis*? But I will not tax your patience any longer, Orthodox men and women. I asked for only fifty nuns, but now that the whole convent is here we shall be finished all the quicker, and so may I ask mesdemoiselles the lady nuns to follow me to the barracks?"

'The crowds stood bareheaded before me and sang in answer: "The heavens declare the glory of God; and the firmament sheweth His handiwork. Day after day He exalts and night after night He reveals the wonders of His works."

'The Abbess stepped forward in front of me. Her aged chin was trembling and she asked me: "In the name of the Heavenly Father, what are we going to do in there? Do not destroy your soul."

' "Orthodox men and women," I shouted to the crowd, "we shall scrub the floors and clean the barracks so that we can put the Petrograd Cavalry Regiment into them. Let's go."

'The crowd followed me and with such a quantity of industrious hands the barracks were in perfect order by the evening.

'The same evening a young and pretty nun brought me a small icon and a letter from the old Abbess containing the simple sentence: "I am praying for you."

'Since that day I have slept in peace, because I know that to this very day there lies hidden in the old oak forests of Bugulma a Convent of the Most Holy Virgin, where an aged Abbess lives and prays for me, wretched good-for-nothing that I am." '

When some of these stories appeared in translation in the Soviet press, veterans of the Fifth Army protested at the sacrilege Hašek had committed. He had disparaged the idealism of the Civil War. But, as one of the editors pointed out, the facts were that the Tver cavalry detachment had actually operated in the Bugulma district, and ingloriously abandoned its position when the Whites attacked. There was also the case of Yerokhim, the corrupt member of a special commission for the Bugulma district. Moreover it was strongly rumoured in Bugulma itself that Hašek really had had the barracks cleaned by the inmates of the local convent as he described in 'The Procession of the Cross'.

The Political Department of the Fifth Army now wanted to employ Hašek themselves and asked the Central Committee of the Czechoslovak Communist Party in Moscow for information about him. They were told that Hašek had left the Czech Corps in March. From that time on he had been in touch with Party organs, but since the fall of Samara nothing further had been heard of him. Thus by the end of December Hašek had become an official of the Political Department of the Fifth Siberian Army, working in the front command of the 26th Division.

According to Sauer, Hašek used to tell an amusing story of how he came to be chosen for the job. (The Russians have no 'h' in their alphabet and have to use a 'g' instead. So Hašek was now addressed as 'Comrade Gashek'.)

'A member of the Central Committee came to Ufa and at once searched for me!

' "You're Comrade Gashek, aren't you?"

'I nodded . . .

' "You're a former legionary, aren't you?"

'He looked at me sternly, straight in the eyes.

' "Yes, I am."

' "You're from Prague, aren't you?"

' "Yes, I am."

' "Comrade Gashek, you're a great drunkard. Isn't that right?"

' "Yes, that's right."

' "Comrade Gashek, everything's all one to you—there's nothing sacred, right?"

' "Quite right."

' "When you were at home they say you were everything—Anarchist, Social Democrat and working in editorial offices all over the place. Is that correct?"

' "Perfectly correct."

' "Khorosho!* You don't deny anything. You're a good man."

'After his departure in about a fortnight, I was appointed inspector of the Fifth Red Army.'[6]

On December 31st, 1918, the Red Army captured Ufa, a town in the Southern Urals lying about sixty kilometres east of Bugulma, and today the capital of the Bashkir Autonomous Republic. The Revolutionary Army Soviet together with the Political Department decided to publish a major daily for Red

* Good

Army men to be called *Our Path* and looked for capable people for its editorial staff. Somebody remembered that a Czech journalist named Hašek was working in the Political Department and he was soon invited to take over the running of the printing department of the daily and contribute to it as well. The big privately owned printing works had been hit by artillery and practically destroyed; the electric motors were out of action and only two machines could be operated by hand. Hašek arranged for what was left of them to be requisitioned and put at his disposal. At the same time he became secretary of the Party organisation at the works. By spending his days and nights in the building he was able to get the first number of the new journal into print by January 11th, 1919.

He found among the employees a young woman named Alexandra Lvova. Born in Ufa, she had worked before the Revolution in the printing works. Her father, who had been a clerk in the wine stores, had died when she was seven years old, so she now lived alone with her mother. She got on very well with Hašek who was her chief and fellow-worker, correcting his Russian manuscripts while he helped her with the type-settings. Food was brought in from outside and they slept at night on bundles of newspapers.

Soon Alexandra, or 'Shura', introduced 'Gashek' to her mother, who used to provide them with hot water for making tea. According to Shura, Hašek was always so 'good and gallant' that he won her mother's heart. He always maintained, however, that he was single and had no children, and she was not allowed to know more of his past than that he had once been an editor and written funny stories which made people 'split their sides with laughter'. According to her account, Hašek at this time looked splendid: he had a ruddy complexion, held himself erect, did not know what it was to be ill and never touched alcohol.[7]

Initially he had had some doubts whether his Russian was up to the requirements of his new assignment, but the chief editor, who was a friend of his, promised to help him draft the articles, and in the third number a *feuilleton* of his appeared, caricaturing the mentality of a Russian reactionary, under the title 'From the Diary of an Ufa Bourgeois'.[8] He followed this up with a story about speculators and black marketeers called 'About

Greengrocer Bulakin, the Ufa Thief'.[9] He also wrote several pieces against the church and clergy.[10] In fact almost all the copy for the paper eventually came from Hašek's pen. Without him it could hardly have continued.

Promotion came quickly. On January 12th he was appointed Secretary of the Party of Foreign Communists in Ufa. A month later the first number of its daily organ, *Red Europe*,[11] appeared, edited and managed by him. Its first and second pages were in Russian, the third in Hungarian and the fourth in German.

As secretary of the Party organisation in the printing department, Hašek took a ruthless line over working discipline. In an open letter to the press he sharply attacked the behaviour of a plenipotentiary of the printing department who drove drunk through the streets of the town, shouting, 'See how a commissar drives round!' 'All unscrupulous workers,' Hašek wrote, 'who treasonably undermine public respect for our government of working people should be mercilessly pilloried. They should be hounded out of their offices and punished with the sharpest penalties of these revolutionary times.' To denounce a commissar publicly for drunkenness was almost the equivalent of passing a death sentence on him. History does not relate what happened to the offender, but in view of Hašek's own not unblemished record, it might have been more appropriate for him to follow the example of the Salvation Army and admit that he had once been a gross sinner himself!

Ufa was at that time a small dirty town, where the hygiene left much to be desired. Now that it was momentarily overpopulated, an epidemic of typhus broke out, which was formented by an unusually warm spring. It was just at this moment that Admiral Kolchak's White armies threatened the town. In March 1919 their pressure was so great that the Red Army, which had only 12,000 men to Kolchak's 50,000, were forced to evacuate. Hašek is said to have been one of the last to leave. He was seen standing by the cart on which the printing machines were being loaded before being stowed on a railway truck and transported to Belebei, some fifty kilometres to the south-west of Ufa, while the troops withdrew to Buzuluk, sixty kilometres further in the same direction. The printing department and its staff of thirty-five managed to escape to Samara which was a good bit further, after which they got separated from the army.

Hašek caught a bad bout of typhus *en route*, as a result of which *Our Path* stopped publication while he slowly recovered.

At the end of April the Bolshevik commander, Frunze, who was later to defeat the White generals Admiral Kolchak and General Wrangel, mounted a counter-offensive and recovered the lost positions. The printing department was able to restore contact with the army. *Our Path* was restarted under a new name, *Red Arrow*,[12] and, while the print was still wet, copies were thrown along the railway track for the advancing troops.

In the middle of June 1919 the printing department moved back into the old building at Ufa. Under the first occupation of the town the Red Army had not behaved too harshly towards the bourgeoisie, but, after the Whites had taken the town and terrorised the population, severe reprisals were carried out by the returning Reds against those thought to have been in league with them: property was confiscated, there were deportations to prison camps and tribunals were set up. The former owner of the printing works and his wife were shut up in the cellar of his plant.

Hašek and a German friend of his took part in the purges. According to Shura (who is not a reliable witness) he did not approve of the brutal way in which people were being treated and felt ill when the death sentence was mentioned. If this is true, he was unconsciously emulating the saint whom he ridiculed, Wenceslas, of whom it is related that he always left the sittings of the court of justice before a death sentence was pronounced. As a member of the Red Army Hašek is said never to have shot anyone; he was convinced that people would themselves find 'the path of righteousness'. Meanwhile Shura, who had not previously been a Communist, had been accepted as a Party member in reward for her services. From now on she began to collaborate with Hašek in his political work too.

Meanwhile Hašek was appointed Commissar for the Austro–Hungarian Soviet of Army and Workers' Representatives in Ufa. According to Sauer, he also exercised the function of commissar for education in a division of the Fifth Red Army operating against Admiral Kolchak, and within a month his sphere of duties was extended to embrace the whole army. He was regarded with such respect that he was treated as a Russian and never referred to otherwise than 'Jaroslav Osipovich

(Gashek)'. His promotion was exceptionally fast, because the Red Army was short of capable organisers and workers in this easterly corner of Russia. Sauer relates:

' "He doesn't only work hard," said the Political Commissar of the Fifth Army, when he came to Moscow and was boasting of the excellent Czech he had succeeded in finding, "he really slogs. He does more than ten people."
' "And he doesn't drink?"
' "Who? Jaroslav Osipovich? Are you mad?"
' "But in Bohemia . . ."
' "No, you must be thinking of someone else. It's certainly a mistake. Jaroslav Osipovich is extremely serious." '[13]

He devoted most of his time and energy to rousing the revolutionary consciousness of the members of the various foreign nationalities who found themselves in Russia—German, Hungarian and Czech prisoners and deserters. Here his knowledge of languages came into play. He spoke some Russian, Polish, German and Hungarian and later learnt some Bashkir as well as a little Chinese. Indeed his 'pidgin' Chinese seems to have had great success with the Chinese prisoners-of-war.

When new units of the Red Army were formed out of former prisoners-of-war, the Party of the Foreign Communists was incorporated into the Political Department of the Fifth Army, and Hašek was appointed head of its International Section. He published multi-lingual journals in Hungarian, German and Russian—*Storm*,[14] *World Revolution*,[15] *Red Europe*—gave courses in the department, and lectured at so-called 'concert meetings' on themes like 'The Political Situation in Europe', 'The League of Nations or the Third International?', 'The Victory in the East Will Liberate the West' etc.

Under the influence of the Bolsheviks his attitude to the Legion and to Masaryk had hardened. While earlier he had regarded him as the rightful leader of the Czech resistance movement and even as 'the old teacher of Socialism', in an article published in *Our Path* he did not hesitate to call him 'the leader of the Czechoslovak counter-revolutionaries'. In his eyes the Legion by its interventionist action had taken the wrong road, one which could not lead to the social revolution in the Republic.

Many of Hašek's friends found it hard to believe that he could really transform himself into a responsible revolutionary. Part of the explanation for his 'conversion' was that for the first time he felt he was doing a job which was needed. In Siberia there was a pitiful lack of revolutionary intelligence and an army printing office needed an educated director. The recognition which he acquired won him back his confidence and self-respect after years of failure. Unfortunately, as a result he concentrated all his efforts on propaganda and published nothing to enhance his literary reputation.

He mentioned several times that he was planning to write a war novel, but no manuscript of it has been found. He told a friend that he wanted to describe in it the metamorphosis of an Austrian soldier into a Red Army man. He also promised he would write a book about priests. After his return to Czechoslovakia he is reported to have said the same to Jarmila, but no such work has been traced. Even the journal *Storm*, of which he was apparently very proud and on which he lavished all his energies, has been lost.

In the course of the Fifth Army's victorious advance against Admiral Kolchak, Chelyabinsk fell, and Hašek and his printing staff, including Shura and her mother, moved there in the middle of August. He was full of initiatives. When there were no lights in the offices, he showed them how to hollow out big potatoes, pour oil in them, stick a wick inside and improvise primitive illumination. In the international department he asked to be allowed to organise a secret counter-espionage section directed against spies from the Legion and foreign Right Wing Socialists who were critical of the Communist line. He adopted the methods of the Cheka and became an employer of Bretschneiders!* He was also responsible for organising detachments of the Red Army manned by the various foreign groups. Once he came in and announced, laughingly, that there would now be a Turkish unit in the Red Army, because he had won over a group of Turkish prisoners.

At the end of 1919 Hašek and Shura followed the advancing

---

* The plain-clothes police spy and *agent provocateur* in *The Good Soldier Švejk*.

Red Army to Omsk in Western Siberia, where he was given more newspapers to organise. But news had at last reached Prague of what Hašek was doing in Russia. Under the heading 'Hašek a Bolshevik Commissar', the *People's Right* of February 25th, 1920, published a sensational report:

'As we learn from a Comrade who has recently returned from Russia, the author of *The Good Soldier Švejk** and other humorous writings, who lacked neither originality nor wit and who was regarded as dead, is quite definitely alive and kicking. He has established himself in Chelyabinsk in the Urals and lives the regular life of an official there. The members of the local Soviet respect him for his industry in the office and honour him as a good Comrade and Socialist. In the evening after his work he returns to his lodgings. The only thing that the Russians have against him is that he doesn't mix much with them, for on principle he does not visit bars any more, and the Comrade from whom we got this information claims that he could not recognise the former Prague bohemian, the figure who previously haunted the night bars and wrote his cleverest sketches over a cup of black coffee, if he did not sacrifice literature to pure enjoyment. Today in Chelyabinsk they regard Hašek as a conservative. Let us hope that our patriotic papers won't turn on him again for having become a Bolshevik.'

In April 1920, Hašek and Shura went on to Krasnoyarsk on the river Yenisei in Central Siberia. Hašek had by now achieved high advancement in the Soviet establishment and his thoughts turned to settling permanently in Russia. He decided to legalise his relationship with Shura, and on May 5th signed a 'voluntary marriage' contract with her, with General Braun, a German Communist, as a witness. He made a false declaration that he was single and had neither obligations nor children. He had presumably made up his mind to burn his boats. But man proposes and God disposes. It was precisely because he had become so prominent that he could not later escape the consequences of his nationality.

* *The Good Soldier Švejk in Captivity.*

Arnošt Kolman, the Czech Communist philosopher, who spent most of his life in Russia, could remember Hašek at this time and wrote afterwards: 'By nature Hašek was conscientious, optimistic, and indeed a promising worker ... After he got back from the office he became a quiet citizen. He had happy memories of Prague and dreamt about beer from the barrel. You couldn't talk to him about politics at such moments. He sat thinking about his friends and told stories. He never read a line but stared all the time at the river Yenisei. When the conversation turned to politics one did not know whether he was talking seriously or playing the fool.'

A member of the Political Department of the Fifth Army told Karel Kreibich, a leading German Communist from Czechoslovakia: 'In Krasnoyarsk I lived in the same house as [Hašek] did, but had very little to do with him. As far as I know he worked well. At that time theory was not necessary. He was neither a theoretical Marxist nor a Communist, but a real revolutionary. He had a clear idea of who would benefit by our revolution. He was prevented from becoming a Marxist by a certain excitability which was at that time the cause of his spontaneous *joie-de-vivre* ... In spite of his stoutness he was very agile. Probably it was his lively temperament which brought him over to the side of the revolution ...'

By the beginning of June 1920 they had moved on to Irkutsk in south-east Siberia, where Hašek became a member of the town Soviet. He went about dressed in an old blouse which had lost its shape, his blue foot-wrappings showing out of his boots. He appeared to have aged and did not seem too cheerful. He occupied a small house on the banks of the river Angara, sharing it with the propaganda department, General Braun and a Chinese. With the help of the latter he continued his study of Chinese. In a journal called the *Fatherland of Labour*[16] he published a report of his work among the Chinese Communists and announced that a weekly journal would be published for them. He also spoke at a meeting of the local Chinese. In his free time he went fishing and could be seen sitting with his collar turned up and humming Czech songs.

In Irkutsk the Political Department decided to publish a journal in Buryat-Mongolian. Hašek was entrusted with the task. Sauer tells how he found a way of getting it done.

'Hašek's soldiers captured a reactionary who in peace time had been a teacher in a Buryat village.

' "Who are you?" Hašek asked.

' "A teacher."

' "Do you know Buryat?"

'He nodded.

' "Can you write Buryat string scripts?"

' "Yes, I can."

' "Very well, then, you're free. You write it for me."

'Hasek went bail for him and from then on the teacher translated into Buryat Hašek's articles written in Russian and prepared the characters which were then transferred on to metal blocks and thus primitively duplicated.'[17]

Hašek appears to have been generous to his former comrades who opted for what was in his view the wrong side. A Czech legionary, who fell ill with spotted typhus when the Legion evacuated Siberia and had to stay behind in a Russian military hospital in Irkutsk after the district had been occupied by the Red Army, related how he got captured and met Hašek:

'They shut me in a stable where there were already huddled together many prisoners of different professions—officers, priests, landowners, teachers etc. I was the only Czech. I reconciled myself to my fate and was looking hopelessly out through the little window in the door across the yard of the building opposite, which was the office of the Commissar, when I heard the sound of the hooting of a car. After a time a collection of people got out of cars into the yard and at its head strode a very familiar figure. Was it possible? Could it be Hašek? It was indeed.

' "Jarda," I shouted. Hašek stopped and I shouted again: "Jarda, I'm here!" And as a proof I stuck my hand out through the hole in the door as far as I could. I was so excited that the other prisoners thought I'd gone mad.

'It was Hašek, who at that time was a high functionary of some political department of the Soviet Army.

'The procession went into the house opposite and after a moment I was ushered into the office.

'When Hašek recognised me, he seized my hand and said:

"*Nazdar*, old chap, what are you doing here? D'you want to go home?"

' "Of course I do!"

' "All right, then, you'll come along with me to Irkutsk and there we'll fix it somehow!" That was the end of our discussion and also the end of my suffering.

'I never went back to prison. In Irkutsk Hašek "fixed it" by giving me documents with the help of which I managed to get across the whole of Siberia and Russia to Jamburg where I left Soviet Russia and with the help of the American Red Cross got home across the Baltic and Germany.'

In the eyes of Soviet officials Hašek was growing in importance and status. He was elected secretary of the Party cell of the staff of the Fifth Army and took the chair at a meeting called to discuss the mobilisation of Red Army units for the rehabilitation of the economy. His department printed leaflets, organised propaganda activities and in addition to its current publications produced a journal called *The News of the International Section* in Russian.

He worked out directives for war prisoners returning to their home countries in the form of leaflets and booklets. At the same time he collected information and passed it on in reports. On the anniversary of the setting up of the Hungarian Soviet Republic he helped to write and produce a play *Back to Home*. It was a straight piece of Socialist realism. Lájos, a backward Hungarian prisoner-of-war, returns home after the war, thinking that he will find everything just as he left it. But his old aunt tells him that his wife died in a famine in 1917, his children have died too and his small shop has been ruined. However, his brother Ferenc, also an ex-prisoner-of-war, has turned into a revolutionary worker in the underground. The police arrest and imprison Ferenc and Lájos as people who have returned from Bolshevik Russia. On his release from prison Lájos, tormented by what he has gone through, in a fit of anger kills a bourgeois who has insulted him. The play ends with the victory of the people over Hungarian reaction.

In August 1920 Hašek came across a copy of *Countryside*[18] from January of the previous year, the organ of the Czech Agrarian party. It presented him with the unique opportunity of being able to read his own obituary notice, which was published under the unflattering headline 'Traitor' and contained the words 'a clown and drunkard with chubby hands, who was always ready to betray everything he had—his wife, his country and his art'. It wounded him deeply because it came from the pen of a friend.

He immediately sat down and wrote out his 'confession' in the form of an amusing but rather bitter *feuilleton* 'The Little Soul of Jaroslav Hašek tells its Story'.[19] He did not publish it in Russia, but kept it and sent it to the *People's Right*, where it appeared after his return to Prague. Hašek's soul is speaking:

'When they shot my body in Budějovice for high treason which the two of us committed in *delirium tremens*, I flew to heaven ... Before the gates of heaven there was a long queue. I tried to infiltrate myself somewhere near the front so as to be one of the first to taste its joys, when one of the military police— a cross between an archangel and an Austro–Hungarian cop —seized me by the shirt.

' "You," said the divine apparition, "you infantryman! Are *you* on the casualty list? Show me your papers." ...

' "Humbly report," I said, clicking my heels together according to regulations, "they shot me a moment ago at Budějovice. I didn't know I had to have it confirmed by anyone."

'The celestial one scowled at me. "Who d'you think you're talking to? I wasn't born yesterday, you know! I've stood here since the time when the proud angels broke discipline. I've been on duty at the receiving end since the Flood ... I tell you, as far as you're concerned, you're not dead yet. You made a bad choice with Budějovice. D'you think I don't know my geography? Why, those people there come from that dove-like nation who are always brawling somewhere or other. Do the likes of us have to do overtime for them? And every snivelling little angel'll tell you that at Budějovice there's no front at the moment. This is no place for shirkers. About turn! Back to your march battalion!" '

Hašek's soul then made a pilgrimage to all the various places where, according to press rumours, Hašek was supposed to have met his end: Hašek's body was found, but the only written confirmation of his death was the obituary notice '*De mortuis nil nisi bonum*'. The soul goes on:

'I was insulted by being described as "a drunkard" and "life's acrobat". He even used the word "clown", *Hašek—Šašek* [clown]. These were the insulting words they used to call after me on the streets, before I started going to school, and so I was not in the slightest surprised by them . . . I too gladly hit out at people and said caustic things about my fellow-citizens, but out of principle I aimed my shafts only at living people. I may have criticised them sharply and made fun of everything they dared to do publicly, but I never touched private dirty linen. I never got on to Mr So and So for having a lover or having got drunk at such and such a place. It was quite enough for me that he had said this or that in public.'

The soul comes up to the gates of heaven once more and has to satisfy the angels about its identity.

'After thirty-five years I had behind me eighteen years of industrious, fruitful work. Up to 1914 I deluged the Czech journals with my satires, sketches and stories. I had a large circle of readers. I filled whole numbers of humorous journals, using the most varied pseudonyms. My readers, however, generally recognised me behind them. I thought then in my simpleness that I was a writer.

' "Don't make long explanations here. What were you really?"

'I gave a start. I felt in my pocket for the obituary notice and gasped out in confusion: "With apologies, I was a drunkard with chubby hands." '

In the government* of Irkutsk there were many Czechs who left the Legion and settled down as workers in industry or agriculture. For their benefit Hašek helped to produce a weekly journal in Czech, *Commune* (the name seems familiar), of which 5,000 copies were printed.

Arising from this Hašek started to correspond with the Czechoslovak Central Bureau of Agitation and Propaganda, which was attached to the Central Committee of the Russian Bolshevik Party and was under the presidency of Jaroslav Salát-Petrlík. The Bureau kept in touch with events in Czechoslovakia and

* i.e. province.

pursued intensive propaganda activity among the Czechs in Soviet Russia, whose presence was required at home to reinforce the growing power of the Marxist Left within the Social Democratic Party. In May, with the help of two members of a delegation from Czechoslovakia, Dr Bohumír Šmeral the war-time leader of the Social Democrats in Bohemia and Ivan Olbracht the left wing writer, the Bureau had published a pamphlet about the mobilisation of Czechoslovak Communists on Soviet Russian territory, explaining how vital it was for all Czech and Slovak Communists working in the Soviet Union to return at once to their country.

In June the Bureau asked to have Hašek recalled from Siberia to Moscow. From the records it is obvious that they knew about his journal *Storm* and had formed a favourable opinion of its quality. They wanted him to edit their newspapers and pamphlets and be a member of the commission responsible for the recruitment of Communists for revolutionary work in Czechoslovakia.

But the Regional Bureau at Irkutsk—certainly with Hašek's approval and possibly at his instigation—refused to part with him and so the Central Bureau together with the members of the Czechoslovak delegation, headed by Antonín Zápotocký,* applied to the Central Committee of the Russian Communist Party for his release.

His case came up once more at a meeting of the Bureau on October 2nd, 1920, where a report was made of the situation in Czechoslovakia with particular reference to the revolutionary movement in Kladno, the important mining town near Prague, and a resolution was passed—evidently thanks to the personal intervention of his friend, Hula, who was also a member of the delegation—that 'Comrade Hašek from Irkutsk be sent to Kladno forthwith'.

Irkutsk having refused to discharge him, the Bureau came back with a renewed request for his immediate release. 'We've already asked for Comrade Hašek several times through the Central Committee and the Army Revolutionary Soviet,' they said. 'You cannot therefore have any excuse for keeping him

* After World War II he became President of the Czechoslovak Federation of Trade Unions (1945–50), after the Prague *coup d'état* of 1948 Prime Minister (1948–53) and President (1953–57).

with you any longer. Abroad in Czechoslovakia we must show our faith in revolution and Communism.'

Up to the last moment Hašek was deep in his work for the Political Department of the army, where he had become the responsible editor of the journal publishing army orders and reports (an ironic assignment for someone who in the past had debunked such things). In the period from October 7th to 13th he even deputised for the head of the department.

Meanwhile in Czechoslovakia the political temper had become more and more radical. The Social Democratic party had openly split into two and the left seemed to have acquired a dominating position. The Central Bureau had no intention of waiting a moment longer. And so by order of the Central Committee Hašek was relieved of his duties on October 19th and left with Shura for Moscow five days later.

When the time came for him to go he had less and less taste for the prospect. Shura recalled:

'In his first fit of delight at the knowledge that the leadership was counting on him, he wrote a letter to Salát-Petrlík, in which he agreed to his return, but the more he thought about it, the less he believed in the idea that there could be a revolution in Czechoslovakia as there had been in Russia. He said the Czechs were a nation of doves and every one of them played on his own little sand-pile . . . We go for long walks in the neighbourhood of Irkutsk and Jaroslav is always pondering whether he should go or not. He smiles sadly and says that the situation is different in Czechoslovakia and that it will be more difficult there than it is here.'[20]

On their way they spent three days seeing their friends in Ufa. The trains did not go regularly and at some stations they had to stop several days. Once during a walk in a wood, wolves appeared and Hašek and Shura climbed up separate trees and waited till they ran away. When they had gone Shura tried to locate Hašek. Suddenly she heard a snoring from a tree. Quite unruffled he had fallen fast asleep in this uncomfortable position. But when they arrived in Moscow on November 27th he was in a bad temper because his Russian–Chinese dictionary had been stolen on the train.

On the questionnaire they had to fill up, in the column: 'Where do you want to work?' he wrote: 'Wherever I am needed.' In the corner of the registration form was added: 'To Kladno by the agency of the Comintern.' He was provided with the necessary money and propaganda material and sent off via the Baltic ports and Danzig *en route* for Czechoslovakia. It was to be a fateful journey for him.

[III]
CZECHOSLOVAKIA

(16)

Back in Prague

On December 19th, 1920, Hašek and Shura arrived in Prague. Hašek hated and feared nothing so much as the thought of returning home. On the railway journey he had repeated over and over again to Shura that he would get out and return to his friends who had stayed behind.

They embarked at Narva in Estonia and travelled on false documents in the name of Herr and Frau Josef Staidl, taking with them a copious stock of Communist propaganda material. When Shura asked him about his future work in Czechoslovakia, he said he would be making propaganda, arranging political meetings and writing for the papers. In a year's time he would keep the promise he had made to her mother and return to their home at Ufa, where he still had work to finish. At Tallinn Hašek heard some people talking Czech and at once felt happier. When Shura was sea-sick and confined to her cabin, he went out and came back slightly tipsy for the first time in several years. When some of the Czech passengers joyfully recognised him and pressed him to come and drink with them, he could not resist it. When Shura tried to persuade him not to go, he looked at her with a strange expression in his eyes and said: 'We should never have gone back. Now I am quite certain about that.'

On reaching Czechoslovak territory they were held in quarantine in Pardubice for a week. Once more the temptation to sneak off occasionally and snatch a drink was too strong for him. As soon as they were let out, they took the first train for Prague. They made a strange pair—Hašek in his Russian fur cap, long dark overcoat and dirty grey *valenki** talked excitedly in Russian to the dumpy and dowdy Shura, totally oblivious of the effect it was having on their fellow passengers.

On arriving at Prague on December 9th, Hašek called a cab

* Russian felt boots, reaching up to his thighs.

and drove round the city. When he reached the former Ferdinand Avenue[1]—now rechristened the National Avenue[2]—he
called out joyfully: 'Our National Avenue.' Then he ordered
the driver to go on to his former haunt, the Union, where the
waiter joyfully recognised him and soon collected as many of his
former bohemian friends as he could. There was a lot of laughter
and talk but no one spoke of revolution or seemed interested in
it. Fortunately for Shura one of Hašek's friends spoke Russian
and came up to talk to her. He asked her if she was an aristocrat
or princess, as Hašek was claiming. She answered stiffly that she
was a worker in a printing works and a member of the Russian
Communist Party. Her husband had come here to give the
Czech bourgeoisie a sound thrashing. After that they would return to Soviet Russia, where Jaroslav had a lot of work to do.
'I'll teach him to call me a princess!'

Langer came to the Union a day or two later. The head
waiter led him to a room at the back near the kitchen. He could
not understand why they had put Hašek there. Was it because
they did not know what kind of a reception he might get or was
it because of the condition he was in? He was sitting there, in
the kind of mood and tousled and bedraggled state which was
normal for him in the small hours of the morning. On the floor
there was a row of empty beer bottles and round a table with
Hašek were squeezed a number of young men in various stages
of drunkenness. By Hašek's side sat a blond buxom woman.

Hašek's greeting was effusively affectionate and even to such
a good friend as Langer he did not hesitate to present Shura as
'a relation of Prince Lvov'.* The one-time anarchist seemed
now to be proud of her spurious aristocratic origin. Later the
embarrassed Shura whispered to Langer that she had no idea
what had come over Hašek. She had never seen him in this
state before.

Hašek was most anxious to find out from Langer what sort of
reception awaited him in Prague. He had heard they were
punishing all deserters from the Legion and, as he was considered a deserter, what would happen to him?

Langer tried to comfort him by assuring him that there was
no question of his being punished. People might talk against

---

* The prime minister of Russia after the February Revolution.

him, but in the end everyone who really knew him would be only too glad to see him back.

When Langer met him again at a party a few months later, Hašek was reluctant to talk about his time with the Red Army in Russia except to claim that he had made it up with the 'brothers'* and had even buried the hatchet with Medek. They had met in a wine-cellar somewhere and Medek had told him straight out that if he had caught him in Siberia, he would have had him executed as a traitor straight away.

'Wouldn't you have offered me a drink first?'

'No, certainly not. I'd have had you executed at once.'

'Well, now, if you had fallen into *my* hands, I'd have given you a drink first.'

'And then?'

'Then I'd have pardoned you.'

At that, or so Hašek would have had Langer believe, Medek burst into tears and fell on his neck, after which they drank together until the small hours.[3]

Reports of Hašek's arrival soon filtered into the press. The *Tribune* of December 20th, 1920 published under the column Small News from Home: 'Yesterday there was a little surprise in store for the Union. Jaroslav Hašek suddenly dropped in there out of the blue after a five-year stay in Russia, where it had been reported so many times that he either was dead or had become Bolshevik Commissar . . .'

But *Time*'s† comment was more barbed:

'The People's Commissar Hašek, having recently returned married from Russia, is now busy studying republican Prague. For the time being he is propagating his Communist ideas in a very idyllic way. Among that circle of old friends, with whom he once formed the Party of Moderate Progress within the Bounds of the Law and with whom he has now had a happy reunion after a separation of many years, he is distributing and selling brochures and autographs, which are said to find a ready market. Quite recently, a certain Prague paper claimed that the humorist and Communist Hašek has joined the Salvation Army.

* Members of the Legion called each other 'brother'.

† *Čas*. Now a daily but still expressing the views of President Masaryk and those close to him.

Like the Good Soldier Švejk, he has recently started carrying the flag in street processions.* Being a People's Commissar has obviously become so much a part of his life that he cannot apparently live without an army. It is a pity that the Red Guard at Kladno have all dispersed . . .'

This was perhaps not too far-fetched. Anything could be expected of Hašek: he might easily have become a Major Barbara.

Unfortunately for him, ominous events had just taken place within the Social Democratic Party in Czechoslovakia. A struggle had been going on for some time between its right and left wings and in the autumn of 1920 there was an open breach between them. The Party leadership, who were members of the coalition government, belonged to the right wing, but the Marxist left, which planned to take the Party into the Comintern and set up a Soviet republic in Czechoslovakia, would be in the majority at the forthcoming Party Congress. Feeling unable in these circumstances to remain head of the government, the Social Democrat Prime Minister, Tusar, resigned and President Masaryk appointed at his suggestion a government of officials, headed by a former senior civil servant Černý as both Prime Minister and Minister of the Interior. The Marxist left then staged a *coup* and took over the Party headquarters and printing press. When the courts ruled that this action was illegal Černý, after consultation with Masaryk, ordered the police on December 9th to expel the left and to restore the premises to the party leadership. Not to be outdone the Marxist Left then organised street demonstrations. When these were dispersed by the police, they called a general strike and proclaimed a Soviet republic at Kladno as had been previously planned in Moscow. But the President and the government refused to negotiate until the strike was over. In the end, after police intervention resulting in some casualties, the left had to climb down and call off the strike and the Kladno 'Soviet republic' collapsed. Thanks to the energetic action of Masaryk, Černý and the Social Democrat leadership, the long prepared attempt to set up a Bolshevik republic in Czechoslovakia, in which Hašek had hoped to play an important role, had failed—four days before his return.

* Švejk never did this!

The ringleaders of the leftist *coup* were now put on trial. Had Hašek arrived earlier he might have been among them. The contact man for the returning Czechoslovak Red Army men was gaoled with the rest, who included Alois Muna from the Legion and Antonín Zápotocký, a future Communist President of Czechoslovakia. Throughout the journey back Hašek had been waiting impatiently to hear news of the revolution and had been depressed to find that no one talked about it. Now he understood why.

Shura described the effect the news had upon him:

'On the second day Jaroslav stayed long in bed and it was about noon when he started to dress. He put on his Russian shirt, fastened a leather belt round it, stuck his trousers into his *valenki*, buttoned round him the overcoat he had got in Moscow and put on a peaked cap. He kissed me goodbye and said he would be back soon. And he was indeed back in about three hours' time.

'He looked depressed and banged his cap on the bed. "And so we've lost everything, Shura. We've come too late. The people I was supposed to get in touch with have all been rounded up and put in gaol. And those who are still free don't seem to trust me any more. They pretend not to know anything and say I'm not Comrade Gashek but the editor Hašek, who used to write all those funny stories."

'He looked as if he was going to burst into tears. I comforted him as best I could. "Let's go back to Russia. There's heaps of work to be done there, and there they were really fond of us, Mama and all of them. Here there isn't even a proper winter. Outside it only rains and rains, and it's all muddy." But Jaroslav just sat there apathetically. Then he got up, changed his Russian tunic for a shirt without a collar, put on his shoes, his jacket and coat, and said he'd be coming back. Only this time he didn't come back for three days, and when he did he was a sight—all tousled and dishevelled. He brought with him a Mr Longen and his wife, Xena, and introduced them to me. They were very kind and asked us to spend Christmas Eve with them. Meanwhile Jaroslav fell asleep and the Longens went away.'[4]

They had been recommended to stay at the Hotel Neptune, but the unfortunate Shura could find no one there whose language she understood except some Russian emigrés, who shunned her like the plague when she said she was a Bolshevik. They told her triumphantly that there would be no revolution, the police had given the strikers such a hiding that they would remember it for a long time, and the Communists had all been clapped in gaol.

As usual Hašek had been naively optimistic about his reception in the Republic. On three counts he was an outcast, not to say a criminal. First, he was a deserter from the Legion and so a traitor in the eyes of Czech patriots. Next, he had been a Commissar, a Red, at a time when there were well-grounded fears of a Bolshevik take-over. Finally, he was a bigamist. He was cold-shouldered publicly on all sides and one of his writer-friends even refused to shake his hand because of his alleged implication in the barbarities of the Red Commissars in Russia. Not even the Marxist left wanted to have anything to do with him. They either distrusted him or refused to take him seriously. 'I should never have returned. They hate me here,' he lamented and talked of suicide.

The self-discipline which he had observed in such a miraculous way during the three years he spent in Bolshevik Russia crumbled as soon as he left that country. He was back on alcohol again, but it did not bring him the same sweet release as before. Longen thought that something had gone out of him. He was surprised by Hašek's manifest anxiety to give the impression that he was the old bohemian of pre-war days.

'But there was no trace of it left. His roguish smiles had lost their gentleness and apparent cordiality and his eyes blinked foxily with sullen derision. His mouth spouted amusing words, but all the time his eyes were obviously mocking his listeners. His appearance and movements had acquired a ruthless angularity and from time he to time had a burst of ill temper and his features were distorted by a wry contemptuous grin. He would quickly gulp down his drink, drink nervously and incessantly without enjoyment, often taking several gulps in quick succession, as though he wanted to throw off an unpleasant fit which had seized him . . .

'He did not want to talk about Russia. When he was asked about his Soviet activities, he said nothing and only went on drinking and drinking. He drank and sang and swore. He swore at us and at the whole world.' . . . 'He became terribly wild after he had taken alcohol, showing no consideration at all for anyone, not even for Shura, whom he pushed away so roughly that she fell over. Before the war I never saw him in a state like that. In his worst drunkenness he still retained some portion of his consciousness and preserved his wit, even if it was drastic and not very elegant . . .

'I tried to interest Hašek by talking to him. "Jarda, why don't you write a comedy for our Revolutionary Theatre?[5] Perhaps something from Russian life? We'll pay you well." '

Hašek's rejoinder was explosive. 'Revolutionary theatre! Who's a revolutionary? You're just common idiots, so you shut up about revolution.' And with a violent blow he knocked the glass off the table and gave a laugh. 'You have a "Revolutionary Avenue", a "Revolutionary Square", a "Revolutionary Theatre", but what you've none of you got is revolutionary spirit!'[6]

Hašek told Shura that the gendarmes and police had broken the big strike which the workers hoped would bring them to power. Now it was only the traitors who were left and they would go on doing just the same as they did under Francis-Joseph. 'Chatter rather than action. That's always been our tragedy,' he said bitterly.

Again Shura suggested they should return to Russia, but Hašek would not hear of it. 'The authorities know I've come back and now they'll never let us out again. We should have to try to run away. Besides, the Soviet comrades would never understand our position. They'd regard me as a traitor who had run away from the battlefield.'

Hašek blamed it on the traditional weakness and spirit of compromise of Czech politicians. Shura recalled:

'I didn't want to sit down under this, but Jaroslav just shook his head and wouldn't listen. I reminded him how in Russia we had not given up heart even when Kolchak drove us out of Ufa. I did not know the Czech character, he retorted. If anyone brandished his fist at him, the Czech took fright. It takes a long time before he pulls himself together and then he rushes blindly ahead. And the worst enemy was the Czech bureaucracy. In Czechoslovakia it wasn't like in Russia, where for hundreds and hundreds of miles there were only a handful of Tsarist officials. Here a certain group, and a pretty big one at that, were living very well indeed and didn't want to take any risks. They'd be afraid of losing what they had. He called them toadies. Literally shaking with anger and hatred, he said that a large number of Habsburg bureaucrats were still holding office in the Republic. He explained how he had ridiculed them all and they would now want their revenge . . .'

Terribly short of money and unable to afford to stay at the Neptune any longer, he asked friends to help him find rooms somewhere else. He used to go to the Union every day to do his writing, just as he did before the war. According to Longen he gave the 'The Revolutionary Theatre' permission to dramatise any of his works they liked in return for an advance. He had said that he himself was not able to write for the theatre and Longen should adapt some of his stories. Typically enough, he forgot all about this and later accepted an engagement at the Red Seven, a cabaret which had started before the war and was now working again. Its manager offered him a hundred crowns in advance and billed him to talk about his Bolshevik past, but when the performance came Hašek only read out some of his 'confessions' and a *feuilleton* called 'How I Met the Author of My Obituary Notice',[7] which had already appeared a few days before in the *Tribune* under the sub-title 'The Secret of my Stay in Russia'. The manager was naturally upset.

One day Hašek's old friend Ladislav Hájek read of Hašek's appearances at the Red Seven and decided to go with his wife to his performance. Hašek came on the stage looking tired and out of sorts. It was depressing to hear him read his story 'How I Died'; they felt he should not be performing at a cabaret at all —certainly not in the condition he was in. Either he had been overtired by the journey or the impressions on his return had been too much for him. The Hájeks decided to put off meeting him until a more favourable time. They met by chance in Wenceslas Square some time later and Hašek came up and kissed him. 'That's not a Judas kiss,' he said. But he would not talk about his time in Russia. It was as if he disliked being reminded of it. When they met the same evening in company in a restaurant he seemed strange and distant.[8]

At the beginning of January, Michal Mareš, an old Anarchist friend of his, saw Hašek at a rehearsal in the theatre. He was sitting in a box with a bottle of soda water and a glass beside him. Mareš presented him with a copy of some poems he had just published.

'Hašek took no notice and turned over the pages absent-mindedly. Then his face grew stiff. "Ah, yes, little poems . . . They want to make a clown of me here," he sighed. "In this world you can only be free if you're an idiot." He stroked his face slowly with his hand, as though he wanted to wipe off a stray drop of sweat, and between clenched lips muttered the word: "*Svoloch!*"* I told him I had to go to the manager's office, but he didn't even answer me. He just looked stiffly through me for a few moments and then shut his eyes and leant back in his chair.'

When Mareš went round to the box again some twenty minutes later, Hašek was leaning with both his elbows on the balustrade with his face hidden in his hands. Was he asleep? Was he crying? What was plain was that he did not want to see or hear anything.

Hašek's appearances in the Red Seven began to resemble more and more those of Professor Unrath in *The Blue Angel*. He grew careless about his person and often came on the stage look-ing tired, dishevelled and dirty. The manager finally lost pati-ence with him and asked him point-blank whether he would say something about his Bolshevik past. When all he could offer was a very boring lecture on the geographical curiosities in Siberia, instead of the jokes about the Soviet government which his audience were waiting for, he lost his job.

Ever since her separation from Hašek, Jarmila had had a job in the Chamber of Commerce and was still living with her family, of whom little Richard had become the darling. In spite of the many rumours in Prague that Hašek was dead, she told her friend, Vilma, that she knew for certain that he was alive

* A common Russian word of abuse meaning 'vermin'.

and well, and had a high position with the Bolsheviks. He had completely given up alcohol, she claimed, had become popular and famous in Russia and would certainly return home. 'And so I think that after my seven lean years could come seven fat ones,' she said.

But when Hašek finally did return, it was a great blow to her that he had brought a Russian woman with him. She had been counting on his getting in touch with her. Indeed, long before he actually returned, she had told Vilma that he was already in Prague.

' "I was sewing yesterday evening by the window and suddenly I heard someone whistle the fanfares from *Libuše** under my windows. It went straight through my heart. I thought I was going to faint, because it was Jaroslav's whistle."

' "But how can you be certain that it was him?"

' "He whistled out of tune, as he always did."

' "And didn't you go down and look?"

' "I looked down but didn't let myself be seen. I only caught a glimpse of a pale face."

' "But are you absolutely sure it was really him? And what happened next?"

' "Nothing. I didn't go downstairs or answer, and a moment later he had gone."

'She paused for a moment and then continued in a surge of emotion:

' "I must get away from Prague. I shall have to get myself transferred to Bratislava."

' "Why?"

' "He'll force me to return to him. He has the right to do so. We're not divorced. And he could take little Richard away from me."

' "But what on earth would he do with him? You've brought him up. The child belongs to his mother." '

Meanwhile Jarmila waited to see what Hašek would do. She wanted to try and help him and, when he failed to get in touch with her, she wrote to him asking him to come and explain his

---

* Smetana's opera of that name. The fanfares are still played in Czechoslovakia today on formal occasions as the presidential fanfare.

ideas. She claimed she had the right to do so, because since they parted she had made no new friendships.

Finally Hašek arranged to see her. According to Vilma the first meeting was far from straightforward. Hašek described his remarriage in Russia as 'a frightful misunderstanding'. After that they met in secret several times without the knowledge of the Mayers.[9] Shura was told about it and naturally did not approve. She has given a totally different account of the first meeting. According to her at the beginning of 1921 Jarmila came to the hotel to find Hašek. 'She . . . threatened to make a scandal and prosecute him for bigamy and his failure to pay her alimony for their child. At first she even threatened me as well, but afterwards she offered me money several times to induce me to go back "where I came from".'[10]

On January 12th, 1921, after meeting Hašek Jarmila wrote:

'Míťa

'I am sending you a few photographs of the hero of the novel, *The Little Bourgeois*,* and some pages from his exercise book of last year. The contents will interest you.† If you can, please give me that little photograph which you brought from Russia. I shall keep it as a memento to show Richard that he was not so utterly forgotten as he'll certainly one day imagine he was. I think you can send it to me in exchange for what I enclose.

'I'm sorry. I didn't mean to be so bitter, but the bitterness has been stored up for eight years. Richard isn't going to be a theologian. If I have my way, he'll be a doctor or a lawyer. I shan't encourage love of art in him.

'I think it would be right if you were to tell Mrs L.‡ that you have a son.

'Don't show the photograph to your friends. There's no need for anyone to look down on Richard. If you would like to see him I'll arrange it.

J.'

When Shura first heard the news that Hašek was married and had a son already it hurt her deeply.

* Richard.

† '. . . Our concierge is a tailor. My papa is a writer and is a Legionary in Russia. He may be dead.'

‡ Shura.

'At first I could not understand. Only later I felt able to ask him why he had not told me before, why he had married me, why he had returned to Czechoslovakia at all and why he had taken me with him. It was one big Why?

'He replied that during his life before the war he did not admit any responsibility to anyone or anything. He never found anyone who had understanding of him, or so he said . . . And so he just did what he thought was proper without regard to other people.'[11]

Hašek's first premise was undoubtedly the key to his behaviour all his life, including his marrying Shura, bringing her back with him to Prague and then paradoxically immediately demonstrating once more his love for Jarmila. His second was totally unfounded. There were many who showed him understanding, his mother, Jarmila, Hájek, Lada—to mention only a few.

Later Jarmila brought Richard along for him to see. She did not tell the child that he was meeting his father and introduced him as the editor of *Tribune*. When Hašek first saw Richard he stroked his hair shyly and addressed him in the polite form of the second person plural!

Hašek had asked Jarmila to help him with her contacts. As soon as he had re-established connections with the various editors he tried once more to persuade them to publish her stories. He affected to forget that their relationship had been broken and that much water had flowed under the bridge since their marriage. In his letters could be heard once more the old promises and pleadings for forgiveness.

On February 3rd he wrote:

'After your letter, which I only got today, because I go to write *feuilletons* only once a week, I promise you that I will be a respectable person. It will be the first promise I shall keep, and I ask you, if you have any influence, to help me to get any job anywhere—however unimportant. I shall give up drinking completely, which I can easily do, because in Russia when I was in the service of the Bolsheviks I didn't touch anything for years. Don't think, Jarmilka, that I didn't love you. I still love you. How everying you described in your letter happened at all is one of life's enigmas. It is such a damned zig-zag. Please believe me today for the first time. It's a puzzle even to me why I never answered you. I wanted to write, but hadn't the courage to. How could I write that I wanted to see you and my son, when I was really as shabby and ragged as one of the vagabond brethren, who are after all human beings too. Don't go away from Prague, Jarmilka! Please let me meet you, if you are not ashamed of me. I'm no longer appearing in the Red Seven. My photograph is from a forged Russian passport, made when I was running away to come home. Please be assured that I love my son. I am sending you the picture of him I carried about with me when I was in Russia. Unfortunately I didn't have your photograph, otherwise I'd have carried that with me too. It's a terrible misunderstanding about that girl.* Please, advise me what to do. Kiss my boy from me.

'Míťa, who has thrown up the sponge, or "The End of the Tramp".'

At first he had wanted Jarmila to believe that he had run away from the Bolsheviks, but soon he had to confess that he was really being pursued by the Czechoslovak police. Shura relates how they came several times to see how they lived and where they got their money from. Hašek was desperately afraid of going to prison. He knew it would mean moral disaster for him. How different he was now from the careless young bohemian of other days who had been quite happy to spend a night or two in the cells!

Another letter from Hašek to Jarmila has been preserved from about the same time. On February 19th, 1921 he wrote:

'You are so much in my thoughts and, believe me, I love you more than before our marriage. It's a lovely fairy tale of the heart—the month of May in my declining years! And at the same time it's such a frightful tragedy. Last time after seeing you I got back home at 9 p.m. The landlord had fortunately kept dinner for me. That's a small detail of my private life. Tomorrow I shall have another Bugulma story in *Tribune*. Yesterday you had a *feuilleton* about Richard in the *People's Right*. He'll grow up into a fine fellow.

'I didn't see him on Thursday. I was afraid he was ill, and

* Shura.

231

was very happy to know that he was well, when I was with you yesterday.

'I shall stop now, so that you get this letter. I kiss you, dear Jarmilka, and our Richard too. I am waiting for a letter from you on Monday.

Your Míťa'

In another letter, this time undated and cryptic, Hašek wrote:

'My dear friend,

'During the last few days, when fate has separated us again, some very interesting things have happened.

'First, I have been carrying in my pocket the photographic equipment, which I return with cordial thanks. The same day, when I returned home, I found this interesting document:

> '*Summons of accused in penal charge Vr* XXXIV *6948/21 against you under paragraph 206.*
> *You are summoned to appear for interrogation at 9 a.m on April 28, 1921, at this court 90/2nd floor in respect of the charge laid against you. If you do not present yourself, you will be fetched by the police.*
> *Regional Penal Court. Prague* XXXIV
> *April 8, 1921*'

'Paragraph 206 is not political. It's only the crime of having two wives—also called by the poetic name of "bigamy". The following day a detective came again and in spite of his protests I threw him out, because he had no official credentials with him to prove his identity. And so here it is. Paragraph 206. My legal representative, Dr Papoušek, will have a lot of work again if it comes to any proceedings, which it probably won't, because I go on repeating in a mechanical way: "I know nothing. I was never in a church or register office and I can't remember anything."

'I definitely hope it won't come to proceedings, because I wouldn't like a public scandal. As far as the sentence is concerned, the lightest would be six months. Today I'm going to

Ondřejov* where the painter Panuška has given me a recommendation for summer holiday accommodation . . .

'I hope I shall find something suitable. Panuška maintains that it's prettiest of all around Ondřejov, because the village is surrounded by woods and there's a lake nearby with a sandy bottom and very clean water without any mud. Every peasant in the neighbourhood is a poacher and poachers are always very nice people.

'I am convinced I shall find something and I think I shall be back by Wednesday.

'Now our friend from Russia† has received a summons too in the penal charge against me under paragraph 206.

'I send you the second instalment [of *The Good Soldier Švejk*]. The third comes out next Wednesday. I suspect that that declaration didn't come from your side and in that case it's really only a question of the offence of false registration, because today I have two summonses, and on each of them there is something different. And so perhaps the whole of my bigamy case will be recorded as nothing more than the misdemeanour of false registration, costing me a fine of ten crowns, because I didn't commit licensed bigamy, legally supported by official documents and all that will remain of the honourable prosecutor will be the memory of a lazy bourgeois epoch and a few scribbled papers.'

Hašek had apparently sent this letter by messenger and not by post, and had started it with 'My dear Friend' instead of 'My dear Jarmila', because he was under investigation by the police and felt he had to be cautious. He may have been fearing a 'political' trial and was relieved that the paragraph which was invoked in his case excluded this.

Meanwhile he had resumed the role of the wandering Jew. After leaving the Hotel Neptune and taking rooms at Žižkov, he had to move again because Shura did not get on with the landlady and they were given notice for not having paid their rent. It was at this time that he was helped by his old friend, Franta Sauer, who took him in to his home which was in the same suburb. They had together formed a joint 'publishing

* In the valley of the river Sázava.
† Shura.

house' which published his latest book *Three Men and a Shark and Other Instructive Stories*.[12]

After his dismissal from the Red Seven he began to publish his Bugulma stories, the first of which was *The Commandant of the Town of Bugulma*. But the public, who had expected revelations about the horrors of life under the Bolsheviks, were disappointed with it in spite of the humour and charm of his description of his encounters with the impulsive commander of the Tver Cavalry Regiment, Yerokhymov. None the less the series had success and Hašek received advances for further stories, this time purely Švejk adventures: *Švejk among the Bolsheviks* and *Švejk in Holy Russia*. They were never written.

Relations with his fellow writers were bad. Hardly anyone from Left to Right had a good word for him. The poet S. K. Neumann described him as a traitor to the revolution. 'The clown has returned from Russia,' he wrote in *Stem*.[13] 'J. H., back in his old milieu, is still the old J. H. and remains convinced that life's nothing more than a lark.'

When he was on the brink of destitution and despair, he suddenly had a brilliant idea. He would write a new and longer version of *The Good Soldier Švejk*. Shura recalls how the thought came to his mind about the end of February 1921.

'Jaroslav and Sauer came home in a good mood. They laughed and hugged each other, and Jaroslav said that he'd had an idea: he would write about the soldier Švejk again. I did not know that he had already written about him before the war and during it. He only told me it now, but he went on to say that this time it would be something different; it would be real literature. "I shall laugh at all those idiots and at the same time show what our real character is and what we are capable of doing."

'They started by sending to the pub opposite for beer and getting properly drunk. They slept until the afternoon of the next day and then Jaroslav started to write, while Sauer kept on going out to fetch beer. Jaroslav wrote very quickly without a draft and when his hand hurt him he dictated to Sauer. They both had a fine time while they were doing it and forgot all about the beer. They went on writing throughout the whole night.'[14]

Hašek did not trust publishers and brought out the book himself in instalments in a joint venture with Sauer. Later they both persuaded the owner of an estate office in Žižkov named Čermák, as well as Sauer's brother Arnošt, to join the partnership.

The book was advertised on a strident yellow poster, which was put up in the windows of pubs and at the street corners in Žižkov. The text ran:

LONG LIVE THE EMPEROR FRANCIS JOSEPH I!
exclaimed
THE GOOD SOLDIER ŠVEJK
whose fortunes in the Great War are described by
JAROSLAV HAŠEK
in his book
The Fortunes of the Good Soldier Švejk
During the World and Civil War Here and in Russia
With the Czech edition there will simultaneously
be published translations of it in
FRANCE, ENGLAND, AMERICA
The first Czech book to be translated into world languages!
The best humorous and satirical book in world literature!
Great Victory for a Czech Book Abroad!
The Czech original is published by A. Sauer and
V. Čermák in Žižkov, Kolárovo Nám. 22
Weekly in Instalments at 2 Crowns (32 pages)
The cheapest Czech book!
FIRST IMPRESSION 100,000 COPIES!
Ask for it at all booksellers or direct from the publishers
A. SAUER AND V. ČERMAK IN ZIZKOV, KOLAROVO NAM. 22.

Hašek and Sauer then sought out the artist Josef Lada and asked him to make an illustration for the cover of the first instalment. Lada's account of his experiences with the two bohemians is typical of Hašek's way of doing business.

'In 1921 Hašek visited me in my apartment and asked me if I would make a sketch for the cover of *The Good Soldier Švejk* which was coming out in instalments. I started to do so. I did not create the figure of Švejk after any definite person, but according to Hašek's concept, as described in the book. I drew the figure of Švejk filling his pipe in the midst of a rain of shells and bullets and exploding shrapnel. I tried to depict his good-humoured face and calm expression, which showed that he had all his wits about him, but could if necessary act stupidly. On the pre-arranged day I brought my sketch to the wine cellar, where we were to meet. Hašek and Sauer were very pleased with it, and after lengthy consideration Hašek promised me a fee of two hundred crowns.

'Sauer thought that this was too little and raised it to five hundred. Hašek, after a long silence, ended the discussion by banging his fist energetically on the table and deciding that I should get a thousand crowns. Instead of getting any money, however, I had to pay the restaurant bill for both of them. The cover was printed, but I never got any money at all for it. But I had never had great expectations of getting any, but after I had forgotten all about it the accountant came from Sauer, who kept some kind of shop for underwear, and brought me some pairs of underpants and stockings with a message that his chief presented his respects and that this was the fee for the cover. He had not been able to send it before, because he had gone bankrupt.'[15]

The publisher, Edvard Weinfurter, had refused to undertake the sale and distribution of the novel: 'We won't have anything to do with scurrilous literature of this kind,' he wrote. 'Its sole object is to teach people to be coarse and foul-mouthed, rather than to be intelligent, and we shall certainly not soil the name of our firm by touching it. It is not for Czechs, but only for Communists.' Some of the first few press reviews were unfavourable and scared off Hašek's partners who decided to opt out.

A historic account of how the book was born, published and distributed was given to Ančík by Karel Šnor, the owner of a Žižkov tavern:

'Because I was a publican by trade, I took over a small tavern in Žižkov . . . with a tap-room and three tables. In the cellar I had three casks containing each about twenty-two gallons of

beer and in the tap-room a bottle of rum, two pound of frankfurters, a jar of pickled gherkins and some small cheeses.

'Across the street . . . Franta Sauer lived with his sister on the
second floor and in one of their rooms our hero, Jarda Hašek,
was lodged with his lady wife, Shurinka . . .

'I opened the shutters and displayed my wares so that everyone should know that it was a proper tavern . . . Everything
could be seen from the opposite side of the street, because I had
a big window with a fine lot of room for my wares.

'Then I waited for customers and, sure enough, as though by
a miracle, my best ones came in—Hašek, his wife Shura and
Franta Sauer. And I shall never forget them to my dying day.
When I greeted Hašek politely, he answered: "Dear Karel, I,
my wife and Franta here have decided to come and see you as
often as we can, because—don't you think so, Franta?—what's
the point in our walking any further when we've got you so
close at hand?" Then his eye caught a bottle of rum and he
went on: "So now pour out something for all four of us, there's
a good fellow, and let's have a drink." (The fourth one was me
—he was a real gentleman and most considerate to his fellow
men.)

'I opened the first bottle of rum and served them four glasses
at a crown a glass. After he had drunk his up, Franta said:
"Your food's marvellous and the rum's excellent, so another
round for me, please." Again four rums disappeared and now it
was another round for Hašek's wife, but she didn't want any
more, so it was only three rums, and after that it was three
again for the house.

'And then at last they sat down and ordered one beer and
two frankfurters each with onions and vinegar. I rushed down
right away to the houseporter for onions and vinegar, and then
they ordered cheese and more beer again. At this point Madame
Shura tactfully left to go home after saying goodbye to Hašek
with a nice kiss and a warning to him to come home for supper,
although it was only half past ten in the morning (how well she
knew him!).

'When she had gone, Hašek said: "Karel, as you see, we're
your first customers, and so you have to respect us. Here are
twelve crowns in cash for those three rounds of rum, at one
crown a glass, which makes twelve crowns together. The rest

must be on tick, because it won't be long before the first instalment of *Švejk* appears and you'll be the first to get two hundred
copies of it. You'll be able to sell them for two crowns apiece
and so you'll get four hundred crowns for them, and that'll be
for yourself. Now, may we have two more glasses of rum,
please? Today, I'm going to sit and write until the morning,
and now we're going to Prague." '

Šnor looked ruefully at his window display and calculated
that already considerable havoc had been made of it. Six frankfurters with onion and vinegar, six portions of cheese, three
large gherkins, twelve rolls, nine glasses of beer and half a bottle
of rum—all gone, and he'd only got twelve crowns for the lot
and the rest on tick.

'I was looking pretty blue, but when I remembered that I
was to get two hundred copies of *Švejk* free and how much cash
I could get for them, I brightened up a bit. Customers dropped
in one by one, the crossing-sweeper came in for beer and cheese,
then a customer from the spirit-shop opposite, a tradesman or
two, a house-porter from next door and some young lady returning from her nightly trade. And so it went on day after day.
The debt grew bigger and bigger, business was slow and I
thought Hašek and Sauer were beginning to look rather
dejected . . .'

And so one day Šnor asked Sauer how things stood with the
book.

'My dear chap,' Sauer replied, 'it's like this. Yesterday I was
at uncle's and hocked Hašek's overcoat. It's quite warm now,
you know, and Hašek was afraid that the moths would get at it
. . . He's already got the first instalment of *Švejk* practically
ready and it's terrific! Now he must finish it and, you know, you
can't get him to write a word without rum and cigarettes. But
don't worry. When the book comes out, there'll be a God
Almighty rumpus among all the top brass and the other nobs,
because he's hit out at them for all he's worth; there are a lot
of them still here who'd like to carry on in the Republic just as
they used to before the war . . . Maybe next week we'll give *our*
work (he said "our") to the printers and then we'll all do jolly
well out of it, so don't refuse Hašek anything, but serve him
whatever he asks for.'

'And the customers came,' Šnor continued. 'They were all

Hašek's acquaintances . . . and listened to what he told them, how he'd soon have the first book of *Švejk* ready and needed more money to get it printed, and who had got that money? "I know, boys," he said, "that if you'd got it, you'd put it into the business without a moment's thought, and I know we're all of us glad to be able to keep our heads above water . . . Now, Karel, may I have a glass of rum, please, and you'll get those hundred copies as sure as my name is Jarda Hašek."—"But, Jaroušek, you promised Karel two hundred," Sauer put in.— "Quite right. Very well then, we'll give him two hundred." . . .

'Then they went away and the customers slowly followed. I added up my takings and knew for certain that I only had enough to pay my rent till the end of September and the next month I'd have to live on what they owed me!

'The next day Franta came in triumphantly at eleven o'clock and said that they were going to make a contract in the afternoon and the next day they would have the first instalment of *Švejk* printed. And he took a crown out of his pocket and ordered one rum, cash down. I took this as a definite sign that something was going to happen. But they didn't come back at all that day, and the next morning Shurinka came along in tears and told me in heart-breaking tones that they had not been home since the previous day and she had prepared fried *škubánky** for Jaroušek. ("My darling adores them although he always tells me that he's had enough of them.") I consoled her by saying that perhaps Mr Writer was getting on with his *Švejk* somewhere on the quiet side, but she wouldn't believe it and said he hardly wrote at all. When he came home at night he was nearly always sick; he had an illness and we were only mortal and she loved him very much. I gave her a glass of liqueur and two frankfurters with mustard just to get her to go, because she was crying to break my heart. And it was not until ten o'clock in the evening that Hašek and Sauer arrived in a cab and with the help of the customers I got them into the tap-room and pumped into them black coffee without sugar and soda water . . .

'After some time, one day in the morning at about nine, Franta arrived with a parcel, banged it on the table and said: "Karel, the day has dawned for you at last. Here you have for

* Potato-paste dumplings fried in hot butter and served with sugar, poppy-seed and cinnamon sugar.

the time being one hundred and fifty copies of the first instalment of *Švejk*. Things aren't yet quite all right with the money for the printing, you know, but we'll keep our word to you. And so as not to forget, you're to send Jarda three portions of soup, six rolls, three bottles of soda water, twenty cigarettes and half a litre of rum, and in the evening he'll settle the bill.''

'I gave him everything, because I was going to go bust anyhow and after warning him that my very life depended on *Švejk* and that I needed money for beer or I'd have to close tomorrow, Franta gave me his promise. He saw how things stood, the last barrel already opened in the cellar, only two dry frankfurters, ten stinking cheeses and half a bottle of rum left, in fact—utter disaster.

'I took the copies, read them at once and I liked them very much. Twenty of them I put in the window so that the passers-by could see that *Švejk* had at last come out. I had prepared a caption on cardboard saying SEE NAPLES AND DIE, READ ŠVEJK AND LIVE! and various other slogans so that anyone who went by would be struck by them. And indeed that very day I sold twenty copies to customers and passers-by and got forty crowns for them in cash, which revived me a bit. And then Franta came to see me in the evening, again bringing me a hundred crowns in cash, saying that it was for the fifty copies which they had not delivered to me and that Jaroušek was at home writing the next instalment.

'But later I learnt from Franta's good sister that Hašek had had an attack of gout. He had been quite drunk and had only recovered that day. They were cooking garlic soup for him. He was once more completely broke and was going to hunt for money. That afternoon they both came back sober and sad, and after ordering one beer and one rum each, asked at once whether the sellers hadn't left any money here for the copies of *Švejk*, because—as Franta explained to me—when they were pub-crawling in Žižkov, they gave various acquaintances they met fifty copies each and one copy free, on condition that they sold them to their friends for two crowns and brought back here to my pub one crown fifty hellers for each copy, as well as the unsold copies. And here was the list of names of the sellers. "Yes," I said, "I do have money here from a certain gentleman, thirty-five copies returned and twenty-two crowns fifty in cash for fifteen copies." So I gave them the money and at once took off the amount owing for two beers and two rums. Hašek said that they were all idiots. Franta said: "Look, Jarda, we gave them these copies to sell and the condition was that they should have ten days to do it in, so there's nothing to be done. According to the list there are twenty of them, which makes a thousand copies. So, let's wait and you, Karel, keep the copies that have been returned."

'At that moment [one of the sellers] came in carrying some copies in his hand, and when he saw the well-known couple, he said: "Boys, here you have eighteen copies returned and the money for thirty-two." "Hurrah," Jarda shouted. "Serve us rum all round. That'll be all right. There's a whole fortune for me in those copies. Give us just one more rum for the journey . . . We'll go and get some money." And so they went away together.

'Then I knew for certain that it was a bad look-out for me. It was going to be very difficult for me to get my money for all the drink and food they had consumed. In my pub it was just like *The Shop Where Everything Had Been Eaten** and out of those hundred and fifty copies of *Švejk* they had given me I still had more than a hundred and ten left. I started to pack the frank-furters and cheese in them. From the sellers I had got about seven hundred copies, of which Hašek took thirty each time. In Prague he exchanged them for cash and very quickly spent it on drink. And one day they came again and took away all the copies from me saying that they were going to the larger towns in the Republic and that the book was starting to sell like hot cakes. In October the second and third instalments of *The Good Soldier Švejk* were published. People who had not read the first instalment now tried to get hold of it and asked for it.

'I told Jarda and Franta this, and they assured me that the first instalment would be reprinted. Now they were both very respectably dressed and seemed to be doing better. They had not forgotten me and gave me some cash, but the time for pay-ing my quarter's rent was approaching and so I ceremoniously shut up my shop. In short, everything had been drunk up and my customers together with Hašek and Franta had the last

---

* *U snedeného krámu*, a novel by a Czech humorous writer Ignát Herrmann, born 1854.

drink with me. *The Good Soldier Švejk* had started to make his triumphant way through the world.'

Meanwhile Hašek went on seeing Jarmila clandestinely. In the summer of 1921, probably at the end of June, she wrote to Vilma in the country that she would like to visit her one day and would bring Hašek with her.

They came together one Sunday in early July. Hašek did not look well: he was pale and emaciated, and his clothes hung loosely on him. Both the guests enjoyed a lunch of chicken prepared with sour cream and Hašek persuaded Jarmila to take a second helping: 'Let's eat, Jarmilka,' he urged. 'We're getting it free.'

After lunch Hašek spent some time making a mill on the stream for Vilma's little boy. But when he bent down, he felt pressure on his stomach. He had severe pains, turned even more pale and said anxiously: 'I've got cancer.'

Vilma and Jarmila laid him on his side on a narrow bench under the window with his hands under his head. His position on the bench seemed rather insecure: he might easily fall and hurt himself. They wanted to make it more secure, but did not know how to do so. Finally they supported him with two huge logs. And so he lay there and slept—'a poor sick human being'. He was no longer the handsome young man with the pink complexion whom they had known long ago.

While he was sleeping Jarmila sat with Vilma on some logs a little distance away and talked quietly. She confided to Vilma that Hašek had been asking her to come and live with him again. She would have been ready to do this, had it not been for Shura. What was to be done about her? After all she was nothing more than his nurse.

'And a nurse is just what he needs,' said Vilma. 'You wouldn't be able to be one. You should leave him in her care. Besides, it wouldn't be decent of him to abandon her.' But Jarmila made no reply.

After Hašek had had a good sleep, they gave him a cup of black coffee and he felt better, although somewhat chilly. Finally they left together. It had turned cold, and Hašek began to have shivering fits. 'I shake like an aspen leaf, only to get as hot as a blacksmith's tongs a moment later,' he had written to her a month before. Jarmila said it was due to his having contracted malaria in Russia. Now she took off her jersey and put it on him. As they went off, Hašek said: 'You see, you thought Jarmilka and I wouldn't meet again, that they had separated us for ever. But, luckily enough, we've found each other again.'[16]

Hašek's health had long worried Jarmila. The Prague climate did not suit him, he had written, and he and the painter Panuška were looking for somewhere to stay in the summer. In June he had complained to her that he was suffering from ague fits, having caught cold at a Socialist May Day rally.

On July 5th, 1921, he wrote to her:

'My Dearest Jarmilka,
    'Fortune favoured me, so I was able to return from our trip [to Vilma] and be well thanks to the way you looked after me. But on Monday I had the misfortune to be exposed to torrential rain for more than half an hour, and my feet were wet through when I waited for you in vain and so now I've got a pain in my chest and a violent cough.

    'I thought that you might have been very tired after our expedition and probably had not gone to the office, and it was only this morning that I learned the truth, when your express letter arrived.

    'I slept until nine o'clock on Monday. My disappearance [from Sauer's flat] and my return did not cause any sensation. People saw me acting as though I were drunk when I was playing cards at the Valhans's wine cellar.

    'Today I have a little fever and I can't come and see you. Please, my darling, send me those prescriptions, so that I can follow them.

    'My return in a jersey caused a sensation and it was especially Sauer's Běta who noticed it. I told her that I had won it at cards on Sunday.

    'Now I've had a little nap and I dreamt we were together on the Petřín. Instead of Prague that village where we were together on Sunday lay at our feet, and to get to Prague we had to go by train. The station was down by the Kinský Garden. I dreamt I was kissing you, kissing you unceasingly and we were quite alone on the Petřín.

    'And now that I have woken up, I kiss you again in my heart.
        Your Mítuška'

In the holidays when the 'editor' came again, Jarmila told Richard the truth. Hašek brought with him his collection of short stories *Three Men and a Shark* and wrote in it: 'To my dear son from Jaroslav Hašek.'

On August 16th Hašek wrote to Richard.

'My own dear Richard,

'I am expecting you, my dear boy, with Mama at the Palacký Bridge this afternoon. Do be sure to come. I am sending you some chocolate. Mama has eaten a little bit of it.

'Keep well and don't forget to guard the Secret* very carefully.

Your Papa'

This was the last extant letter which Hašek wrote to his family, and the meeting was the last time Richard saw his father alive. After that Hašek left Prague and the old sweet romance 'in his declining years' came to an end. When Vilma met Jarmila later in the autumn she and Hašek had separated again—not at their own wish, nor at the orders of her parents, who still did not know about the relationship, but because Shura had insisted on it, saying she was pregnant.

Vilma was sceptical about Shura's story. The pair had lived together for years and had no children, and now suddenly as though by order, they were getting one, and at a time when Hašek was so ill. Jarmila said nothing, but it was obvious that she had given way to Shura.

* That he was Richard's father and that they saw each other.

(17)

Lipnice and the End

In the summer of 1921 Hašek suddenly disappeared from Prague. The person responsible for whisking him away was the landscape painter, Jaroslav Panuška, a great hulking man of enormous strength, who would have been a good 'chucker out' at a pub and had indeed proved himself as such. Among his eccentricities was to address everybody in the familiar second person singular, to save himself the trouble of distinguishing between his closest friends and the rest. He had an *atelier* in Vinohrady and was at one time friendly with Lada, the illustrator of *Švejk*. A great drinker and gourmand, he combined just those qualities which were dear to Hašek's heart. More important, he was a kindly person who took a real interest in Hašek's welfare.

The road from Prague to Vienna via Jihlava and Znojmo crosses a long, high plateau on the frontiers of Bohemia and Moravia. These are the Bohemian–Moravian Highlands, where Panuška was born. Although he had painted some attractive landscapes of this beautiful region, he was, curiously enough, better known for his paintings of ghosts and archaeological remains—a rather odd combination. Langer said that the chalets in his pictures always leaned to one side, the roads were full of boulders, the forests ghostly with twisted trees; one felt that out of them some hideous monster might appear at any moment. Once, in order to achieve the right perspective of a castle, he hired a bomber and cruised over it.[1] His language was highly seasoned, but somehow or other in his mouth it sounded natural and acceptable—like Palivec's in *The Good Soldier Švejk*.*

Hašek had been so slow in getting on with his writing of *Švejk* that Sauer had become seriously worried. He told Panuška that if the book was ever to be completed Hašek must be spirited away somewhere in the country, where the climate was healthy

* *The Good Soldier Švejk*, p. 6.

and food plentiful (unlike at Prague at that time). Panuška had immediately thought of Lipnice, which lay near the valley of the river Sázava and commanded a magnificent view of his native highlands. 'That place is just made for him,' he said. 'I go there every summer and in winter too, when there is snow. I can paint, and he can write in peace somewhere in the woods. We shall mutually restore each other's zest for work.'

Hašek's departure from Prague was typical of him. On August 25th, while Shura was out shopping with Sauer, he sallied forth scantily dressed in an open-necked shirt and without a hat, carrying a jug to fetch beer. By chance on the way he happened to run into Panuška, who was dressed for a journey. 'It was obvious that he was not well,' Panuška recalled. 'His eyes had not lost their famous sparkle, but his face was more pinched than usual.' 'One thing led to another' as Švejk might have said, and both went off to Lipnice together. But in fact the move must have been more carefully prepared than that; as long ago as in May, Hašek had been writing to Jarmila of his intention to find somewhere to go for the summer and the Sázava valley was one of the spots mentioned.

He had every reason to wish to escape from Prague—the disdainful frowns of the establishment, the disparaging remarks of the press, the unpleasant sensation of being tailed by the police, his failing health and possibly too, some agitated scenes at home after Shura had found out that he was seeing a lot of Jarmila.

Hašek and Panuška walked from the railway station to Lipnice, but spent most of the journey in the shelter and comfort of wayside inns. In this way a walk which would have normally lasted only an hour and a half took them five, because Hašek continually complained of being footsore and thirsty and ordered rounds of beer for all the guests at every inn they visited. 'Man proposes, but an inn transposes' was his cheerful comment. But in spite of this they were able to see something of the beauty of the surroundings before darkness fell. The black and jagged silhouette of Lipnice castle stood out against the purple horizon and Hašek was captivated by the sight.

Invald, the landlord of the Czech Crown, Lipnice's one decent inn, had prepared a small room for Panuška, who told him that Hašek could sleep with him for the first night and after that a bed should be made up for him in the adjoining room. The landlord had never seen Hašek before and eyed him with some suspicion, because he was shabbily dressed, had no luggage with him and did not look at all like a 'writer gentleman', but Panuška soon convinced him that the stranger was someone to be properly cared for. Later the landlord was to become devoted to him.[2]

The peace and quiet of Lipnice appealed to Hašek: it was exactly what he needed. But his reaction was typical. 'Now I live bang in the middle of a pub. Nothing better could have happened to me.' Panuška prevailed upon Invald to grant Hašek a credit of up to 500 crowns, which was a great relief to him, as he not only had brought no money with him, but was in fact penniless. Both friends enjoyed themselves hugely, eating, drinking, going for walks in the neighbourhood and swopping stories. Panuška painted and Hašek carried his easel and palette. Hašek grew very fond of the artist and missed him very much when he went back to Prague, which he did at intervals. In order to lure him back he appointed himself Panuška's 'meteorological agent'. At first he carried out the assignment conscientiously, but later in the typical Hašek fashion sent him bogus weather predictions in the hope that they would induce him to come back to Lipnice.[3]

One of their favourite haunts was Lipnice castle, with its sweeping views on the one side of the beautiful Sázava and its woods, and on the other of the undulating Bohemian–Moravian Highlands. Its custodian at that time, the Chief Forester Bohm, lent them the key, so that they could get in whenever they liked. Later they would light fires in the courtyard, grill sausages and potatoes, and sing old Austrian songs.

Hašek made the castle the scene of some of his idiosyncratic pranks, and once held a drinking party in it with Panuška and a local schoolmaster. After darkness had fallen the schoolmaster fell asleep in a befuddled state somewhere in a corner and was forgotten. None too steady on their feet, Hašek and Panuška locked up the castle and went back to the inn. Shortly afterwards people came running up to say that the castle was haunted; a white figure had been seen running along the battlements and calling for help. Hašek suggested it might be a deserter from the former Austrian army and sent word to Bohm to bring his gun. One would have thought that he would have taken a more merciful view of deserters. As soon as he saw the excited figure on the battlements, he shouted out that it was the White Lady of Rožmberk (an apparition supposed to haunt all castles in Bohemia) and loudly urged Bohm to shoot the phantom and 'liberate' her. When they finally unlocked the castle gate, the unhappy schoolmaster was literally trembling with fright.

Hašek's more colourful version of this episode is given in one of his letters to Sauer in Prague. 'On Monday I arranged a huge festival of chivalry in the castle, where everybody got so frightfully drunk that a schoolteacher fell from the bridge and broke his neck. His widow has just been to see me and asked me to pay the expenses of the funeral. I gave her a copy of *Švejk* to assuage her pain and grief.' Here speaks the Hašek of earlier days.

He often used to sit in the big old hall of the castle and write. Anxious to study its history he sent out one day for a guide book. The local bookseller brought it to him at the inn himself. A discussion then took place, in the course of which the bookseller spoke slightingly of Lenin and Trotsky. For a long time Hašek took no notice, but when the bookseller became more and more impassioned he suddenly shouted at him: 'Shut up or I'll slap your face. Do you really know them? Have you actually read their writings? Did you ever hear *me* insult Kramář or Rašín?'*

But the bookseller refused to give in and so Hašek carried out his threat. There was an embarrassed silence afterwards. Invald looked darkly at Hašek: 'I can't forgive you for that, Jarda. You really shouldn't have done it. He didn't mean it badly, and he's many years older than you are. I'm not going to let you have any more drink.' Hašek paced nervously up and down the room, his hands behind his back. Suddenly he stopped, put his head in his hands and said: 'I ought never to have done it. I shouldn't have hit him.' Then he rushed towards the frightened bookseller. 'Listen, you must give me one back.' 'Better forget about it,' said the bookseller crossly. 'You're a fine one, I must say, but at least I'm glad that I've learned the sort of chap you are.' 'I ask you for the last time to give me one back,' Hašek insisted. 'If you don't do so this very instant, I'll smash your jaw again.' Invald, seeing more trouble brewing, lifted up the bookseller's right hand and somehow brought it down gently on

* Political leaders of the bourgeois parties in Czechoslovakia.

Hašek's cheek. 'All right, now we're quits,' said Hašek with a happy sigh.[4]

Meanwhile, while Hašek was enjoying himself at Lipnice, Shura and Sauer were turning Prague upside down hunting for him. But glad as he was to be away from Shura, he could not shut her completely out of his mind for long. And so one midnight he sat down and wrote her a letter, giving her his address and suggesting she should come and join him. Impulsively he took it off immediately to the post office, which happened to be on the first floor of the inn, waking up the postmistress who slept in the hotel. But by the next morning he had had second thoughts and tried desperately to retrieve the letter but in vain. The deed had been done.

Shura's arrival with all her nagging and fuss put paid to Hašek's halcyon days. It was some relief that Sauer came with her, but he did not stay long. And when in the end Panuška had to return to work in his Prague *atelier*, Hašek felt doubly miserable. Another reason for his gloom was that the credit he had received was now exhausted and he was hard pressed for funds. On October 22nd, 1921, he wrote an appealing letter to Sauer in Prague:

'Dear Franta, my golden boy,

'I am sending you for the present five pages (of *Švejk* of course) and tomorrow there will be more. I am utterly alone here. Panuška is in Prague and so it is only now that the real work begins, because I have got through all my visits. For God's sake, I implore you by all the saints and in memory of the Emperor Francis Joseph, send me some money, because we are two of us here now, Shurinka and I. I haven't got a single heller and if I want to post a letter I have to borrow the money for the stamp, and it's a frightful disgrace for me, because I am, as you well know, a very orderly man . . .

'. . . If you can, my joy, come here some day. I'm frightfully sad here . . .'[5]

Sauer sent him 400 crowns, but insisted that Hašek must in return supply him with further instalments of *Švejk*. This produced the following reply:

'My dear, dear Franta,

'I am sending you for the time being nine pages, which I wrote yesterday and today till twelve o'clock, when the post went. In the afternoon I shall go on writing and I shall certainly send you further pages tomorrow. I have developed an unusual appetite for writing and please don't forget me, but come and see me definitely as you promised—not on Monday, but, better still on Sunday! You must admit that I am in a very disagreeable situation: I don't want to be in debt to anyone and undermine our reputation, when I've got to remain here until I've completed the book. Now I have really recovered my zest for work and I assure you I shall make every possible effort to make it a success. Do come and you will see what an energetic mood I am in . . . I am longing so much to see you, Franta, because I am sincerely fond of you.'

In spite of this appeal Sauer did not arrive until the Monday. He had only come to get out of Hašek further instalments of *Švejk*, but he had to return to Prague without them, utterly exhausted as well by the pub-crawling Hašek had dragged him off on. But Hašek could not or would not write on order. Panuška suggested to Sauer that they should get Bohm to lure him into his forester's lodge with the bait of good food and drink and then lock him up until he had done his 'homework'. Bohm tried this on, posting a second forester on guard and refusing to allow Hašek out until he had produced the prescribed number of pages. But when they opened up, they found the prisoner happily enjoying a bottle of cognac. He had not written a single line. This trick would not work on him. The explorer Frič had already tried it.

When Hašek scalded his hand, it seemed at first likely that this would prove yet another obstacle to his getting on with the job. But it probably speeded things up, because he had to engage a secretary and chose the twenty-year-old son of the local police officer, Kliment Štěpánek. They made an agreement to work from nine till twelve every morning and from three till five every afternoon. The conscientious Štěpánek, who became Hašek's devoted slave and addressed him as 'Maestro', related:

'The next day I came punctually at nine o'clock, as had been agreed. Hašek was still asleep. Because Mrs Shura was also sleeping, I could not get into the rooms. When I knocked at the door, Hašek woke up and, when it dawned on him at last that it was me, he asked me to come again in an hour's time. And so I did, and it was the same story all over again. Hašek called out from his bed: "Jesus, I want to sleep. Come back in an hour's time—or perhaps even better, come in the afternoon!" '

Štěpánek often came and left again without being given any work to do at all. Sometimes Hašek did not even get up in the afternoon, and when he did, wrote very little. 'I tried to catch [him], so that I could remind him of his work, but he seldom listened to my suggestions. It depended mostly on his mood.'

Štěpánek soon stopped coming in the morning, because he found it a waste of time. And then of course one day he found Hašek already sitting at the table, waiting for him and smiling. 'We're early for once, aren't we?' he exclaimed. But before they could get started, Shura had first to bring tea from the Invalds and pour out *slivovice* for Hašek. Only then did they eventually settle down to work. Štěpánek was looking forward to his new assignment and was curious to know how Hašek would actually set about writing *Švejk*, but on that day he did not learn anything.

' "Today we'll let Švejk sleep a little and write something shorter," Hašek announced to his disappointment.

'We went on talking about quite everyday things and in the meantime I prepared paper, pen and ink. Then Hašek suddenly got up, began to walk up and down the room in a very small space, put his hands behind his back and said, "All right, now we're starting! Don't write any title. Just leave a space and we'll fill it in later, according to what it turns out to be." '

'Once he dictated to me in the inn while at the same time having a quarrel with a guest. In situations like these I often had to ask him repeatedly about a sentence.'

Or he might sit in the company of Panuška and other local friends including a schoolmaster who was teaching Shura Czech, when he would talk very excitedly with them and simultaneously dictate.[6]

At this rate things did not look very promising for Sauer, whose position was desperate: he was already practically bankrupt, creditors were hot on his heels and the whole publishing business was gradually grinding to a halt. Not only was he left by Hašek to bear the brunt of all this, but he was exposed in addition to the reproaches of Hašek's friends for not having given the author the money he was allegedly entitled to. Shura had her knife into him as well for having smuggled letters to Hašek from Jarmila. In the end Sauer got tired of Hašek's repeated begging letters and his failure to send him further instalments of *Švejk*, and the publishing house of Hašek, Sauer and Co. was dissolved by mutual agreement. The printing and distribution of *Švejk* was henceforth to be in the hands of another publisher, Synek. But Sauer lived to regret his hasty action: he had opted out just as the book was beginning to catch on. After the appearance of the first volume interest in it had grown, and more and more copies were printed. Next year the first volume would appear in five editions and the second in four. The third volume, which Hašek was to write in the spring of 1922, would appear at the end of the year in two editions. The fourth volume would be published in 1923 after Hašek's death.

After breaking with one of his friends Hašek now picked a quarrel with another. Sauer had told him that in Prague he had gone to see the première of a dramatic version of *Švejk*, put on by Longen at the Adria without the author's permission and now enjoying a great box-office success. Hašek immediately wrote Longen a letter of protest, couched in his own inimitable style.

November 4th, 1921

'Dear Friend,

'I've just learnt from some newspapers of November 1st that on the 2nd of this month the première took place in the Adria of *The Good Soldier Švejk in the World War* by J. Hašek. This has been confirmed to me by my friend, Sauer, who was present at a performance.

'He praised the production and assured me that it was very well done and that you had taken great care that everything, down to the smallest dialogues, should be faithful to the text.

'To the best of my memory, however, we have had no contact at all since December last year, and our chance meeting in the Union a little later concluded with very odd behaviour on the part of both of us, by which we apparently wished to make it clear that we did not know each other any more.

'I am therefore all the more surprised that you suddenly remember me and are putting on the stage a work which at that time I did not even know I should ever write.

'I remember very well that I promised to write something for you, which I shall certainly do, and that I signed a receipt for 300 crowns in advance for it. But you must admit that it was not for you that I wrote *The Good Soldier Švejk* and you are therefore putting it on without my knowledge. You did not even ask me about it. You have just done nothing but shit on me. I shall forgive you under the following conditions, which are hard and inexorable:

1 You are to write off those 300 crowns and send me back my receipt by return of post. This is a fine imposed on you for not having asked my permission.

2 You are to send me at once a substantial amount in advance (because you've already given Franta Sauer one) and you are to do it by telegraph . . .

3 The sum of money you are going to send me (and don't think in terms of a paltry 500 crowns!) is to be an advance on the daily receipts from each performance which you negotiated with Sauer to the amount of 10 crowns.

4 The postal receipt for the advance sent to me under the above conditions can be regarded as my permission for you to produce my play.

'Otherwise, if I do not receive the money at once by Tuesday, November 8th, I shall forbid the performance. You know that I am a swine!

Yours,
Jaroslav Hašek

'Love to Xena! Shura sends her love and remembers the fish soup.'

What had happened was that on that first Christmas Eve after Hašek's return to Czechoslovakia, when Hašek and Shura were guests of the Longens, Hašek had promised Longen to write some sketches for his Revolutionary Theatre and accepted a small advance from him. When the first volume of *Švejk* appeared, Longen remembered this promise and put on a dramatised version of it. At first he had wanted to produce it at the open air theatre at Šárka near Prague with the famous Prague comedian, Vlasta Burián, as Švejk, but as he was unable to engage him, he put it on in the Adria with Karel Noll in the leading role. But Longen had jumped the gun: his dramatisation of *Švejk* had nothing to do with Hašek's promise.[7]

On receipt of this menacing letter Longen decided to go to Lipnice with his wife and talk things over. Recalling the impression Hašek's physical appearance made on him he wrote:

'He had become surprisingly fat since his flight from Prague and gave the impression to people who didn't know him of a crank who was tramping round the world. His legs were stuck right up to the knees in huge felt boots. On his body he wore a jersey, a long-tailed black coat of old-fashioned cut and an overcoat which was so tight that he could not button it up. His face had acquired a fleshier and tubbier appearance and an unnatural shininess, as though from frost-bite. He suffered from great lassitude and every movement seemed to tire him.'

Longen hoped he would be able to get from Hašek if not the dramatic sketches promised to him, at least some fresh ideas for a New Year's programme. Hašek offered him two pieces. The first of them, *The Minister and his Child*, was banned by the censors shortly before it was going to be staged. And so as a substitute Hašek quickly wrote the second—*From Karlín to Bratislava in 365 Days*. Again the performance was vetoed at the last minute. Neither of these plays or sketches has in the final count been attributed to Hašek. *The Minister and his Child* is now to be found among Longen's collected works, Hašek's original piece having been considerably adapted by him, and the other play is attributed to E. E. Kisch, on whose original work it was based.[8]

Hašek could not surely ever have imagined in his most optimistic moments that *The Minister and his Child* would be allowed in Prague. It dealt with a supposed row between the Czechoslovak Foreign Minister and an explorer A. B. Frik, a character who was obviously drawn from Hašek's one time benefactor A. V. Frič—another example of Hašek's ingratitude.

In the play the Foreign Minister refuses to appoint Frik ambassador in some faraway country among the Indians. In revenge Frik bombards the public with scurrilous leaflets abusing the Foreign Minister. When these have no success, he resorts to occult means which he had learnt from the Indians, and turns the Minister and his staff into fantastic animals. To stop this the chief of the secret police breaks into Frik's villa in disguise, but himself falls a victim to the explorer's occult powers. Frik then writes another scandalous leaflet called *The Minister and his Child*, in which reference is made to the 'rotten fruits' of the Minister's foreign policy. This is taken literally by the Foreign Minister's wife, who suspects her husband of infidelity, she herself having been made pregnant by the Minister's secretary.

The chief of the secret police orders the leaflets to be confiscated and this leads to the arrest for incitement of the Foreign Minister's greengrocer mother-in-law, who has bought up a hundredweight of them to wrap her vegetables in. The error is explained and the lady is released, after which she gives her son-in-law a piece of her mind. Finally the explorer achieves his aim and is appointed ambassador in New Zealand, where he becomes a dutiful citizen, loyal to the government of the Republic. The references to the greengrocer mother of the Foreign Minister's wife were meant to point to Mrs Beneš.

The story of the Kisch play was also topical. It dealt with the adventurous voyage of a small steamboat which sailed from Prague to Hamburg along the Vltava and Elbe, crossed two oceans and returned to Bratislava via the Danube. Hašek made his own embroidery on Kisch's narrative.[9]

It was in December, while the Longens were still at Lipnice, that Hašek's old friend Hájek suddenly turned up. He had been sent to address a political meeting at Lipnice and knowing that Hašek lived there wrote and asked him about the local political situation. In reply he received a long and excited letter from Hašek about the local political groups in which he urged Hájek to come to Lipnice, hold a meeting there and put things right. But as the letter bore the mark 'secret' Hájek suspected the mark of the old hoaxer's cloven hoof.

When Hájek finally arrived at the Czech Crown his attention was immediately caught by a poster of a huge drawing of Švejk. It was a theatre poster from the Adria.

'How did that poster get here?' he asked the innkeeper. 'Why, Mr Hašek lives here and at the moment Mr and Mrs Longen from the Adria theatre are staying here too. Mr Longen is writing a new play with Mr Hašek about a Mr Minister. But Mr Hašek is waiting to see you. I'll tell him at once that you are here.'

When Hašek appeared, he looked like a Russian *muzhik*. He had his *valenki* on, which reached up to his thighs, and he was so fat that it almost took Hájek's breath away. Overjoyed to see his friend again Hašek wanted very much to come and hear him speak at the meeting, but Hájek was not having any and made him promise to stay away. He was scared of a practical joke. After the meeting they spent a happy evening together exchanging memories of their days at the Commercial Academy.[10]

After Hájek had gone back to Prague Hašek began arranging evening parties, for which he usually brewed his famous 'sailors' grog' (so strong that 'after taking it you could swim the English Channel'). His special recipe was as follows (in his own words): 'Bring to the boil half a litre of water together with two or three allspice corns, six to eight peppercorns, ten cloves, a piece of cinnamon, a small piece of lemon peel and the juice of one whole lemon. Add a pound of sugar. After boiling add six pints of white wine and bring to the boil. Then add two pints of cognac and bring it near boiling point again. Be careful not to let it boil over. Then put it on the table close at hand. Take the lid off for a moment, light the aromatic vapours and put the lid on again. That's the end of the ritual. And if someone tells you to add vanilla give him one across the jaw.'

He also went on writing *Švejk* and when friends like Panuška came to see him sometimes read part of it. Panuška would pat him on the back and say appreciatively: 'You've got something good there, you old cow.'

On New Year's Eve Hašek was busy making preparations for a special performance. Local amateurs had come to ask him to write some couplets for it, but when he found to his disappointment that they wanted him to buy tickets and provide some songs but not perform himself, he decided to stage a rival evening of his own at the inn. When the day arrived, he went repeatedly to the kitchen to see whether there would be enough wine for the midnight drink. But the festivity proved a flop as very few guests turned up. In the end he was reduced to acting before a few workers from the local quarry who had come to the inn late in order to play cards. He could only induce them to leave their game and listen to his couplets by promising that he would pay for everything they ate and drank.

His desire to make cabaret appearances, so misjudged, only distracted him from his literary work. None the less, all things considered and for all Sauer's complaints, one cannot help admiring the speed with which he wrote. He probably started the second volume of *Švejk* in Lipnice in about mid-September 1921. In a letter written on January 16th, 1922 he said he was just beginning to write the third volume.

In the New Year Hašek and Shura returned with the Longens on a short visit to Prague. When they arrived there they found that the Revolutionary Theatre had been closed by the police. Hašek and Longen went round the ministries trying to get permission for it to go on and for *The Minister and his Child* to be presented. But after several failures they gave up and thought out other ways of getting money. In the course of their discussions Hašek quarrelled with Longen once again and their collaboration came to an end.

Shura went to see Synek, to whom she could talk because he knew Russian. Hašek refused to see him, declaring to Shura that he was not going to beg for what he was entitled to. Both were convinced that he was robbing them.

During his week in Prague Hašek could not resist revisiting some of his old haunts. In one of them he had an argument with a Czech general about the role of the Czech Legion in Russia and at Šnor's he persuaded the proprietor to let him have some drinks on tick with the help of a merry pseudo-nursery rhyme: 'Šnor, Šnor, you're from Baltimore.'[11]

Thanks to his new agreement with Synek he was now obtaining a regular income and his economic position was better. Even if he felt he ought to be getting more, he was at least able to pay off his debts and modestly improve his wardrobe, which up to that time had consisted of shabby clothes preserved from Russia and some others given to him by Bohm. Most of the time he went about in a dirty grey Russian soft tunic, a peaked cap and the inevitable *valenki*. Towards the end he took to wearing an extraordinary pyramid shaped 'homburg' hat with a broad coloured band. From Prague he brought back with him a new blue suit, a grey hat and a stick with a silver knob. He had two suits made in Lipnice, one for himself and one for his secretary Štěpánek, but they were made of thin lustre wool and there were soon two enormous patches on his trousers which became a stock joke. People told him he looked like a miner about to go down the pit. Since he was so fat and sweated a lot in the summer, he had a comfortable check shirt made for him which he fastened with a blue cord and a tassel.

After the row with Longen, the actor Karel Noll asked Hašek for the rights to perform *Švejk*. He had been the leading member of the Revolutionary Theatre and after its dissolution decided to form his own group out of the actors who had been dismissed. Hašek, who was still in financial straits at the time, gave his consent to Noll's production in the nearby town of Německý Brod.*

The performance, which was in three parts and lasted for three whole evenings, had great success with the public. At the première Hašek, Shura and his best friends in Lipnice sat upstairs in the gallery, but Hašek could not see properly and had continually to lean forward, so the management cleared the whole of the first row of the stalls for them, and they moved down. After the performance, exhilarated by the success of the piece, he appeared several times on the stage hand in hand with Noll to thank the public. He also held a small reception in the local hotel and even offered to act the part of Sapper Vodička himself, although the offer was not taken up.[12]

In his excitement Hašek had forgotten that nearly a year previously he had given the rights to another theatre director, Antonín Fencl. When the latter learned of the infringement he rushed off to Lipnice and negotiated a contract for the exclusive dramatic and film rights for the sum of 5,000 crowns, of which Hašek obtained an advance of 1,500 crowns in cash. The contract was finally signed on August 13th. In the appendix to the agreement it was specifically stated that the play must not be performed without Fencl's permission. Noll was passed over.

The Longens' relations with Hašek were now finally terminated. Shortly afterwards they ran out of money and emigrated

* Today Havlíčkův Brod.

to Germany. They never saw Hašek again, but Longen wrote and illustrated a fanciful and not very charitable book about him in 1928. However, Hašek's business inconsistencies could not escape their judicial consequences. The conflicting claims between the three claimants were heard in the district court. Each of them had apparently sued the other!

Other contenders for Hašek's, or rather Švejk's hand who came to Lipnice were: Rudolf Mařík, who later dramatised Švejk's adventures for Fencl in the Adria and brought them up to date by introducing contemporary events (one scene for instance was called *Švejk at the Peace Conference in Geneva*); the film director Rovenský, who came to discuss a Švejk film; and Synek and his wife, who brought Hašek money with which he could pay his debts to his old friends Opočenský and Kuděj, who came to Lipnice to spend their holidays and relive fellow vagabond days of old. Finally in the middle of June Hašek's younger brother, Bohuslav, came for the first time. This alcoholic's stay was celebrated by a gargantuan drinking bout.

According to Shura, Hašek went and addressed a political meeting for gypsies at Humpolec which was enlivened by gypsy music. She claims that he spoke to them of the way the Soviet government had solved the problem of nationalities by giving them the same rights as the majority enjoyed and providing them with newspapers in their languages or dialects. The meeting did not turn out too well for Hašek, because he ended his speech with the words: 'When there is Communism in Czechoslovakia we shall show the world', and the gypsies were not impressed.

Signs of serious illness were becoming apparent in Hašek. Invald recalls that his legs had begun to swell and that he had difficulties in going upstairs. He had always been fat, even when he was young, but now his body appeared unhealthily bloated. Shura remembers that he weighed nearly twenty-four stone when they moved in. Moreover a very unusual and alarming thing had happened: he had lost his appetite. He tried to conceal this from the Invalds and went on ordering heavily spiced dishes, only to leave them untouched or smuggle them away somehow. His gluttony was a source of vanity to him (after all, had he not persuaded Panuška to make a personal book-plate for him of a boar's head on a dish?) and any sign of weakness on this score was like a confession of unmanliness.[13] Sometimes when he was dictating he was overcome by a fit of vomiting. He was indeed seriously ill, although he continued to deny it, attributing the swellings of his legs to rheumatism and his stomach ailments to overdoses of aspirin.

A year earlier Jarmila had noticed on one of the last expeditions he made with her that he got tired and out of breath at the slightest effort. Longen, on his first visit to Lipnice, had observed that when Hašek drank black coffee with rum a thick sweat formed on his flushed face. 'He walked round the room choking with his cough and then rushed out of the door into the fresh air . . . He couldn't sleep on the bed in his room, but sat down in the inn near an open window, where he slept until dawn. Naturally we tried to persuade him to stop drinking and go for walks, but he wouldn't listen.'[14]

It had always been hard to persuade him to accept advice. He refused to see a doctor and have himself examined. Nor could Shura persuade him to keep to a diet. 'He should never have eaten spiced and acid dishes,' she recalled, 'but he was very fond of gherkins and the brine from them. He even crept down in the night secretly to drink it in the Invalds' larder.' His favourite dish was what he liked to call 'The Cat's Dance' which consisted of chopped boiled potatoes, chopped grilled frankfurters and chopped hard-boiled eggs mixed together and fried in fat. It was heavily seasoned with pepper and salt and washed down by beer.

It seemed too that the bohemian was at last tired of being a vagabond. Shura said of him: 'He got sick of living and eating in an inn. He said that in his declining years he'd like at least to have a roof over his head.' When he had secured himself financially by his contract for *Švejk* he bought a small house just below Lipnice castle in the summer of 1922. It was a curious building which had grown out of the knocking together of several outbuildings and was set on a slope, so that on one side Hašek could get straight out on the road from the top floor without going down any steps. It had four exits, one at every point of the compass. He liked the idea of being able to get out easily and talk to passers-by. His friends had tried to dissuade him from buying it; it would probably be cheaper, they said, to build a new house than to try to restore it, but he would not listen. He thought that he could make a work-room for himself upstairs, while Shura could have the rooms below. As the local builder worked too slowly for his taste, he even hired two extra bricklayers under his own personal control. Once he took Štěpánek with him to the site, sent him back at once for writing material and made him write on a barrel not far from the bricklayers.

When in the autumn of 1922 he finally moved in, he occupied only one room on the lower floor, which was study, sitting room and bedroom all combined. His new bedroom furniture of larch-wood was stored away on the floor above. He claimed that he did not have enough money for the time being to buy mat-tresses and so until the very end of his life he slept on a spring bedstead near the window, which he used to rest on during the day and dictate *Švejk*.

From the windows of his room he had a glorious view of one of the most picturesque corners of the Bohemian—Moravian Highlands, the same view he had enjoyed from the castle, which was indeed the reason for his having chosen the site of the house. The table and chair in his room were copied from old Czech furniture in the castle too. Unfortunately they could not stand up to the strain imposed on them by his drinking parties.[15]

In the late summer Hašek had made a journey in the region with Shura and a friend of hers in a carriage with a coachman lent by Bohm. On a postcard to Panuška he wrote: 'My com-panions can hardly cry, they are so tired . . . Today I've done twenty-two miles.'

So keen was he to have company that he was quite offended if any of his friends declined an invitation. There is a story that on one occasion he took out something like a revolver and aimed it at one of his guests shouting: 'Jesus Mary, Tonda, I shan't let you go anywhere else. You'll stay here and you'll drink!' Al-though it proved in the end to be only the big key from the castle, the guest turned pale and gave in.

Although his health continued to deteriorate, neither he nor anyone else seriously thought that his life was at risk. He was looking forward to planting flowers in his garden in the spring and various other activities.

His conviviality persisted almost to the end. If there was any feast on in the neighbourhood, he could not resist going there. When in the middle of November he heard that a Martinmas

Feast was to be held in the inn at a nearby village, he hired a conveyance and set out on the journey with Štěpánek, who recalled:

'We had to carry Hašek out to the carriage, and, because it was very cold indeed, we wrapped him up well. We came to the village and arrived at the inn, where the feast was being held. Hašek ordered the driver to stop and tried to get up, and, when he found he couldn't, Shura and I helped him and supported him so he shouldn't fall. As he stood up in the carriage he suddenly felt an urge to perform his lesser needs. There were quite a lot of spectators around and indeed at that very moment a group of girls were passing. When they saw Hašek's unconventional behaviour they ran away tittering. Hašek thought it was great fun and called after the girls: "Now then, girls, what about it?" '[16]

Although his health did not permit him to take a full part in the feast he enjoyed himself playing cards with his friends all night and was in high humour the whole time. The party returned home at five o'clock in the morning, put Hašek to bed and had to light the fire in the stove quickly so that he could get warmed up a bit.

By the end of November any further journeys were out of the question. He could not even get from his house to the inn. He arranged instead an inn in his home. He had a servant by this time and would send her to invite his cronies to come for a drink (and not only just a drink). If she could not get hold of any of his friends, she was ordered to go to the inn and invite everybody who was sitting there. Sometimes this included the inn-keeper himself. Hašek hardly ever went out now except for a few steps which he took round the house.

On Christmas Day Mrs Invald went to see him and noticed that his condition had strikingly deteriorated. His face was ashen grey and he had difficulty in talking.[17] Shura said that he had great pains and was often silent for hours on end. He used to say to her: 'Švejk is suffering.' None the less a lot of snow had fallen and putting on his *valenki* he sallied forth to shovel it from the path round the house. He even sent Štěpánek to Humpolec on Boxing Day to buy sledges so that they could go sledging, as

Shura and he had done in Russia. After Christmas however his condition took a serious turn for the worse. At last he consented to a thorough examination by a doctor. But even so he refused to follow the doctor's instructions and made repeated efforts to struggle up and down the room. The doctor complained that if he did not observe the treatment, he would never complete *Švejk*. Hašek replied that he would only die when he allowed Švejk to die and this he would never permit because Švejk would live for ever among the Czechs.[18]

By New Year's Eve the snow had melted and he was looking forward to the usual celebration in the evening. He dictated for a whole morning in a recumbent position, sitting up for a while in the afternoon, but he was very fidgety. He continually went into the kitchen to try to direct the preparations for the feast and to send the servant to fetch some small things from the inn. In the evening he suddenly began to feel worse. His guests noticed that he had difficulty in breathing and was making an effort to conceal it from them. He apologised to them for being unable even to speak and promised he would be better by Twelfth Night, when he would arrange a proper entertainment.

But by now his condition was grave. He could not keep down anything he ate. The doctor ordered him to drink nothing but milk. Visitors who came to see him for a short time saw on his table no other liquid than a bottle of mineral water, used as a laxative, and milk. As he drank the milk he is supposed to have said: 'Lightning strike the cow that first let herself be milked.'

The next day he was so ill that he would have nobody with him except Shura, nor could he get anything down. The doctor was summoned and they brought his bed down from the room above. Up till then he had gone on lying on the spring bedstead pushed near the window.

During the night he lay in agony. He breathed with more and more difficulty and had the death rattle. The doctor advised that his relatives should be immediately informed.

He woke up and fell into a coma again. When he regained consciousness, he began to weep. In the night he is said to have begged for a sip of cognac, but the doctor refused and offered him a glass of milk instead: 'But you're cheating me,' Hašek said reproachfully, and then his breathing stopped. This was on January 3rd, 1923.

The doctor gave the following account of his last hours:

'I treated Jaroslav Hašek for about four weeks before his death. The day before he died I was called to him at eleven o'clock in the morning and found his heart was failing. I was with him several times that day and stayed with him the whole night. He was lying down. In the night he got up and wanted to make his will. He sat at a table and took a pen in his hand. But when I saw how difficult it was for him to write, I told him I would do it for him. He dictated his last will and I took it down in the presence of the cook and servant. Then I read it out and Hašek himself read it again, signed it and corrected two mistakes. Then the two women and I signed it as witnesses. He was calm and in his right mind. At five o'clock in the morning I went home and woke up the mayor. When I came back at eight o'clock Hašek was already unconscious and the Mayor signed his will in my presence.'

On the death certificate the cause of death was given as pneumonia and heart failure. Hašek had apparently contracted pneumonia from lying in bed so long and not from shovelling snow outside at Christmas as some people had imagined. But the cause must have lain deeper—probably it was cirrhosis of the liver.

Among the draft letters which he left behind was one addressed to the district police:

'I, the undersigned, ask respectfully to be kindly given the necessary passport for a stay in Spain (Barcelona, Calle Rosellos) with a view to improving my state of health on the urgent advice of the examining doctor, Dr Novák, and the district doctor, Dr Ressel. I intend to stay in Barcelona with my brother-in-law, A. Bejček, in the hope that adequate home and medical care and a mild climate will permit me to return cured after three months. I shall travel via Germany and France. I hope that the police will not delay the granting of my request, so that I can escape as quickly as possible from this harsh climate which is so bad for my health.'

Hoaxer to the last, Hašek had no brother-in-law in Barcelona.

He was referring to one of his former Anarchist friends who often used to take refuge in Spain. According to Longen he had some idea of writing a play set in Spain on the model of a piece which a painter friend from Barcelona had sent him. One of the main characters was to be a mendicant friar and Karel Noll would play the role. Hašek wanted to show the world that he could write serious drama. He would call his piece a newly discovered play by Calderon, and only if it had good reviews would he disclose that he was the real author. He never got round to writing it, but the idea may have prompted the letter.

The Good Soldier Švejk remained unfinished. No doubt he could have completed it, if he had taken care of his health in good time, and if he had changed his way of life. But as Pytlík has aptly said: 'If he had done so, there would not have been the same Hašek and perhaps not the same Švejk either.' In the morning and afternoon of New Year's Eve he had dictated his last story, about a collector of taxes for pig feasts. He never finished it and the manuscript cannot be traced.

(18)

The Bad Bohemian Hasek

If Švejk is a cryptic character, his creator is for most of us even more of an enigma. Can we understand him any better after following him through all the stages of his turbulent life?

After reading the testimony of Jarmila and his best friends, we find that much is left unexplained. One reason for this, of course, is that he wrote so little himself about his inner feelings and very few witnesses were interested enough to want to probe beneath his captivating and often bewildering exterior. Why should they spoil the fun by encouraging introspection either on his part or theirs?

To most sober-minded readers he must appear unbelievably reckless, the architect of his own unhappiness and final doom. Even Jarmila, who knew him better than anyone else and was his most indulgent critic, blamed his misfortunes on his ir-responsibility, although she excused it as the inevitable price which had to be paid for originality.

There is a tendency among Czech critics to shift the blame from him to the circumstances of his youth. But the misfortunes and possible deprivations of his boyhood pale before those which Dickens suffered, with his father in prison and his mother left to support eight children. Indeed Hašek was in some ways lucky to have had so many chances offered him. Clearly the careers of chemist or bank official were not for him, but it would not have harmed him to try them out a bit longer. It did no harm to Dickens to have to earn his living by doing menial jobs or to work for a short time as a solicitor's clerk. Nor did Gogol's or Ostrovsky's humour suffer because one worked in an office and another in the law courts. Indeed, since Hašek's stories deal so much with people in stereotyped jobs, more experience of the humdrum daily round might well have provided him with a richer fund of material. Finally, there was no reason why, like

Dickens did with Pickwick, Hašek should not have tried to anticipate his success with Švejk by publishing in his twenties a humorous novel in instalments. At that early period it could not have been *Švejk*, because Hašek had had no experience of military life, but it could have been something else. But this is only one of the many 'whys' and 'why nots' which keep on intruding themselves when one tries to unravel the mystery of his life.

What principally clouds our vision of Hašek is that he was a dual, if not multiple personality. On the one hand there was the joker and hoaxer—light-hearted, irresponsible and incorrigible —and on the other the over-sensitive inner man who was full of resentment about his failure in life but who would not apparently accept the blame for it. And there was perhaps a third Hašek, who when confronted from time to time with the full horror of his mishandled life could admit to Jarmila, and only to her, that the blame rested solely with himself.

His friends were only conscious of two facets. The Czech novelist Eduard Bass who had been one of his bohemian companions in his youth, wrote: 'In Hašek there were always two persons: one played the fool and the other looked on. The other Hašek, whom very few managed to look in the eyes, saw with frightening certainty the futility of human existence and, having apprehended it, tried to deny it, muzzle it, escape from it, or beguile it with jokes, which were generated by the first Hašek. His magnificent comedy was, in fact, tragedy.'[1]

Langer, who knew him well for most of his life, said he had two smiles—one human and spontaneous, which reflected his contentment with the world at the time. This was 'the innocent laughter of an infant'. He never roared with laughter or uttered loud guffaws, but laughed within himself. The other smile was that of the clown and mimic, and it accompanied and underlined the ridiculous in what he was narrating: it was a roguish, clownish, cunning and foxy leer. Neither of these smiles was a sign of good-will. On the contrary Hašek's most unkind actions could be accompanied by the sweetest of them.[2] The face Jarmila saw was a different one. 'The basic trait of his character,' she wrote, 'was not gaiety, cynicism or high spirits. It was softness, quick changes of mood, immediate acclimatisation, the urge to attract attention, to ridicule or caricature. Life paid him back all the kicks he gave and he pined for thunderous applause to deaden the cries and groans within him.' The bitter undertone in so many of his stories was to be explained, she said, by the fact that it was his own grief he was really laughing at. 'My life is such a confounded zig-zag,' he wrote to her when he had returned from Russia and was trying to explain why he had not written to her all those years. These words, she said, concealed a deep melancholy. 'His smile was not the smile of a naive and good-natured man, who smiles because he is happy. It said: "I'm smiling so as not to weep".'[3]

With the good intentions he had it seems clear that there must have been something he could not help, something within him he could not control. Did he have to struggle with physical or psychological inhibitions?

He had indeed some peculiar physical characteristics. As his photographs reveal, his appearance changed astonishingly little from puberty onwards. Outwardly he remained the perpetual adolescent with a pink round face, which was almost beardless and seldom needed a shave. He could easily be taken for a girl and sometimes was. There were occasions when he would pretend to be one or act a female part at a cabaret. Inwardly too he seemed to have stayed fixed in the pre-pubertal stage, of which he gave many small but revealing signs. He could not resist getting up to mischief, loved practical jokes and horse-play and seemed to relish lavatory humour. How many of his characters in his short stories are 'caught short' and their succeeding troubles made the main point of the story? In one a patriotic Czech is forced by an urgent call to descend from the cart carrying him to a national rally. Unfortunately the tree he chooses happens to be the oak which the Czech hero Žižka planted and he commits the unheard of sacrilege of defiling this monument. Jarmila argued in his defence that he was not like that with her and that even in the intimacy of the home he never used an obscene word. He had told her that he had to write as he did to please his readers. None the less in his postscript to the first volume of *Švejk* he seems to argue rather too passionately for the right to use four-letter words to be merely satisfying the desires of his public.

Lada said of him that he had a childish habit of putting out his tongue and waggling it as he wrote. Indeed throughout his life, except perhaps under the Bolsheviks, he remained the ever-lasting schoolboy—a kind of black Peter Pan, who had never grown up but would certainly have been no fit companion for Wendy and her small brothers. He lived in a never-never land of his own, which was a harsh and cruel one, more the world of Swift and Gogol than of fairies, Red Indians and pirates.

He was rarely seen to pay attention to women and normally did not seek their company, and yet his letters to Jarmila, in which he wrote straight from the heart, prove that he was deeply in love with her and suffered grievously during their enforced separation. But after enduring so much for her sake, even to the extent of compromising on his principles in order to win her, he treated her shamefully. There is no doubt that he was genuinely fond of his mother too, and yet he neglected her when she was dying, so that it even shocked Jarmila, who knew what to expect of him. Again it was the confounded zig-zag which he could not perhaps explain, although Jarmila may have instinctively divined its meaning.

He had little success with women. His first erotic experiences with them caused him shame, if we are to believe what he wrote to Jarmila. Švejk's experience with the heartless wench in the cornfield, where he played the role of the innocent fool and she of the predatory female may be an echo of Hašek's own. His only real success was with Jarmila. She seemed to understand and forgive his waywardness. But he went too far and lost her. This must have left a final indelible mark on the man. Shura's role seems to have been more or less a platonic one. She was nothing more than a housekeeper or nurse, as Vilma Warausová suggested. This was what Hašek needed, she said, and probably by that time Shura was the only type of woman he stood any chance of keeping.

He was happiest in male society and found in the end that he could not do without it. Jarmila hated his bohemian friends and begged him to stay away from them. This was one of the causes of the breach between them. One of his inseparable characteristics was his sociability, which was bound up with his gift of humour and the words the boys used to cry after him as a child —*Hašek-Šašek*. Langer reminds us that humour does not bubble out of misanthropes or Robinson Crusoes: it is a collective phenomenon rather than a product of solitude. A comedian

depends on an audience and a comic writer on a large readership. Hašek, who lived his own humour and applied it in his
life, needed both an audience and a readership. As Langer said:
'For him his audience was his springboard, prompter, podium
and stage.' In fact he could not live without his 'claque' of
bohemian boon companions and the contribution he could make
to their company was his 'full, concentrated, gay and sometimes
almost gargantuan vitality'.

Parody and horseplay, which were staple elements of the
Hašek form of humour, are the peculiar province of the male.
This at least was Langer's opinion. From some passages in
Švejk and Hašek's stories one might think that the author was a
man of coarse conversation who would be inhibited in any but
male company. But Langer maintains on the contrary that he
would never say anything which could offend a lady. This
seems quite probable in view of his disillusioning sexual experiences and Jarmila's puritanism.

Could he have been impotent? There is no evidence at all to
suggest this. The son which Jarmila bore him so soon after their
marriage was undoubtedly his. Might he have been homo-
sexual? Only one source has suggested it and Jarmila has denied
it. The fact that as a young man he always went on travels with
those of his own sex and never met a woman, that he spent the
first thirty years of his life in the close company of his male
friends, even sharing their beds, might lead to that supposition,
had intersexual freedom been what it is today. There is a reference in one of his letters to the possibility that he may have been
teased by his friends for not going for walks with girls. But he
appears not to have cherished any very deep feelings for his
male friends. Such relationships with him were nearly always
transient and ephemeral. He would often introduce as his
'friend' someone whom he had only just met. He never showed
interest in or compassion for the personal difficulties of his
cronies and had no scruples about leaving them in the lurch.
There seems to have been no emotion in his relationship with
them and certainly no genuine deep devotion to those to whom
he was bound by special obligations, like Hájek, Lada and Sauer.

He changed very little during his life, except possibly in Soviet
Russia (although we know so little about his everyday life there
that it is hard to be conclusive about it). From the age of twenty

to thirty he certainly did not change, and maturity, if one can speak of his ever having reached it, does not seem to have endowed him with a conscience and sense of responsibility, or to have taught him to reflect before acting. And so whenever any-one met him again after a long interval he found just the same Hašek and got into the same 'Hašek situations' with him. Like a child Hašek would rush into the waves just for the sheer exhilara-tion of it without being conscious of the danger, and when he found himself bruised by the rocks he felt surprised and deeply hurt.

It was just this spontaneity, this uninhibited surrender to the emotion of the moment, to which he was always so prone, that negated all principle in him. Because of this he could never be a Marxist, a Communist or a true believer in anything. He would believe for a limited period and then be assailed by scep-ticism. The only creed which he could truly stomach was anarchism, because it had no doctrinal discipline, but the more he suspected latent doctrine or hypocrisy in it the more he felt alienated from it. But he was convinced that if anarchism did not suit him the fault lay with it not with him. And so it was with everything else—the Social Democratic Party, the National Socialist Party, the Czech Legion and, had he stayed long enough, the Communist Party as well. Maybe he gave signs of disillusionment with that too, but, if so, this does not come out in the current Czechoslovak analysis of his character.

And so from being a bitter opponent of the Habsburgs, he became for a short time a partisan of the Romanovs; from being an eager recruiting sergeant for the Czech Legion, he turned almost overnight into an enthusiastic propagandist for Bolshev-ism; while yearning to see his wife again and be taken back by her, he ruined all his chances by marrying another woman whom he certainly did not love; and finally, having seen the light and abandoned alcohol after some seventeen years of it, he went back to his old vice and let it kill him.

His alcoholism—the great menace of his life—was possibly inherited, but we are told that even without drinking he often gave the impression of being under its influence. His high colour, his eyes which watered in a smoky atmosphere, his eccentric behaviour and love of joking and hoaxing often suggested he was tipsy when he was not. In fact he seldom touched strong

liquor and normally drank nothing stronger than beer albeit
plenty of it. Even the wine he liked to sip while writing was
mixed with water. But he seems to have been easily knocked
over by small quantities of alcohol, and under their influence
his irresponsibility and ruthlessness were aggravated.

A characteristic of Hašek unusual in a writer was his indifference to culture, art or scholarship. He took no interest whatsoever in the works of his literary colleagues and gave no signs of
having read them. Indeed he was the first to disparage his own
literary work and often said that the sketches he wrote were
worthless twaddle. But at the same time he was more than
pleased if anyone had read it and his face lit up if they praised
it. In cultural questions he was a sheer philistine. Although he
wrote verses himself throughout his life, he took no interest at
all in poetry and totally. rejected modern trends. He left the
circle of the Modern Review because their ideas were beyond
him. When his friends talked about literature, he remained
silent or tried to switch the conversation to some light-hearted
topic; and, if he did not succeed, he left in search of more con-
genial company. At a time when Bohemia was ringing with the
melodies of Smetana and Dvořák, he was deaf to them, although, as the gaoler says in *Dalibor*, 'What Czech is there who
does not love music?' Art and architecture meant equally little
to him. Instead he was drawn to people, human beings of all
kinds—good, bad, ordinary or exotic.

Strangely enough, it was said of him that he took little interest
in the countryside: when he went out on excursions he seemed
to notice nothing and be bored. In an early story he wrote: 'We
are not concerned only with the landscape, we want first and
foremost to get to know the people.' He was essentially a man
of the town, and yet none the less he was very fond of animals—
especially dogs and cats—and had a good knowledge of natural
history, acquired more from the pages of Brehm* than from life
itself.

He was a voracious reader who absorbed an enormous number of curious facts. In search of them he would browse in a
railway time-table or a medical text book. He loved tourist
brochures, prospectuses of firms and trade and professional

---

* *Brehm's Illustrated Animal Life* was a very popular and readable book on
birds and beasts which could be found in most houses of the period.

journals (even including those published for hoteliers and hair-dressers). He read newspapers from the back, beginning with the classified advertisements. Drawn only to the concrete, ideas, abstract reflections or moral homilies left him cold. He probably never read the leading articles in newspapers, although in the course of his time in Russia he had to write many himself.

He neglected his dress and liked to go about like a tramp. In his early days he could appear quite smart and indeed did, especially when looked after by his mother. In the days when he was courting Jarmila and after his marriage, he could cut a dandy-like figure—thanks to his wife's insistence and his father-in-law's threats. But if he started early in the morning as a model of elegance, his clothes were in a terrible state by the time the night was out.

A psychiatrist would say that Hašek was the classic example of a creative psychopath, who could not help himself. In spite of all his protestations and his probably sincere good intentions, it was impossible for him to improve or change. Had Mr Mayer realised this he might not have gone on cherishing the hope that he would turn over a new leaf. A creative psychopath is so ego-centric that he can seldom be persuaded that it is he who is wrong: he blames everything on other people and the world, and since he cannot attribute any fault to himself, sees no reason to alter his way of life. Although he is not normally prone to suicide, an occasional fit of depression, especially if brought on by alcoholism or heightened emotion, or both, is not to be excluded. Hašek's adventure on the Charles Bridge may have been a genuine suicide attempt, with the object if not of self-destruction, at least of attracting attention to himself.

Where Hašek differed from most other psychopaths was that he had great literary talent. He could not help writing—it bubbled out of him. If it had not been for this gift, which he had in a degree hardly to be matched, he would have been nothing more than one of the many unfortunates who spend their life in and out of gaol and he would never have been heard of except in police records. Indeed, if he had not written *The Good Soldier Švejk* he would have been condemned to comparative obscurity, in spite of those twelve hundred minor works which he penned so assiduously.

Given the lack of reliable information about Hašek's inner

self, we must lend an attentive ear to what Jarmila has to say, even if she sometimes appears to us to be too indulgent with him. Writing of his smile (which seems to have intrigued so many of those who knew him) she said: 'I knew that smile for many years and it went very well with some sharp furrows, which intensive brain work had scored on his brow. He was hard-working and did his portion honestly and gladly . . . Big children and humorists both have their sorrows sometimes. They conceal them, play the clown but none the less sometimes sob out: "I too have a human heart which aches . . ." '

She thought that a poem of his published in '*Cries of May*' offered one of those rare occasions when he lifted the veil and revealed the melancholy in his heart.

> I went into a forest. Spring was singing.
> Two young birch trees, which boys had pierced
> To suck their sap,
> Stood there with heads bowed down,
> Like my ideals.
> I went into a forest. Spring was singing.
> But the fresh grass had all been trampled down
> By people looking for flowers.
> And I recalled how in my life I too
> Had trampled down all sorts of things.
> I went into a forest. Spring was singing.
> It was so beautiful beneath the trees
> I stopped and hid my forehead in my hands.
> The forest smelled sweet. Spring was singing.
> But I was sad and cheerless.

However, this poem was written when he was only twenty, at a time when he had had little experience of the conflict between ideals and life and before he had begun to make real havoc with his trampling. Perhaps he was born with an innate pessimism, with an intuition that he would wreck his life because he could not control his irresponsibility?

And so, if we are to believe Jarmila, Hašek's life was not the merry-go-round we might have taken it to be, nor was he the merry andrew his boon companions wanted to make him. Often he must have had very bitter moments which made his life a Calvary. We can only wish that it had been otherwise and that the man whose books have given such pleasure to millions could have had his share of happiness too, and that his smile had not been a malicious leer or a smile through tears, but a joyful smile instead—the prelude to the full-throated laugh which was his unique gift to others.

A Rough Guide to the Pronunciation of Czech

One simple rule is that all words have the stress on the first syllable. Listed here are some of the names which appear frequently in *The Bad Bohemian*.

Ančík	Unn'cheek	Marek	Murr'eck
Beneš	Benn'esh	Míťa	Meet'ya
Čeček	Chetch'eck	Muna	Moo'na
České Budějovice	Chess'kay	Opočenský	Opp' och enn skee
	Boo'djay ov it say	Panuška	Punn' oosh ka
František	Frunn' tyee sheck	Pavlů	Puv'loo
Grýša	Gree'sha	Poděbrady	Podd' je brudd ee
Hájek	High'eck	Pytlík	Pitt'leek
Jarmila	Yar'mill a	Sokol	Sokk'oll
Jaroslav	Yarr'o sluvv	Štěpánek	Shtyepp'ah neck
Kuděj	Koo'djay	Strašlipka	Strush'lipp ka
Lada	Ludd'a	Švec	Shvets
Libáň	Libb'ahn	Švejk	Shvake
Lipnice	Lipp' nyits ay	Synek	Sinn'eck
Lukáš	Loo'kahsh	Vaněk	Vunn' yeck
Máňa	Mahn'ya	Vinohrady	Vinn' o hrudd ee

ň is pronounced like the French gn in *cognac*
ř is pronounced as in the name Dvořák, i.e. r with a French j as in *journal*
ž is pronounced as though with a French j
Czech family names of German origin are pronounced as they would be in German

Bibliography

WORKS BY JAROSLAV HAŠEK

The Good Soldier Švejk and His Fortunes in the World War in a new and unabridged translation by Cecil Parrott, Heinemann and Penguin London, Crowell, New York 1973. All editions have the same pagination.
  Short stories, articles, poems etc. Very few of these are yet translated. All Hašek's lesser works cited in this biography will be found in the following collections:

1 *Črty, povídky a humoresky z cest.* Spisy Jaroslava Haška, vol. 1, Státní nakladatelství krásné literatury, hudby a umění, Prague 1955
2 *Dekameron*, Československý spisovatel, Prague 1968
3 *Galerie Karikatur*, Spisy Jaroslava Haška, vol. 8, 1968
4 *Moje zpověď*, Spisy Jaroslava Haška, vol. 16, 1968
5 *Dědictví po panu Šafránkovi*, Spisy Jaroslava Haška, vol. 3, 1972
6 *Májové výkřiky.* Spisy Jaroslava Haška, vol. 11, 1972
7 *Panoptikum.* ROH, Prague 1950
8 *Aféra s křečkem a jiné povídky*, Mladá fronta, Prague 1973
9 *Škola humoru*, Svoboda, Prague 1949
10 *Pepíček Nový a jiné povídky*, Edice Skvosty, Prague 1963
11 *Dobrý voják Švejk v zajetí*, Spisy Jaroslava Haška, vols. 13-14, Prague 1973
12 *Zrádce národa v Chotěboři*, Spisy Jaroslava Haška, vol. 4, Prague 1962
13 *Loupežný vrah před soudem*, Spisy Jaroslava Haška, vol. 2, Prague 1958
14 *Velitelem města Bugulmy*, Spisy Jaroslava Haška, vol. 15, Prague 1966
15 *Fialový hrom*, Spisy Jaroslava Haška, vol. 5, Prague 1961
16 *Útrapy vychovatele*, Albatros, Prague 1969
17 *Utrpení pana Tenkráta*, Spisy Jaroslava Haška, vol. 6, Prague 1961
18 *O dětech a zvířátkách*, Spisy Jaroslava Haška, vol. 7, Prague 1960

19 *Praha ve dne v noci*, Československý spisovatel, Prague 1973
20 *Politické a sociální dějiny strany mírného pokroku v mezích zákona*, Spisy Jaroslava Haška, vol. 9, Prague 1963

The lesser works mentioned in this biography are listed here together with the number of the collection in which each is to be found.

Adele Thoms z Haidy, německá učitelka [1]
Adjutantem velitele města Bugulmy [14]
Aféra s dalekohledem [1]
Aféra s křečkem [2]
Aféra s teploměrem [6]
Baluškova zrada [2]
Baráčnická krev pana Potužníka [11]
Cikáni o 'hodech' [1]
Česká panna Orleánská slečna Süssová [20]
Čím jsme povinni ruským Čechům [11]
Den voleb [20]
Dějiny strany mírného pokroku v mezích zákona [20]
Dobrý voják Švejk a jiné podivné historky [16]
Dobrý voják Švejk opatřuje mešní víno [16]
Dobrý voják Švejk před válkou [16]
Dobrý voják Švejk působí u aeroplánů [16]
Dobrý voják Švejk stojí proti Italii [16]
Dobrý voják Švejk učí se zacházet se střelnou bavlnou [16]
Dobrý voják Švejk v zajetí [11]
Dopisy z fronty [11]
Drobílkovo milostné dobrodružství [20]
Dušička Jaroslava Haška vypravuje [4]
Gott strafe England! [11]
Historky z ražické bašty [5]
Hradčany s Rozhlednou pokračují v rozmluvě [11]
Idyla venkova [1]
Jak Hans Hutter a Franz Stockmaynegg hájili německý ráz Vídně [1]
Jak jsem se setkal s autorem svého nekrologu [2]
Jak jsem vystoupil ze strany národně sociální [3]
Jeden den v redakci Českého slova [20]
Když se zametá ... [11]
Klínový nápis [13]
Klub Českých Pickwicků [11]
Kolik kdo má kolem krku [11]
Konec opice [1]

'Krestný chod' [14]
Kynologický ústav [18]
Májové výkřiky [6]
Má drahá přítelkyně Julča [2]
Minulost a přítomnost [11]
Moje zpověď [4]
Na jaře v sadě [6]
Největší den Folimanky [2]
Obchodní akademie [5]
Oslík Guat [1]
Osudy pana Hurta [11]
Otcovské radosti pana Motejzlíka [17]
O ufském lupiči hokynáři Bulakulinovi [14]
Panovník, který se posadí na české bajonety [11]
Pláč gefreitra [11]
Pohádka z východu [13]
Po stopách státní policie v Praze [2]
Povídka o obrazu císaře Františka Josefa I [2]
Povídka o záruce [11]
Proč se jede do Francie? [11]
Prof. Masarykovi [11]
Průvodčí cizinců ve švábském městě Neuburgu [2]
Přišel včas [1]
Psychiatrická záhada [2]
Redakční sluha Šefrna [20]
Schůze politického klubu strany státoprávní dne 20. června 1904
    v Konviktě [6]
Sklenice černé kávy [20]
Smělý pokus útěku dvou dozorců z pankrácké trestnice [13]
Spravedlnost v Bavořích [1]
Superarbitrační řízení s dobrým vojákem Švejkem [16]
Šestého ledna [11]
Temná síla [11]
Tři muži se žralokem a jiné poučné historky [2]
Utrpení pana Tenkráta [17]
Válečná báseň o vších [11]
Velitelem města Bugulmy [14]
Velký den [12]
V reservě [11]
V strategických nesnázích [14]
V Zlaté uličce na Hradčanech [11]
Z deníku ufského měšťáka [14]
Ze staré drogerie [8]

BOOKS, ARTICLES ETC.

ON JAROSLAV HAŠEK AND HIS PERIOD

Ančík, Zdena, *O životě Jaroslava Haška*, Československý spisovatel, Prague 1953

Bouček, Antonín, *Padesát historek ze života Jaroslava Haška*, V. Boučková, Prague 1923

Bradley, J. F. N., *La Légion Tchécoslovaque en Russie 1914–1920*, Paris 1965

Brod, Max, *Prager Sternenhimmel*, Paul Szolnay, Vienna and Hamburg 1966

Červený, Jiří, *Červená sedma*, Orbis, Prague 1959

Deyl, Rudolf, *Písničkář Karel Hašler*, Panton, Prague 1968

Durych, Jaroslav, *Ejhle člověk!* *Český pomník*, Prague 1928

Frynta, Emanuel, *Hašek, the Creator of Švejk*, Prague 1965

Fučík, Julius, *Válka se Švejkem*, Rudý večerník, Prague 21.4.1928

Hájek, Ladislav, *Z mých vzpomínek na Jaroslava Haška*, Čechie, Prague 1925

Hampl, František, *Nejznámější absolvent Českoslovanské—Jaroslav Hašek*, Střední ekonomická škola, Prague 1972

Hašková, Jarmila, *Drobné příběhy*, Krajské nakladatelství, Havlíčkův Brod 1960

Havel, Rudolf a Jiří Opelík, *Slovník českých spisovatelů*, Ústav pro českou literaturu CSAV, Československý spisovatel, Prague 1964

Janouch, Gustav, *Prager Begegnungen*, Paul List Verlag, Leipzig 1959

Kalaš, Josef, *Jaroslav Hašek ve fotografii*, Československý spisovatel, Prague 1959

Kunc, Jaroslav, *Slovník soudobých českých spisovatelů*, Orbis, Prague 1945

Křížek, Jaroslav, *Jaroslav Hašek v revolučním Rusku*, Naše vojsko, Prague 1957

Kuděj, Z. M., *Když táhne silná čtyřka*, Nakladatelství Svět, Ostrava 1948

Lacina, Václav, *Dvě haškovské monografie*, Nový život, vol. 3, 1954

Lada, Josef, *Kronika mého života*, Československý spisovatel, Prague 1954

Lada, Josef, *Můj přítel Švejk*, Svoboda, Prague 1969

Langer, František, *Byli a bylo*, Československý spisovatel, Prague 1963

Longen, E. A., *Jaroslav Hašek*, E. Beaufort, Prague 1928

Ludvík, Břetislav, *Kdo je Jaroslav Hašek*, Orbis, Prague 1946

Lvova, Alexandra, *Jaroslav Hašek ve vzpomínkách své ženy*, Průboj, Prague 24.1.1965

Masaryk, T. G., *Světová revoluce*, Čin a Orbis, Prague 1925

Masarykův slovník naučný, Prague 1925–1933

Medek, Rudolf, *Za svobodu*, Památník odboje, Prague 1924–1929

Menger, Václav, *Lidský profil Jaroslava Haška*, Koliandr, Prague 1946

Novák, Arne, *Stručné dějiny literatury české*, Promberger, Olomouc 1946

Opočenský, Gustav R., *Čtvrt století s Jaroslavem Haškem*, J. Steinbrener, národní správa, Vimperk 1948

Ottův slovník naučný nové doby (Dodatky), Prague 1930–1943

Petr, Pavel, *Hašeks 'Schwejk' in Deutschland*, Rütten und Loening, Berlin 1963

Příruční slovník k dějinám KSČ, Nakladatelství politické literatury, Prague 1964

Pytlík, Radko a Miroslav Laiske, *Bibliografie Jaroslava Haška*, Státní pedagogické nakladatelství, Prague 1960

Pytlík, Radko, *Toulavé house*, Mladá fronta, Prague 1971

Pytlík, Radko, *Jaroslav Hašek*, Československý spisovatel, Prague 1962

Sauer, František, *Franta Habán ze Žižkova*, Nakladatelství politické literatury, Prague 1965

Sauer, Franta and Ivan Suk, *In memoriam Jaroslava Haška*, Družstevní nakladatelství, Prague 1924

Stejskal, Vladimír, *Hašek na Lipnici*, Krajské nakladatelství, Havlíčkův Brod 1954

Štěpánek, Kliment, *Vzpomínky na poslední léta Jaroslava Haška*, Krajské nakladatelství, Havlíčkův Brod 1960

Thunig-Nittner, Gerburg, *Die Tschechoslowakische Legion in Russland*, Otto Harrassowitz, Wiesbaden 1970

Tůma-Zevloun, Ladislav, *Alej vzpomínek. Začátky Jaroslava Haška*, Prague 1958

Vika, Karel, *Z mé staré zlaté Prahy*, Prague 1946

Warausová, Vilma, *Přátelé Haškovi a lidé kolem nich*, Krajské nakladatelství, Havlíčkův Brod 1965

Wohlgemuthová, Renata, *Příspěvek k dějinám českého anarchistického hnutí v letech 1900–1914*, Academia, Prague 1971

Notes

[1] Marie Škodová-Hašková

[2] Emil Arthur Longen ('E. A. Pitterman'), actor, producer, caricaturist, film worker, playwright and author.

[3] Zdeněk Matěj Kuděj, a hobo who tramped over half the globe including all of America, wrote books on American down-and-outs and translated the Tarzan books.

[4] Franta Sauer ('František Kyselý', 'Franta Kysela'), proletarian writer, anarchist, locksmith, commercial traveller and author of a book on the Prague Bohème and the Longens.

[5] Gustav R. Opočenský, fashionable author of prose and ironic verse who ended his career writing erotic pot-boilers.

[6] *Ve dvou se to lépe táhne*

[7] *Když táhne silná čtyřka*

[8] *Franta Habán ze Žižkova*

[9] *Čtvrt století s Jaroslavem Haškem*

[10] *Jaroslav Hašek zajatec č.294217*

[11] *Jaroslav Hašek doma*

[12] *Lidský profil Jaroslava Haška*

[13] *Lidové noviny*

[14] Jan Morávek, popular author and journalist who wrote many novels about the Sázava valley in Bohemia.

[15] *Večerní České slovo*

[16] Ladislav Hájek-Domažlický, poet, writer of short stories and editor.

[17] Josef Lada, painter, illustrator and humorist who specialised in scenes of Czech village life and fairy tales.

[18] František Langer, the leading modern Czech playwright after Karel Čapek, a military doctor in two world wars who served in the Czech Brigade in London during the Second World War.

[19] *Z mých vzpomínek na Jaroslava Haška*

[20] *Kronika mého života*

[21] *Byli a bylo*

[22] Zdena Ančík, Communist journalist of long standing who worked in London as a journalist in the Czech Brigade and in the Communist-run Ministry of Information after the Second World War.

[23] Dr Radko Pytlík, literary critic attached to the Literary Institute of the Czechoslovak Academy of Sciences.

[24] *Jaroslav Hašek v revolučním Rusku*

[25] *Toulavé house*

[26] *Naše vojsko*

[I] *BOHEMIA*

The three main sources for Chapters 1–10 are Menger, *Lidský profil Jaroslava Haška*, Ančík, *O životě Jaroslava Haška* and Pytlík, *Toulavé house*. Unfortunately none of them provide notes on their sources. Only Ančík has a very brief and vague list. These three sources are the chief sources I have used and other sources will be cited in the notes.

(1) *Introduction*

[1] *Tribuna*

[2] Gustav Janouch, *Jaroslav Hašek, Der Vater des Braven Soldat Schwejk*, p. 283

[3] František Langer, *Byli a bylo*, p. 92

[4] *Jak jsem se setkal s autorem svého nekrologu*

[5] *Moje zpověď, Večerní České slovo*, 28.1.1921

[6] *28. říjen.* When Hašek published his story '*Dušička Jaroslava Haška vypravuje*' in *Večerník Práva lidu*, 31.12.1920, the journal published a reply, 25.1.1921, called '*Jaroslav Hašek vypravuje*'. In a further article, published 26.1.1921, the journal denounced Hašek as a 'Bolshevik attaché and diplomat'.

(2) *School Street and School-Days*

[1] *Guide to the Royal City of Prague and to the Kingdom of Bohemia*, p. 5

[2] *Historky z ražické bašty*

[3] *Sv. Štěpán*

[4] *Karlovo náměstí*

[5] *Božena Němcová* (1820–62), one of the great Czech novelists and author of the famous book *Babička* (Grandmother).

[6] *Eliška Krásnohorská* (1847–1926), a leading poet, who wrote the libretti for some of Smetana's operas.

[7] *Nové Město*

8 *Klášter sv. Kateřiny*
9 *Konvent řádu alžbětinek*
10 *Františkovo nábřeží* (now *Smetanovo nábřeží*)
11 *Baluškova zrada*
12 *Největší den Folimanky*
13 *Ze staré drogerie*
14 *Českoslovanská obchodní akademie*

(3) *The Literary Vagabond*

1 *Občan Brych*
2 *Romeo, Julie a tma*
3 *Karikatury*
4 *Jiří Stříbrný* (1880–1955), a deputy chairman of the National Socialist party and one-time Minister of Defence in the Czechoslovak government, who later founded the Fascist *Národní liga* and became its president. In 1945 he was tried and sentenced to a long prison sentence and died in gaol.
5 *Cikáni o 'hodech'*
6 *Idyla venkova*
7 *Přišel včas*
8 *V Tatrách*
9 *Slovenské spevy*
10 *Národní listy*
11 *Konec opice*
12 *Právo lidu*
13 *Ilustrovaný svět*
14 *Liška Bystrouška*
15 Sauer and Suk, *In Memoriam Jaroslava Haška*
16 *Májové výkřiky*
17 *Na jaře v sadě*
18 *Národní politika*, a widely read daily. Hašek's uncle Jan was manager of its printing works and helped to get his sketches published. Pytlík and Laiske, *Bibliografie Jaroslava Haška*, p. 17.
19 Ladislav Hájek, *Z mých vzpomínek na Jaroslava Haška*, pp. 5, 9, 10, 13, 17ff.

(4) *The Would-Be Anarchist*

1 Wohlgemuthová, *Příspěvek k dějinám českého anarchistického hnutí v letech 1900–14*, provides general background information on Anarchism in Bohemia.
2 Stanislav Kostka Neumann (1875–1947)

[3] *Moderní revue*
[4] *Nový kult*
[5] *Šibeničky*
[6] *Pohádka z východu*
[7] *Omladina*
[8] *Česká federace všech odborů*
[9] *Klínový nápis*
[10] *Po stopách státní policie v Praze*
[11] An earlier form of the word '*Čechoslovák*'
[12] *Nová omladina*
[13] *Prodaná nevěsta*
[14] *Spravedlnost v Bavořích*
[15] *Průvodčí cizinců ve švábském městě Neuburgu*
[16] *Jak Hans Hutter a Franz Stockmaynegg hájili německý ráz Vídně*
[17] *Adele Thoms z Haidy, německá učitelka*
[18] *Oslík Guat*
[19] *Aféra s dalekohledem*
[20] *Velký den*
[21] *Světozor*
[22] *Besedy lidu*
[23] *Ilustrované české humoresky*
[24] *Nový Neruda*
[25] *Svítilna*

(5) Jarmila

[1] *Ženský výrobní spolek*
[2] Vilma Warausová, *Přátelé Haškovi a lidé kolem nich.*
[3] *Utrpení pana Tenkráta*
[4] *Ústřední škola dělnická*
[5] A small town about twenty-eight kilometres north-east of Prague, between Mladá Boleslav and Jičín.
[6] *Komuna*
[7] *Chuďas*
[8] *Den*
[9] *Dějiny strany mírného pokroku v mezích zákona*, pp. 42–3
[10] *České slovo*
[11] *Venkov*
[12] *Zlatá Praha*
[13] *Zvon*
[14] *Švanda* was the leading character in the play *Strakonický dudák*, written by the patriotic Czech playwright Josef Kajetán Tyl, who wrote the words for the Czech national anthem, '*Kde*

domov můj ?' The magazine, which was called after Švanda, was
edited for six years by the Czech humorous writer Ignát
Herrmann.

[15] *Mladé proudy*
[16] *Svět zvířat*
[17] *Ženský svět*
[18] *Zlatý litr*

(6) Married Life

[1] *Sv. Ignác* in *Karlovo náměstí*, built by Carlo Luragho, 1665–70
[2] *Sv. Ludmila*, a huge neo-Gothic cathedral which dominates the
Square of Peace (*Náměstí míru*), as it is called today. It was
called in Hašek's day *Purkyňovo náměstí* (Purkyně Square).
[3] *Riegrovy sady*, a park in *Vinohrady*
[4] *Má drahá přítelkyně Julča*
[5] A town about thirty-one kilometres to the east of Prague
[6] *Kynologický ústav*
[7] *Můj obchod se psy*
[8] *Psychiatrická záhada*

(7) The Birth of Švejk

[1] This is the version given to Richard Hašek by his mother. Ančík,
O zivotě Jaroslava Haška, p. 97
[2] Jarmila Hašková, *Drobné příběhy*, 'Domovní prohlídka', p. 125
[3] *Kolik kdo má kolem krku*
[4] *Dobrý voják Švejk a jiné podivné historky*
[5] *Dobrý voják Švejk v zajetí*
[6] *Osudy dobrého vojáka Švejka za světové války*
[7] *Švejk stojí proti Italii*
[8] *Dobrý voják Švejk opatřuje mešní víno*
[9] *Superarbitrační řízení s dobrým vojákem Švejkem*
[10] *Dobrý voják Švejk učí se zacházet se střelnou bavlnou*
[11] *Dobrý voják Švejk působí u aeroplánů*
[12] *Dobrá kopa*

(8) A Most Peculiar Party

[1] See Chapter 5, note 9
[2] *Schůze politického klubu strany státoprávní dne 20. června 1904 v Konviktě*
[3] *Želva*

⁴ *Čas*

⁵ *Josef Mach* (1883–1951), a journalist and writer of cynical verses and satirical sketches, who later became Head of the Czech Press Bureau in Washington and finished his career as a member of the Czechoslovak Foreign Service. He published nothing more after 1937.

⁶ Langer, *Byli a bylo*, pp. 41–2

⁷ *Dějiny strany mírného pokroku v mezích zákona*

⁸ *Směr*

⁹ *Rudé právo*

¹⁰ *Volební ruch*

¹¹ *Strana propaguje své zásady kulturními večery*

¹² These details come from the editors' notes to *Dějiny strany*.

¹³ *Dějiny strany*, 'Drobílkovo milostné dobrodružství', p. 57

¹⁴ *Besedy Vydrovy*

¹⁵ *Dějiny*, 'Česká panna Orleánská slečna Süssová', p. 89

¹⁶ *Dějiny*, p. 155

¹⁷ Ibid., 'Redakční sluha Šefrna', p. 212

¹⁸ Ibid., 'Den voleb', p. 268

(9) The Break-Up of a Marriage

¹ Vilma Warausová, *Přátelé Haškovi a lidé kolem nich*, p. 64

² *Zlatá husa*

³ *Jak jsem vystoupil ze strany nár. sociální*

⁴ *Otcovské radosti pana Motejzlíka*

(10) A Cabaret Star

¹ *Karel Hašler* (1877–1941), a famous Czech *chansonnier* and film star.

² *Červená sedma*

³ Jiří Voskovec (1905–) and Jan Werich (1905–), two students who produced and acted in revues at the *Osvobozené divadlo* (Liberated Theatre). They were the great rage in Prague between the wars. Their sketches had a great appeal both to intellectuals and a wider audience. Much of their performance was improvised. As their revues became more and more political and critical of the Nazis their theatre was eventually closed down in 1938. They both left for the USA, from where Werich returned to Prague but had difficulties in getting permission to act there. Voskovec stayed in America.

⁴ An attempt was made in Communist Czechoslovakia to revive this type of entertainment first at the *Divadlo Na Zábradlí* (Theatre on the Balustrade) and later at the *Semafor* under Jiří Šlitr and Jiří Suchý but they did not last for long. Their performances were a pallid reflection of V+W.

⁵ For background on the Prague cabaret see Jiří Červený *Červená sedma*.

⁶ *Dějiny*, 'Sklenice černé kávy', p. 217

⁷ *Hora Olivetská aneb Výprava Čechů v Jeruzalémě*

⁸ *Pevnost, pružnost a tažnost*. See Langer, *Byli a bylo*, p. 47

⁹ Prokop Diviš (1696–1765), an early experimenter in electricity and musical physics, who is claimed to be the inventor of the lightning conductor.

¹⁰ František Kysela (1881–1941), a leading Czech graphic artist and theatrical designer who was professor at the Prague Industrial Art School. He did the décor for several productions of Smetana's operas.

¹¹ Vlastislav H. Brunner (1886–1928), another leading graphic artist and professor at the Industrial Art School. Specialised in book production and caricatures.

¹² The nickname given to Matěj Kuděj, Opočenský, Hanuška and Hašek.

¹³ Karel Pospíšil (1867–1929), a composer of music for *Sokol* exercises and *Sokol* songs.

¹⁴ *Albert Vojtěch Frič* (1882–1944), an explorer of South America.

¹⁵ Hájek, *Z mých vzpomínek*, p. 63

¹⁶ Lada, *Kronika mého života*, pp. 303–32 and *passim*

¹⁷ Josef Kalaš, *Jaroslav Hašek ve fotografii*, p. 73

(11) *On the Way to the Front*

¹ We know that Hašek went on one of his tramps to the Polish part of Austria, Galicia, and he may very well have crossed into the Polish part of Russia. If we can take his story *Procházka přes hranice* as factual, he was dragged off by a Cossack guard to Kiev.

² Lada, *Kronika mého života*

³ *Aféra s teploměrem*

⁴ *Aféra s křečkem*

⁵ *Gott strafe Engeland*

⁶ *V strategických nesnázích*

⁷ *V reservě*

⁸ *Válečná báseň o vších*

⁹ *Pláč gefreitra*

[II] RUSSIA

The main sources for the story of Hašek's life in Russia are Jaroslav Křížek, *Jaroslav Hašek v revolučním Rusku* and Pytlík, *Toulavé house*. Other sources are cited in the notes. As a corrective to these accounts one should read the official legionary account in Rudolf Medek, *Za svobodu* as well as jorunals and newspapers of the period.

(12) In Russia

1 *Národní rada*
2 *Klub spolupracovníků Svazu*
3 *Čím jsme povinni ruským Čechům?*
4 *Osudy pana Hurta*
5 *Povídka o obrazu císaře Františka Josefa I*
6 *Povídka o záruce*
7 *Panovník, který se posadí na české bajonety*
8 Langer, *Byli a bylo*, pp. 69–71
9 *Dopisy z fronty*
10 *Baráčnická krev pana Potužníka*
11 *Když se zametá . . .*
12 *Dobrý voják Švejk v zajetí*

(13) The Russian February Revolution

1 *Odbočka*
2 Čermák was the representative in Petrograd of a Belgian cigar firm. He was elected President of the League at its first meeting in March 1915. Later he led the pro-Masaryk opposition to it.
3 Maxa was a middle school teacher at one time on the staff of the Commercial Academy. As a member of the Realist Party (Masaryk's party) he came to Masaryk's notice and eventually was given the highest political position in the Czech movement in Russia.
4 Országh was a Slovak merchant in Warsaw who represented the Czechs and Slovaks living there.
5 *Temná síla*
6 *Černá ruka*
7 *Revoluce*. Called itself an 'independent political weekly'. It was against the Petrograd Czechs, the National Council in Paris and later the Branch.
8 *Klub českých Pickwicků*
9 Pavlů was a Slovak journalist who worked for a while on *Time* (*Čas*), the journal in Bohemia founded by supporters of Masaryk. As a prisoner-of-war in Russia he became editor of the

Petrograd *Čechoslovák*. He was one of the pro-Masaryk oppositional group in the League. Later in 1918 he became editor of
the *Czechoslovak Daily* (*Československý deník*), the main legionary
newspaper.

¹⁰ Later to become General Gajda. He had a colourful career in the
Czechoslovak Republic, becoming Chief of the General Staff,
then leader of an ineffectual fascist party which received little
encouragement from the German authorities even after the
occupation in 1939.

(14) *The October Revolution*

¹ A dilettante in amateur theatricals and a minor writer who became a deputy in the Agrarian party.
² *Slovanský věstník*
³ *Svoboda*
⁴ *Světová revoluce* (*The Making of a State*), pp. 216–17. This account
is to be found only in Masaryk's Czech original. Wickham
Steed's translation was very selective and several interesting
passages were left out.
⁵ *Minulost a přítomnost*
⁶ *V Zlaté uličce na Hradčanech* and *Hradčany s rozhlednou pokračují
v rozmluvě*
⁷ *Šestého ledna*
⁸ *Československá revolucní rada dělníků a vojáků*
⁹ *Průkopník*
¹⁰ *Proč se jede do Francie?*
¹¹ Josef Kopta (1894–1962), a leading Legionary novelist who, like
Hašek, went to the Commercial Academy and was for a short
time a bank official, was a writer and journalist during the first
Czechoslovak Republic and after the second a member of
President Beneš's chancellery. *The Third Company* was a trilogy
about the Czech Legion in Russia.
¹² *Průkopník*. 7, 9.5.1918
¹³ *Prof. Masarykovi!*
¹⁴ *Československý voják*
¹⁵ *Plukovník Švec*
¹⁶ *Československá rudá armáda*

(15) *The Commissar*

¹ *Velitelem města Bugulmy*
² *Adjutantem velitele města Bugulmy*

[3] The *Revolutionary Army Soviet of the Eastern Front* (RVSR) was formed on September 6th, 1918. All armies and fronts were under its command. At the head of every one of its armies was a *Revolutionary Army Soviet* (RVS) made up of the Army Commander and two political commissars. Every army, including the Fifth in which Hašek worked, had a similar chain of command: at the apex was the *Revolutionary Army Soviet*. Underneath it came the Staff and its various departments, broadly categorised as operational, administrative and training. These included artillery, engineering, supplies and the *Political Department*, the *Department of Army Control* and the *Revolutionary Army Tribunal*. Education, press propaganda and publicity came under the *Political Department*, which was supervised and supported by the Party organisations within the Red Army. Control of the political organisations was exercised by the *Political Direction of the Revolutionary Army Soviet of the Republic* (PUR).

[4] *Nash put* (Russian)
[5] *Krestný chod*
[6] Sauer and Suk, *In Memoriam* etc., pp. 28–9
[7] Alexandra Lvova, *Jaroslav Hašek*, pp. 3–5
[8] *Z deníku ufského měšťáka*
[9] *O ufském lupiči hokynáři Bulakinovi*
[10] See other stories in *Velitelem města Bugulmy*
[11] *Krasnaya Evropa* (Russian)
[12] *Krasny strelok* (Russian)
[13] Sauer and Suk, pp. 29–30
[14] *Sturm*. The Hungarian version was *Roham*
[15] *Weltrevolution*
[16] *Vlast truda* (Russian)
[17] Sauer and Suk, p. 30
[18] *Venkov*
[19] *Dušička Jaroslava Haška vypravuje*
[20] Lvova, p. 14

[III] *CZECHOSLOVAKIA*

(16) *Back in Prague*

[1] *Ferdinandova třída*
[2] *Národní třída*
[3] Langer, pp. 86–7
[4] Lvova, *Jaroslav Hašek*, pp. 19–20

5 *Revoluční scéna*
6 Longen, pp. 19–20
7 *Jak jsem se setkal s autorem svého nekrologu*
8 Hájek, pp. 99–100
9 Warausová, pp. 71–2
10 Lvova, p. 23
11 Ibid., p. 21
12 *Tři muži se žralokem a jiné poučné historky*
13 *Kmen*
14 Lvova, pp. 23–4
15 Lada, *Můj přítel Švejk*
16 Warausová, pp. 80–2

(17) *Lipnice and the End*

1 Langer, p. 88
2 Vladimír Stejskal, *Hašek na Lipnici*, pp. 26–30
3 Ibid., pp. 75ff.
4 Ibid., pp. 57–8
5 Ibid., pp. 90–1
6 K. Štěpánek, *Vzpomínky na poslední léta Jaroslava Haška*, p. 15
7 Stejskal, pp. 71–4
8 Longen, pp. 193–4
9 Ibid., p. 208
10 Hájek, pp. 100–2
11 Lvova, pp. 28–9
12 Stejskal, pp. 114–17
13 Ibid., p. 69
14 Longen, p. 203
15 Stejskal, pp. 105–10
16 Štěpánek, p. 35
17 Stejskal, p. 69
18 Lvova, p. 31

(18) *The Bad Bohemian*

1 Eduard Bass, *Postavy a siluety*, p. 124
2 Langer, p. 64
3 Jarmila Hašková, *Drobné příběhy*, 'Profil mrtvého druha'

Index